MY LONGEST NIGHT

MY LONGEST NIGHT

*An eleven year old French girl's
memories of D-Day*

Geneviève Duboscq

Translated by
Richard S. Woodward

Leo Cooper
in association with
SECKER & WARBURG: LONDON

First published in the United States of America in
1981 by Seaver Books, New York

First published in France by Editions Robert Laffont, Paris,
under the title BYE BYE GENEVIEVE! in 1978

First published in Great Britain in 1984 by Leo Cooper in association with
Secker & Warburg Limited
54 Poland Street, London W1V 3DF

ISBN: 0 436 37705 5

Chapter openings illustrated by Nerissa Jones
Photoset by Deltatype, Ellesmere Port
Printed and bound in Britain by
Redwood Burn Limited, Trowbridge, Wiltshire

I dedicate this book
to all the veterans of the Allied Armies
and in particular to the paratroopers
of the 82nd and 101st Airborne Divisions
who gave their lives to free us,
to Philippe Jutras, a veteran of Utah Beach,
Curator of the Sainte-Mère-Eglise Museum,
to Robert,
to all my children,
and, of course,
to Papa Maurice and
my beloved mother.

Contents

List of Illustrations

Author's Note

Since the publication of this book in France – especially since it became a bestseller – a few people have questioned some of the facts that I relate. In France there are some who maintain that I did not give their deeds sufficient credit. In America, some veterans of the 82nd Airborne Division, who fought so bravely for La Fière, have no memory of our house and therefore doubt my family's brave actions. The simple fact is that for them La Fière is a small cluster of houses near the causeway over the river, whereas our house – still a part of that township – is several miles north and across the river. This geographical confusion takes nothing away from their bravery nor diminishes Papa Maurice's heroic efforts from June 5th to 7th, 1944. Those who have been upset by my book seem to forget that I am not posing as a military historian; I am not an expert in military affairs. This is my personal story. I was a little girl when the events described here took place, and I have recorded them as accurately and faithfully as I can, relying not only on my vivid memories but also on the correspondence of several witnesses who lived through those times with me.

GENEVIÈVE DUBOSCQ

Prologue

The railway line between Paris and Cherbourg flies straight as an arrow from the capital to the port. Along the entire route – inaugurated three generations ago by Emperor Napoleon III – the French National Railways had constructed a series of small houses. These were provided as rent-free accommodation for the families whose job it was to raise and lower the level-crossing gates and make sure that tracks in their area were clear and in good shape.

Our house was Level-Crossing 104; as the name implies this was the one hundred and fourth such crossing on the Paris-Cherbourg line. It was a pretty little house, regularly repainted in soft ochre by the railway company, and surrounded by a profusion of flowers and climbing vines that my mother had planted. It was itself a proud, bright flower set in the midst of the barren marshy landscape. In fact, few people as poor as my parents were then could boast of living in such an attractive house.

There were four rooms: the kitchen and my parents' bedroom on the ground floor, an attic and a second bedroom on the upper floor. For some unknown reason, the architect who had drawn up the plans for 104 had so laid it out that we children had to cross the attic in order to reach our bedroom. What was worse, the attic was big and airy and faced the marshes – but since it had never been completed it served absolutely no purpose. Our bedroom, on the other hand, was tiny and overlooked the railway tracks. Consequently, whenever a train thundered past beneath our window, my little brother and I would be literally shaken in our beds. The vibration seemed to emanate from within the earth itself – but it never really bothered us; we were used to it.

1

Level-Crossing 104 was over three miles from Sainte-Mère-Eglise, a village lying in the middle of the vast lowlands and marshes that are characteristic of that part of Normandy. I had to make that trip twice a day, on my way to school and back again. It was a pleasant enough walk in the mornings, and even for the first part of the return trip in the afternoons: two miles through peaceful countryside. But the final leg of the evening journey was another matter altogether. Once I'd reached the railway line, I still had a further mile to walk along the narrow path beside the tracks, with only the marshes on either side. The narrowness of the path itself, the unpredictable gusts of wind, the frequent trains thundering past spewing half-burnt cinders and jets of steam: I had to face these dangers every day.

We also had the use of another house, set on higher ground in the middle of a thirty-acre field. In earlier days this had been a sheep pen, and so we called it the Sheepfold. The part that had housed the sheep was enormous, with room for hundreds of animals, but we humans had to make do with a kitchen on the ground floor, where my parents slept, and a small bedroom on the floor above.

It's hard to say which of the two houses I preferred. I liked them both. Life at the Sheepfold was rougher than at 104. Like all the other level-crossing houses, 104 had both a pump and a cistern. In times of severe drought, we could go and fetch our water from the Merderet, the little stream that ran through the marshes, which always dried up in summer. At the Sheepfold, though, water was more of a problem; we often had to share the water in the trough for the cattle and horses that my parents were paid to look after. Whether we stayed at one house or the other depended on my parents' obligations; they needed both jobs to keep body and soul together.

My father's duties included checking the state of the tracks between Crossings 104 and 103. Unless the marshes were dry, he often used to punt his way along beside the tracks in a flat-bottomed boat – and sometimes he let us go with him. For years these little jaunts were the greatest adventure in my life, floating through the marshes in a little boat with my father as captain, Papa Maurice.

September 3rd, 1939

The day war was declared, the church bells were rung in Sainte-Mère-Eglise.

I'd never heard bells ringing that way before; I'll remember it as long as I live. I knew at once that it was some sort of alarm. I leant out of my bedroom window at the Sheepfold, staring transfixed at the church and its belltower.

The Amfreville bell responded immediately, followed by the bells of Fresville, Neuville-au-Plain and Chef-du-Pont. It was a strange, slow melody, even sadder than one of those autumn evenings when dusk is falling. To me, church bells are happy. Of course they do ring at funerals too – but those I'd learnt to recognize. No, this was no funeral. It was a new and menacing sound, a dismal tolling filled with storms and desolation over field and fen.

That day, Mama had left me – at the age of six and a half – in charge of my twelve-month-old baby brother Claude, who lay sleeping in his cot. As the bells began to ring, I was looking down at Mama from the bedroom window. She was wielding a sickle, doing her best to cut down the random tufts of thorny bushes that grew in the field. If a cow ate them, the thorns could do terrible damage in the stomach. Some people called them 'cursed thistles' but we knew them simply as 'cow-killers'.

Mama was in charge of both the large herd of beef cattle and the thirty acres of pasture in which the cattle grazed. She had more than enough to do, even without two small children to look after. My father managed to spend every penny he earned drinking with his mates. So, as usual, my mother was working. The ordinary work of an ordinary day. As for Papa Maurice, he was nowhere to be seen. But we knew what he'd be up to: downing his daily draught of rough cider or Calvados.

Mama had been up at the crack of dawn, as always. Before leaving for the Leroux dairy farm where she and another woman shared the task of milking some twenty cows, she had come and laid my baby brother in my arms. He was fast asleep and I'd hardly dared to breathe for fear of waking him.

Little Claude was not just my brother, he was also my protégé – and my refuge. He was the only person in the world I felt really at ease with, apart from Mama. I watched him sleeping, attentive to every breath, fearful yet impatient for him to wake up, so that I could see him open his eyes and gurgle.

When she had finished milking the cows, at about nine o'clock, Mama came back to the Sheepfold. Upstairs in the bedroom, she took Claude from me and started to breastfeed him while I went downstairs to light the fire for breakfast. Our breakfasts were very simple, usually consisting of two slices of bread from a huge loaf, toasted over the fire and dipped in hot milk. Breakfast over, it would be time for work: out into the fields for Mama, cleaning the house for me. My elder sister and brother, Denise and Francis, both had jobs at the Leroux farm, doing general chores during the summer holidays.

So today had begun just like any ordinary day. Outside, everything was still. As I gazed from the upstairs window, away to the left I could see the tall elms along the fence bordering the road. They cast almost no shadow: it was noon. To my right, beyond the line of trees marking the end of the field, were the marshes through which the railway ran. The marshes were still dry; winter was a long way off. I could see some cows and horses grazing there – not ours, I knew. I wondered if Papa Maurice was watching them too, leaning up against the gate at Level-Crossing 104, making sure that none of the animals strayed on to the tracks as a train approached. Or maybe he was strolling along the line, looking out for any rails that might have buckled in the heat.

All was peace and serenity. Nothing bad could happen.

So why were the bells still ringing? I glanced at the baby and saw he was still asleep, then ran downstairs and out of the house to find Mama. She straightened up as she saw me coming. I noticed the tears on her cheeks and flung myself into her arms.

'Mama! Mama! Why are the bells ringing?'

She held me tight. 'It's an alarm,' she said. 'They're telling us that war has been declared.'

4

War? In my mind, war was something that happened far away, in some corner of France where neither my mother nor I would ever go. 'War is when men go out and fight each other – kill each other,' she said. Then she added sadly: 'You'll find out soon enough what war is. We're going to get poorer and poorer, more and more unhappy. . .'

I pondered about this for a moment. I hadn't realized that we were unhappy. Life was hard sometimes, and I already knew what it was to work, for I had my own share of responsibilities and chores. But I saw no reason to be sad.

'Come on, Mama, let's go into the house and I'll make you a cup of coffee,' I smiled, doing my best to cheer her up.

'No, Geneviève, I can't stop now,' she told me. 'I must finish my work.'

'Oh Mama! The baby's been such a poppet today. . .'

I knew that would do the trick. The minute I mentioned little Claude, a smile lightened her face and she followed me back into the house.

We made the coffee, and while she sat there sipping it I settled myself on her lap.

'Don't be sad,' I urged her. 'Why don't you teach me a new song?'

For as long as I can remember, I have always loved singing. Sometimes I think I must have learned to sing even before I could talk. It was a pleasure that Mama had passed on to me; she used to teach me a new song every day, or at least a new verse to add to yesterday's song. She had a very pretty voice, and so did I, I'm told. We both derived endless delight from singing. I used to sing to myself all day long – in the house after Papa Maurice had left for the day, or on the road to market with Mama, or meeting my sister Denise on her way home from school. Once or twice I even caught myself breaking into song in the middle of lessons.

But that day, Mama could hardly bring herself to sing. Looking at me sadly, she asked, 'You really want me to teach you a new song – today of all days?'

Suddenly I remembered a story she'd once told me, about how King Louis XIII had put our country under the protection of the Holy Virgin. In time of danger, it was to Her we should pray. She couldn't refuse our prayers. And I knew there was a song about this.

'Teach me the one about the Virgin Mary and France,' I said.

'All right,' she agreed. 'But listen carefully. I'm only going to sing it once, then I must get back to work.'

5

Very softly she began to sing, with me repeating every line after her:

> *Holy Mary,*
> *Our sole salvation,*
> *Lend us your loving hand.*
> *Save our nation,*
> *Save our beloved land.*

Certain memories remain forever engraved in your mind. Nothing will ever erase my memory of that first day of war or of that song, the words so simple yet full of meaning, like a prayer.

Mama patted my cheek and smiled, then went back out to the field, leaving me alone again with baby Claude. But not for long.

Papa Maurice arrived home earlier than expected that evening. His cap askew, his eyes glazed, his expression even more ferocious than usual, he stumbled across the threshold, grasping at the door frame to steady himself.

I knew what this meant – time to make myself scarce. I edged towards the stairs, hoping to sneak up to the bedroom before he spotted me. Too late. He focused his eyes on me and bellowed:

'*Trying to hide, are you? Come here!*'

I had no choice but to obey. I knew what was in store for me. No one could protect me, not even Mama, who by now had returned from the field. Small and slight, she was no match for Papa Maurice.

'*Come here!*' he roared again.

Shaking, I walked over to him. The first slap caught me square in the face. Again, that huge hand – bigger than a washerwoman's paddle – struck me full force. A trickle of blood ran down from my lips. That was enough. As he brought his hand down a third time, I jerked my head away at the last instant, and his hand crashed against the corner of the massive oak cupboard just behind me.

He let out a howl of pain. Then he collapsed into a chair, nursing his hand, and launched into a diatribe – only partly coherent – about the evils of war. '*Madness!*' he thundered. '*Total madness! Ought to be a law against it!*'

I knew it was only a lull in the storm, so I sneaked quietly upstairs to my room. I would be safe there, for my father was scared stiff of the staircase. Even in his drunken stupor he seemed to sense how dangerous it would have been for him to climb those thirteen steps; he'd have fallen and cracked his skull in the attempt. So upstairs meant safety for me, at least until the next day.

A little later, Mama brought the baby up to me. Then she left for the Leroux farm to milk the cows again, as she always did each evening. As payment, she'd return home with three or four pints of fresh milk.

Night was falling. I thought back on the events of the day: the church bells spreading the dreadful news; my mother crying; the baby sleeping through it all; my father coming home drunk. These would be my memories of the first day of World War Two.

September 1939—June 1944

Jean Leroux was the most important man of the district. His farm, Noires Terres, was vast and imposing. I often used to go there with my mother, whom Monsieur Leroux and his wife Marguerite had known for many years, even before Mama married my father. They always found some work for her on the farm, and this was a godsend to us because they usually paid her in food rather than money. It was like the relationship between feudal lord and peasant in the Middle Ages – except, of course, that Mama worked voluntarily. And the sort of work that had to be done was pretty much the same as in medieval times. The grain, for example, had to be threshed by hand. Men and women alike would sit on the stone flags of the farm courtyard, each armed with a flail – an implement consisting of two pieces of wood, one long and one short, joined by leather thongs about four inches long – and all of them threshing the grain with steady rhythmic strokes. It was hard, laborious and tiring work, just as it had been for hundreds of years.

The Leroux farmhouse and its outhouses had been built in the form of a square around the courtyard. I remember wandering wide-eyed among the various buildings. You entered the courtyard through an archway between a cattle barn and some stables. To your right were more barns and storage sheds. Facing you across the courtyard was the farmhouse itself, only one storey high, but so vast it must have had ten or twelve rooms at least. I used to think how nice it would be to live in a house like that.

Back at the Sheepfold there was a big fireplace, built in such a way that we'd been able to install a wooden bench beneath the mantel, and little Claude and I used to sit in there on cold winter evenings. The

8

other side of the hearth was reserved for baby chicks born in the off-season, for we raised chickens and rabbits to supplement our needs. At the back of the fireplace there was a heavy hook that held the big pot in which my mother always kept soup simmering. One winter evening I'll never forget. I arrived home from school, frozen after the long walk, and sat down at my usual place by the fire. I was bending forward, warming my hands in front of the fire, when the hook supporting the soup pot suddenly came loose, and the whole pot of boiling soup spilt all over me.

I was so badly scalded I had to spend the rest of that winter in bed. A whole winter of endless days in the house alone, with only my little brother for company. To help the days pass, my mother gave me a doll, the first doll I ever had.

The doctor used to come twice a week to change my bandages. I dreaded his visits because it was a painful business having my dressings changed, and I could barely hold back the tears.

'If you cry,' the doctor would say, 'I'll take your doll away!'

He was no fool, that doctor. I had one toy, one real toy, a doll such as every little girl in the world dreams of having. And he knew I would never let him take it away.

So, when he leant over me to start removing my bandages, I would close my eyes and clench my teeth. Not a sound would escape my lips. That doll was my dream; pain was a part of life. If I wanted one, I would have to endure the other . . .

Meanwhile, we had more or less grown used to the presence of the Germans. Most of the fighting seemed to be far away, and the news of what was happening, brought to us by word of mouth, was vague and filled with rumours. Anyway, war was a serious matter, not for children's ears, so the subject was rarely discussed when we were around. And yet we knew more than the grown-ups realized. We knew that war was, as Papa Maurice had said, total madness, but also that it was very complicated. For instance, we saw that some Frenchmen, our own people, actually wore armbands bearing the swastika – indeed, they seemed proud to wear them. They worked for the Germans, and the ones we most often met had the job of patrolling the railway line. They used to invite themselves to lunch with us whenever they felt like it, and they ate all our best food; they seemed to think it was their due.

As for those other Frenchmen, the ones who continued to fight for our liberation, we didn't even know they existed. The Resistance? We'd never heard of it. But everyone had heard about a man called de Gaulle, the general who spoke on the wireless – we heard the grown-ups whispering about him. We didn't have a wireless in our house, of course; even if we could have afforded one, neither 104 nor the Sheepfold had electricity. All we could do was listen to the rumours and pray. Every night before we went to bed, we prayed for this man de Gaulle, we prayed for bombs to fall on Germany, we prayed for the soldiers who were dying all over the world, and most of all we prayed for victory.

But while we waited for victory to come, we still had to survive. Necessity is the mother of invention, they say, and I had learnt the truth of this before I'd reached the age of ten. Monsieur Leroux used to let us pick over the fields after the harvest was in, and in this way we managed to gather enough grain of one sort or another to feed our chickens and turkeys for the following winter. And I used to go to the farm every day after school, to pick two big baskets full of dandelions for our barnyard friends. In summer they could fend for themselves, scratching about in the fields around the Sheepfold.

Food for ourselves was another matter. Government rations could not meet even our basic needs; somehow we always had to supplement them. One summer's day I had the bright idea of going poaching. Little Claude was now big enough to come with me on my expeditions, so whenever I could find a free moment between chores, off we went, hand in hand, to explore the area around La Fière.

La Fière – 'The Proud' – what a grand name for such a tiny hamlet! There was only a handful of houses, which in winter stood a bare couple of inches above the water that inundated the surrounding swamps. People say, in fact, that the name La Fière came from a German or Anglo-Saxon word meaning 'ferry' and that it didn't mean 'proud' at all. Apparently one can trace its origins back to the Norman pirates of old. According to the records of the fiefdoms of Normandy, a certain Gauthier de Sainte-Mère-Eglise and Thomas de la Fière each held a knight's fiefdom under a grant from one Lord Lithaire. But that was all a long time ago, and there was nothing now to recall those days when the area was infested by fierce pirates and warlike knights. On the contrary: the utter peace, the wildfowl and other birds, the serenity of the countryside made La Fière a tiny corner of paradise. And, in 1943, it was our favourite spot for explorations.

On one particular day, our foray took us to a small river, the

Merderet, that had all but dried up; in some places, all that was left of the stream was a series of muddy pools. Yet it was a real gold mine, this stream, for it was swarming with eels. Delicious! I knew at least three ways of preparing eels: fried in the pan, smoked in the fireplace (in which case you eat them guts and all) or salted. My mouth already watering, I began to think about how to catch them.

My father's boat happened to be moored nearby and I knew he kept a pail in it, to bail out the water after it had rained. That pail was just what we needed to catch the eels. I scooped the pail into the stream, and up it came, brimful of the squirming eels.

That was the easy part. Now we had to carry our booty home. The pail was heavy, the river banks were steep and high. With every step we sank waist-high in the mud. But abandoning our treasure was out of the question. Luckily a willow tree bent down and lent us a helping hand so that we could scramble up on to firmer ground; but as for the pail, there was no way we could hoist it out of the mud without sinking back in ourselves. So we covered it with some large leaves from one of the wild plants that grew in profusion at the edge of the swamp; its sap is a magic balm against the sting of nettles. With the leaves protecting them, the eels would not suffer from the hot sun. Then, covered from head to foot in that foul-smelling mud, we ran home to the Sheepfold.

Seeing us arrive – filthy, out of breath and stinking to high heaven – my mother let out a shriek of alarm. But while she washed us down, combed our hair and dressed us in clean clothes, I told her of our miraculous discovery. At first she refused to believe me; to her it sounded too good to be true – or honest. But we finally persuaded her to come and see for herself. She saw, and was convinced. Effortlessly she lifted the pailful of eels from the mud and carried it home. The rest of that afternoon she spent cleaning and cooking or salting the manna that had come to us, not from heaven above but from the muddy waters below.

When we'd exhausted our provision of eels, I went back to the river and explored other pools near the one where I'd made the initial discovery. But miracles only happen once. The eels had gone. Still, there were other fish in the pools . . . I sat in Papa Maurice's boat considering how I could possibly get those fish out of the water and into my mother's frying pan, and I said a little prayer.

God must have been listening and smiling that day, up there on His throne, for He wasted no time in producing a solution to the problem. It wasn't quite the solution I'd hoped for, but it would do.

I had discovered how to open the padlock that kept my father's boat secured to a willow tree beside the stream. So now I could borrow the boat for fishing trips without permission. No one would have to know.

I set off to explore a section of the Merderet that I'd never visited before. For a while I used the heavy pole to punt the boat along, but it was exhausting work and I soon resorted to pulling myself forward by grabbing at the tall reeds at the river's edge. My arms were growing more and more weary when suddenly it happened: another miracle! Just under the surface of the water, cleverly concealed by some poacher anxious to add to his own larder, lay several reed fish traps. And the traps were full!

The Merderet is so situated that from almost any spot on it you can see in all directions for miles around. No one, not a soul in sight. The stream was calm, the sun shining brightly. The only sounds I could hear were birdsong and the slap of water against the hull of my boat. I leaned over, plunged my arm into the water and came up with two traps, whose contents I tipped nonchalantly into the bottom of the boat. Lots of good lunches and dinners coming up! I managed to get the boat back to its mooring place, tied it up and returned home with my arms literally filled with fish and eels, which I proudly dumped on the kitchen table.

It was only then that the awful thought crossed my mind. What if those traps had been laid by Papa Maurice himself? What if he ever caught me poaching his fish in his boat? I knew what he would do: he'd kill me on the spot.

One night soon afterwards I asked him several discreet questions about fish traps. When he had not been drinking, Papa Maurice acted more or less normally. He was kind and thoughtful towards everyone – everyone except me, that is, though he only resorted to violence when he was drunk. He answered my questions, and I soon learned that the traps had not been laid by him. So now I could poach to my heart's content.

From that day on, Mama was able to add fish to our menu twice a week. I had become an honest-to-God little poacher. Mama never guessed how I came by the fish, and she very wisely refrained from asking; the pleasure of seeing food arrive on the table was enough for her. As for Papa Maurice, he never said a thing – not even a grunt or a grumble in his moustache. I suppose he simply thought his wife was managing especially well.

My little game went on for several months. As a precautionary measure, whenever I poached from the poacher's traps, I was careful to take the fish from only every third or fourth trap. That way, I thought, I stood a better chance of remaining undetected. There were fifteen traps in all. One more, one less: what did it matter? The poacher who was unwittingly feeding our family would never notice; even if he did, he still had plenty of fish and eels left for himself.

But poachers are by nature an observant breed. Although the poacher never actually caught me red-handed, he did notice some vestiges of what looked like his traps in the bottom of Papa Maurice's boat. And one day he hid among the reeds and waited, thinking to surprise my father. Instead he saw me, and it was he who got the surprise.

My fellow poacher's name was André Cuquemelle; he lived with his wife and two sons on the other side of La Fière. When he caught me going to the boat, he gave me a thorough spanking. Then, more amused than angry, he gave me a lecture to boot.

'Silly little so-and-so!' he scolded. 'Don't you realize you could have drowned?' He pointed out all the risks I had taken in my poaching expeditions. 'I don't care how clever you are,' he added, 'you can't even handle the pole to punt the boat along!' And he made me promise never to go poaching again – at least, not on that part of the river.

No more fish, no more eels. What could I poach now, I wondered. Then the answer came to me: rabbits. Wild rabbits cost nothing and tasted just as good as our tame ones. I asked my older brother Francis to make me some rabbit snares and show me how to lay them. Then, every day on my way to school, I would check the hedges where I'd hidden my snares. But rabbits, it seemed, were smarter than eels: my snares lay empty for weeks. Then one day I discovered a rabbit caught by the neck in one of the snares.

My joy was short-lived, however. I took the rabbit that I had killed in my arms. He was beautiful, his coat was soft and silky, and he was dead. I burst into tears. Still sobbing, I took him home and laid him on the kitchen table. Mama took me on her lap and did her best to console me, but nothing she said could help. With all the wisdom of my ten years, I knew in my heart that I was a criminal. And I've never, since that day, been able to take an animal's life.

I was nearly ten years old when I discovered the French language – and I fell in love with it. It was a language I'd hardly known when I started school, since at home we spoke the local patois. Another of my

13

favourite subjects at school was history. I used to daydream sometimes about the strange quirk of fate that had, through a misalliance,
made me the child of a poor family. My paternal grandfather had been
of a very old, influential and wealthy family. Unfortunately for him,
however, he fell in love with one of the servant girls, and he decided to
marry her. His father tried to dissuade him, threatening to disinherit
him if he persisted. But my grandfather was adamant; the marriage
went ahead, and his father not only disinherited him but refused ever
to lay eyes on him again. My grandfather and grandmother lived in
great poverty, for all his father's friends also refused to help him in any
way, or even give him a job. My grandmother shared his fate bravely
and, despite all their financial difficulties, they still managed to raise a
large brood of children. My father was their last child, their 'baby'. By
the time he came along, their meagre resources were reduced to
almost nothing. They were so poor they could not even buy him a pair
of wooden clogs, and he could never go to school. To this day he still
cannot read or write. Yet in his own way, Papa Maurice is a kind of
genius. He has a remarkable memory; he taught himself how to count,
and he can do sums in his head faster than anyone I've ever met.
Whenever they put him to the test, he can beat anyone in the region.

My teacher at school was Mademoiselle Burnouf. A confirmed
spinster, she was thin and kind, and she rarely if ever raised her voice,
even when provoked. She was affectionate and sympathetic, and
when – as so often happened – my mind wandered away from the
blackboard and classroom into other wonderful worlds, she would
gently bring me back to earth.

I had another friend, too, called Madame Mantey. She was much
older than Mademoiselle Burnouf, but just as nice. I met her by
chance one day – in a cemetery, of all places.

Each morning when I went to school, I took my lunch with me, and
I used to scoff it as fast as I could in the school yard. All the other
children either went home for lunch or ate with one of the local
people, under an arrangement made so that children who lived in the
more distant villages could profit from a hot lunch. Like me, many
children lived several miles from the school. But I had always refused
this solution, preferring my freedom and solitude to the comfort of a
proper meal. So I always had two hours to myself at lunchtime. I used
to wander through the streets of Sainte-Mère-Eglise, virtually
deserted at that hour. I loved the village's quiet charm. My favourite
building was the church, which had been built in the twelfth or

thirteenth century and had managed to last through wars and troubles without a scratch.

In the cemetery one day I found a tombstone of pink marble topped with an almost life-size angel. According to the inscription, it marked the grave of a little girl called Geneviève, like me. I sat on the grass beside the grave and thought how lucky she was to be dead. No one could hurt her or make her suffer any more. The night before this, my father had taken his whip to me, and although I usually took his beatings in my stride, I was still very sore and feeling rather sorry for myself.

I didn't hear the old lady approaching, and I jumped when she touched my shoulder. She didn't ask me any questions, but seemed to sense how miserable I was, for she simply sat down beside me and began to talk, softly and slowly, about everything and nothing. After a while I realized it must be time to return to school, and I told the old lady that I had to go. She asked me if I would walk with her back to her house, which was quite near the school. She was old, very old; and worn out by the walk, at one point she rested her hand on my shoulder. I gave a cry of pain.

The old lady stopped. 'What's the matter, child?'

I told her that I'd hurt my shoulder.

'Is it very bad?'

'No, not really.'

But she was not convinced. She wanted to take a look at it, she said, and asked me to go into the house with her.

'I can't, Madame,' I told her. 'I'll be late for school and Mademoiselle Burnouf will be cross with me.'

'Don't worry about that,' the old lady said. 'I'll go back with you and explain to your teacher.'

So I followed her into the kitchen, where she asked me to take off my jumper, blouse and vest. What she found left her open-mouthed. My torso and ribcage were black and blue, and my father's whip had left ugly red welts across my upper body. Two wounds, one on my shoulder and the other on my hip, were open and festering.

Madame Mantey – she'd told me her name by this stage – gently cleaned the wounds and bandaged them. She seemed to know what she was doing; she had been married to a doctor, she said, who had died many years before. Then she asked who had been beating me.

I hesitated for a moment, then it all came pouring out. How I had arrived home late the previous night. How Papa Maurice had asked

15

Mademoiselle to note in my book the exact time I left school – he allowed me half an hour to get home, not a minute more. How it had been my own absentmindedness that had let me down yesterday; I had been about halfway home when I realized I'd forgotten to buy the bread, so I had to turn and go back to the village, though even as I did so I knew I'd never make it home in time and that Papa Maurice would be waiting to punish me. Depending on how late I was, he inflicted one of two punishments on me, both of his own devising. Generally he made me kneel down on two pieces of irregularly shaped flintstone and hold my arms straight out in front of me. Then he would place a brick in each of my hands, and as soon as the weight of the bricks made me lower my tired arms, he would take up his bull whip and thrash me across the back, as though I were a galley slave. He always made me bare my back before he beat me, which was how I came to get all the scars and welts.

Madame Mantey listened in silence, her head lowered. When she raised her eyes, I could see tears spilling down her cheeks.

'Listen,' she said, 'I'm going to teach you to pray in a very special way. . .'

I believe that her way of praying was responsible for the fact that I was never punished like that again – except once, when I'd forgotten to do it properly.

Madame Mantey accompanied me back to school, which was just across the street. Mademoiselle Burnouf met us at the door. She told me to go in and sit down quietly, then she closed the schoolhouse door behind me and I couldn't hear what my new friend said to her. But from that day on, Mademoiselle Burnouf was even more attentive and patient with me than before. I'm sure that old Madame Mantey must have repeated to her what I'd said about my unhappy home life with Papa Maurice; but Mademoiselle Burnouf never mentioned it, and I was glad of her discretion. She often invited me to have lunch with her, in winter filling me with a good hot soup or a special dessert she'd made herself. She never had to ask me twice. We never had such luxuries at home. I tried to show my gratitude to her by working even harder in French lessons, and forced myself not to daydream in class.

Papa Maurice wasn't always so brutal with me. I remember one evening when I had climbed up the tall elm tree near our house, postponing as long as possible the time when I'd have to go to bed. Papa Maurice passed underneath the tree, and I called down to him:

'Hey, Papa – bet you're too old to climb up here!'

16

To my astonishment, he promptly clambered up the tree to join me, displaying an agility I'd never thought him capable of.

'What are you doing up here all alone in the dark?' he asked.

'Waiting for the stars to come out,' I told him. For the stars always fascinated me; I used to spend hours studying them.

'Did you know they've all got names?' Papa said.

I thought he was joking. There were so many stars; how could they all have names?

'Well, maybe not all of them,' he admitted; 'but some of them do. Look – see that bright one over there? That's the North Star. Sailors use it to navigate by. And there, you see those stars below the North Star? That's the Big Dipper. And over there is the Little Dipper. . .'

'Is there a star called Geneviève?' I asked him in all seriousness.

'I don't think so,' he said, equally seriously.

But in the gloom I suddenly caught the smile that crossed his face, and he put his arm round my shoulders, drawing me close. It was the first tenderness he had ever shown me. Timidly I said as much.

His reply was puzzling – and what's more, he said it in French, rather than in the patois we normally used; I'd never heard him speak French before.

'You know, child,' he said, 'between you and me, nothing will ever be possible. I am close to you solely to add to your burden.'

I didn't understand; what burden was he talking about? But something in what he said somehow touched my heart. Here we were, snuggled together on our unstable perch at the top of this great elm, watching the stars, father and daughter . . . I shivered. He mistook my emotion for cold, and told me to get back down the tree.

'I'm not cold,' I protested, wanting to prolong that magical moment.

'*Down!*' he ordered.

I got down.

Madame Mantey's conversation with my teacher certainly led to an improvement in my life. Before I left school each afternoon, Mademoiselle would check my basket to make sure I hadn't forgotten anything, and she would go over the list of errands I was to run. And only after all that would she write down the time of my departure. As a result, I never again got beaten for forgetting my errands or for arriving home late.

Not that my life turned into a bed of roses overnight. When he had been drinking too much, Papa Maurice's imagination knew no bounds. He found many another excuse to punish me. But I had two new friends now: my schoolteacher and Madame Mantey. I felt less lonely than before.

It wasn't long after this episode that we moved from the Sheepfold back to 104. As always, we moved from one house to the other by boat. It was the easiest way. Both houses were furnished with all the basics, so we only had to transport the smaller items like household utensils and clothing. We piled everything into a barrow and wheeled it down to the bank of the Merderet, which ran just beyond the line of trees marking the northern border of the Sheepfold property. When we had loaded everything into the boat, Papa Maurice would punt it upstream for about half a mile, to a spot only two hundred yards from 104. One of us children would go with him to help him unload. Then we would reload the wheelbarrow and make the final stage of our journey to 104. The whole move took less than a day; by evening we would be settled into our new quarters and new routine.

Only a few days after we had moved back to 104, in the late summer of 1943, the Germans arrived for a visit. We'd seen plenty of German soldiers passing on the troop and munitions trains, but these Germans arrived by plane. The handsome metal bird swooped down out of the bright blue sky and landed only a few yards from our house. I fell madly in love for the first time in my life – not with the Germans but with the glorious machine that had brought them. I caressed its gleaming wings and fuselage. One day, I promised myself, I too would fly among the clouds. I who had watched the birds dip and soar in joyous freedom would be jealous of their powers no more.

But the plane had not landed there to bring pleasure to a ten-year-old peasant girl. I watched the haughty Germans, resplendent in their impeccable uniforms and highly polished boots, emerge one by one from the plane. They didn't strike me as particularly friendly. But then why should they be? What did we represent to these fair-haired, grey-eyed men? We were poor French peasants, whose lives were spent in back-breaking work, eking out a bare existence from the land, whose main duty was to raise and lower the level-crossing gate as trains filled with soldiers sped past. We were nothing more than slaves, ants in a conquered ant-hill.

I watched my father respond to their questions, and was surprised at how polite and deferential he was. I'd never seen him so friendly and courteous. Anyone would have thought he was a fawning milksop – or worse, a coward, anxious to save his skin by collaborating with the Germans.

But I knew Papa better than that. For all his faults, he was no coward. In fact, he was an old bandit really; no one ever got the better of him. He hated the Germans. But he also knew that he was playing David to their arrogant Goliath, and that in such an unequal contest the only weapons were guile and cunning. His deference was a trap, and the Germans fell right into it.

One of the German officers pointed out towards the swamps. 'We're going to build an airfield here,' he announced.

One could understand why this wide flat plain struck the German engineers as a good place for an airfield. Papa Maurice knew they were quite right in their assessment. He squinted and nodded, as though he completely agreed.

"I know these swamps like the back of my hand,' he told the man. 'I'd be happy to take you through them, if you like.'

The German officer accepted his offer. Whereupon Papa earnestly set about explaining that, for six months out of the year, the swamps were flooded.

'Terrible, these floods,' he said sadly, shaking his head as though remembering the annual catastrophe. 'And the worst of it is that we can't do a thing about it. Not a damn thing. . .'

He lied with amazing calm. He was risking his skin, and he knew it. In winter the Merderet did indeed overflow its banks, but no one ever tried to stop it. On the contrary, when it was high tide, the brackish water of the Douve, into which the Merderet flowed, brought alluvial soil and sometimes kelp that enriched the surrounding pastures. Yet if anyone wanted to prevent the flooding, there was a simple enough remedy: dredge the river bed and build up the banks. But Papa omitted to mention this. He took the Germans on a tour of the area, leading them to all the very wettest places. Every so often he would stop and dig a hole, and of course the hole would immediately fill with water.

The Germans wanted to see everything: the Big Swamp, near the Château d'Amfreville and Fresville; the Little Swamp, near La Fière; the higher ground around the Sheepfold. And, with the same servile courtesy, Papa Maurice led them into all the muddiest places he could find. In no time at all, the Germans were spattered with mud up to their epaulettes, and their gleaming boots were caked with dirt. And this was in high summer . . .

But the Germans refused to admit defeat. For a whole week they took soil samples from various spots in the area and sent them away for analysis. Papa Maurice was with them from dawn to dusk, constantly offering his help, constantly sabotaging their efforts. Whenever they decided to take a sample, he would smile and say: 'Allow me. You don't want to get your uniform all dirty.' And inevitably they would let him do it for them.

Afterwards Papa would offer to wipe down the sample bottles, and he'd take them back to the kitchen of 104, where he'd get my mother to add a little water to each of the samples. Then he'd take the doctored bottles out to the waiting plane.

Papa's little game paid off. The Germans finally dropped their plans to build an airfield. But they reckoned the Allies might get the same idea, so they decided the swamps had to be rendered useless. Field-Marshal Rommel, in charge of German defences against a possible Allied invasion, gave the order to flood both the Big and Little Swamps, and all the people who lived in those areas were hastily moved out. The Germans then closed the floodgates that controlled the flow of the Merderet. These gates, situated beneath all the bridges over the river, were normally never closed except in years of severe drought. But in the summer of 1943, by order of Field-Marshal Rommel, the countryside around us was changed almost overnight. By the end of a week, the swamps were completely inundated. The water lapped at our cellar door; it was as if the house now stood in the middle of a peaceful grey lake. Only the railway line stood above the shimmering water, like a causeway across the sea.

We asked the Germans why they had flooded the area.

'To prevent the Allies from landing,' they answered.

Which meant that the Germans were afraid of an Allied landing. And that in turn meant that the Allies were very probably planning an invasion. The logic was irrefutable, and cheering. Now there was reason to hope again.

Winter settled in. I still went to school every day, but now I had to go all the way by a path alongside the railway tracks. Our headmaster, Monsieur Leblond, made us practise air-raid drill. He would take us out of the schoolhouse and lead us along back roads towards La Fière, and whenever he blew his whistle we all had to dive into the ditches beside the road. The ditches were full of stinging nettles but Monsieur Leblond assured us that a few nettle stings were infinitely preferable to a single piece of shrapnel.

As for my friend Madame Mantey, she had left Sainte-Mère-Eglise. Because of her age and growing infirmity, she could no longer look after herself properly, and so she had moved north to spend the rest of her days with her children. I often thought of her, and the kindness she had shown me. But I was never to see her again.

Winter slowly gave way to spring. On April 9th, 1944, I celebrated my eleventh birthday. I was a big girl now, almost a grown-up, and I felt closer than ever to my mother, who still worked day and night with never a complaint to provide for her family. I felt I had said goodbye to my childhood, and I tried harder than ever to be less of a dreamer and more of a help to my mother.

In this part of the world, children were too poor to enjoy the luxury of adolescence. We passed directly from childhood to the world of adults. The event that marked the transition was First Communion, and it was indeed a major event in our lives. Father Roulland, the priest of Sainte-Mère-Eglise, had set June 25th as the date of our First Communion. Only two months for me to prepare. I studied my catechism every day, with the help of my mother, who added her own touches to the memorizing sessions. Be slow to judge others, but quick to judge yourself. Kindness is the highest virtue. Even Papa Maurice deserved our kindness and understanding, she told me.

'Don't believe everything people tell you,' she used to say, 'even about those who drink too much. People poke fun at them, but they shouldn't. Alcoholics aren't criminals, they're sick. They shouldn't be blamed or scolded, they should be helped.'

I didn't hate Papa Maurice. I've never hated anyone. On the contrary, I tried hard to understand him. But I never did work out why he disliked me so much. To me he was a puzzle, sometimes terrifying, sometimes admirable, especially when he managed to outwit those who thought they were cleverer than him.

On Sunday, June 4th, Father Roulland reminded his parishioners to buy their candles for First Communion. The candles were on sale at Mademoiselle Lepresvost's, and the biggest and prettiest ones were prominently displayed in her window. She had all kinds and sizes of candles, something to suit everyone. But some people were so poor they couldn't even afford her cheapest candle. And as for us, it was out of the question; we would just have to rely on charity.

There is a tradition, still practised in some places, that involves the

21

children of poor families visiting local landowners to ask for money to buy their candles. In fact, there used to be several times of the year when this sort of soliciting went on. On January 1st you could go to the farms and wish the farmowner and his family a Happy New Year, and you would be given a coin or two in exchange; and on Shrove Tuesday all the children used to go begging for eggs. And then there was the custom of knocking at doors and asking for money for candles. The egg-begging practice is the only one that still continues in our area today; the other customs have died out. And a good thing too, in my opinion. But in those days I'd never have got my candle if I hadn't gone round begging for money. Poor as we were, we simply had no alternative. We had to display our poverty on the streets; all the world would know we were too poor to buy a candle. I used to get furious about this. The Church seemed unconcerned; the Church of Christ, who loved the poor more than anyone, allowed us to parade our shame in the streets, begging for the right to be allowed to receive one of its sacraments. Every time I thought about it I'd burst into tears.

My mother did her best to comfort me. 'It will teach you humility,' she said. 'Think of it as a penance you're offering our Lord.'

But I kept thinking how this penance could have been avoided with a little bit of organization on the part of Father Roulland. And as for humility, I already knew what that was. Still, there was nothing I could do about it, so I just had to accept the situation.

That Sunday night, on my way home from vespers with my mother, I suddenly started to sing at the top of my voice. It was a song that I'd heard other people singing, a new song that people hummed or sang under their breath. It was a sort of prayer, but a profane one, a prayer to the English:

> *When English planes fly overhead*
> *Our hearts leap up with joy, not dread.*
> *Fly on, fly on, night after night -*
> *Our hearts go with you on your flight!*

I thought Mama was going to have a heart attack.

'Shh! Shh! For heaven's sake be quiet, child! Do you want us all to be shot?'

I laughed. 'Why? There's nothing to be afraid of. There aren't any Germans in the swamps.'

'Never mind that,' Mama said fiercely. 'I don't want you going

22

around singing that song. You're so dreamy you might start singing it on your way to school one day, just as a German patrol is passing.'

But I couldn't go to school the next day, I reminded her. I had to go begging for my candle.

'Tomorrow morning I have to do the washing,' she told me, 'but in the afternoon I can come with you. We'll leave right after lunch.'

Where should we go, I asked her.

Over towards Pont-l'Abbé, she said; she knew some farmers out that way and she thought they would be willing to help us. And then she added, 'It won't be so bad then. No one from round here will know you've gone begging.'

I flung my arms round her and kissed her. When we got home she began to pluck an old chicken, too old to lay any more. Our food for days to come, poor old hen. Or so we thought.

Monday, June 5th, 1944

It was cold out. It wasn't raining, but threatening clouds covered the sky. You'd have thought it was All Saints' Day rather than two weeks from Midsummer. I was helping my mother do the laundry. But it didn't take long to fill up the two big wash tubs; we had a good pump. And after that I found myself at a loose end.

I decided to go egg-hunting. This was something I'd thought up myself. Since the beginning of the war, the wildfowl and game of the swamps were no longer hunted. The German and French authorities had confiscated the peasants' guns, including their hunting rifles. Officially, that is. In fact, there was many a crafty peasant who had hidden his gun under the mattress or in the woodshed, waiting for better days when he could use it again. Better days were surely coming. But for the time being, it wasn't worth wasting good bullets on small game when there was a risk you might be shot yourself if you were discovered. So the wildfowl had learnt to relax. As long as men went on killing each other, the ducks and moorhens and teal were safe. And as a result, the riverside bushes and reeds were full of nests – and the nests were full of eggs.

I had a special egg-hunting routine. First I would dress myself in a bathing suit and put on a pair of good stout shoes. Then I'd head for the river with my basket. I'd wade into the water carefully and search the reeds and bushes along the banks. But even when they are covered by a foot or two of water, brambles can still prick your legs, and those bushes with black thorns are worse: if they prick you, they can give you sores or even an abscess. So I used to keep a very wary eye out for them on my egg-hunts.

'You'll catch your death of cold,' Mama warned me this particular morning, seeing me prepare to go off on my egg-hunt.

I told her I'd take a coat to wrap round me when I came out of the water, but she wasn't reassured.

'I don't want to lose my little Geneviève,' she smiled, and put some hot milk into a flask to take with me. Then she waved me off with the reminder to make sure the eggs were fresh.

She was right. The week before I had come home with a basketful of eggs that were on the point of hatching. Our omelette was on the thin side that day. She had told me what to do in future: I should take one egg from each nest and break it open. If it was fresh, then *allez-oop!* All the eggs from that nest could go into my basket. If it wasn't, then I shouldn't take any. One egg missing from the nest would not prevent the rest from hatching.

I usually managed to collect between sixty and a hundred eggs on each expedition. And since I went egg-hunting two half days a week, we always had a plentiful supply. With the numbers of wildfowl nesting in the area, I never ran out of new nests to poach from.

It really was bitterly cold that morning, and the water felt icy. I left my coat and the flask of milk on the bank, and slowly eased myself into the water, until it came up to my chest. In a strange way, I rather enjoyed being alone there in the water, particularly with that flask of hot milk waiting to warm me up afterwards.

Despite the abundance of nests, it always took me several hours of searching and many trips back and forth before my basket was full. The eggs were so small, that was the trouble. At one stage, I came upon a nest just as the baby moorhens were pecking their way out of their shells. I stood and watched as the chicks emerged from the eggs, tiny balls of black fluff that could swim within minutes of being born. It filled me with awe to realize that life went on even as war and anguish and terror filled the world. And I said a quiet prayer asking for forgiveness for having to keep some of those chicks from being born.

I've always loved birds. Sometimes I even think that they understand me, that I can communicate with them.

I remember once when I was returning by boat from the Sheepfold. I was about halfway across the Little Swamp when something suddenly struck me hard in the chest, knocking me backwards. I'd been so busy manoeuvring the heavy punt pole that I hadn't seen whatever it was that hit me. I fell back on to the pile of wood I'd been collecting, and when I tried to sit up, I felt a sharp pain in my chest, so

25

acute that I couldn't help crying. When I'd cried myself out and my breathing was a bit easier, I looked around to see what had struck me.

At the far end of the boat lay a duck – that's what had hit me. I was sure he was dead. Moving gingerly down the boat, I picked him up; he'd obviously been knocked out by the collision. Almost automatically I started massaging his chest, as though applying artificial respiration. Much to my surprise, after a few moments he opened his eyes. I set him down on the pile of wood, watching him to make sure he was all right. The duck stared back at me, cocking his head from side to side as if trying to get a better view of me.

He looked so comical that I burst out laughing.

'I tell you, Mister Duck,' I said, 'you're going to be in trouble for not following the rules of the sky. You're not supposed to fly into people, you know. I'm going to fly myself one day, so I know what I'm talking about. Aren't you ashamed of yourself, making a little girl cry like that?'

The duck, a splendid adult ringneck, then did an astonishing thing. He edged across the pile of wood, clambered on to my lap and then up into my arms until he lay against my chest, and he rested his bill against my neck. His feathers against my cheek felt like a gentle caress. We stayed there without moving for several minutes: a strange sight for anyone who looked out across the swamp and saw us. The marsh waters shimmered in the sunlight; clouds drifted lazily overhead; the air vibrated soft and luminous in the warmth of early morning. The first day of the world could not have been more beautiful.

I suddenly felt so overwhelmed with joy that – as usual – I began to sing. The duck didn't stir. I could feel the rapid beating of his heart against my own.

When I'd finished my song I took him in my hands and told him what a fortunate duck he was; any other duck would have ended up in my mother's pot.

'But I've got to go now,' I told him. 'And you'd better get back to your family too. Next time I'm here I'll call out for you – "Mister Duck!" I'll cry, and I hope you'll come and see me.'

Again the duck cocked his head to left and right, as though he understood every word I was saying. Then I stroked his soft feathers one last time and sent him on his way.

A few days later, retracing my route in the opposite direction, I did indeed call out to my duck, never expecting to see him. He arrived within a matter of seconds: not just him, but his whole family too. A whole flock of ducks and ducklings settled on the water around my boat. Only Mister Duck himself was bold enough to venture on board. Without being asked, he came over and once more sat on my lap, and responded to my petting with apparent pleasure. Which of us was the more delighted I'd be hard put to say.

From that day on I was adopted. Whenever I crossed the swamp on any mission, I always called out to 'my' birds. At first only the ducks responded; but, little by little, other birds joined them – moorhens, teal, other waterfowl whose names I didn't know. They even escorted me when I disembarked and walked up the hill to the Sheepfold. I had taken to bringing a supply of grain with me – borrowed from the chicken coop at the Sheepfold – and this I distributed to my newfound friends. Each time they came to my call, I felt a renewed sense of delight and exhilaration. Yet I still felt guilty, as though by continuing my egg-hunts I was betraying their trust in me. Still, I had a good excuse; we were so often hungry, whereas they hatched three or four broods a year, and there was always plenty of food for them.

Such were the thoughts that were going through my mind that morning in early June as I filled my basket with eggs. When I got home, Mama massaged me briskly with a concoction that was part Calvados and part eau-de-cologne, in which she steeped a plant that looked to me just like a stinging nettle. Within minutes my chilled body was warm as toast, and this delicious sensation lasted for several hours.

I told little Claude about the birth of the baby moorhens, and he laughed and clapped his hands as I described how the little downy balls of fluff had gone swimming off down the stream. I often took Claude with me on my egg-hunts, but it had been too cold that morning. Actually it was he who had made the decision:

'Too cold for little boys!' he had told me.

After a hasty lunch, Mama and I set off on our mission to get money for my candle. She fastened a basket to the handlebars of her bicycle, so that we could gather food on the way for our rabbits. Since there were two of us and only one bicycle, we took turns pushing it, the way we did on market days at Sainte-Mère-Eglise.

Passing La Fière, we headed towards Pont-l'Abbé-Picauville. We reached a place called La Patte d'Oie de Cauquigny, where we paused for a moment. I looked back towards our house. It seemed so small

27

from there, so solitary, standing above the watery marshes in the light mist with only the railway line for company. I've always loved mist and fog; it seems to fit in with my dreamy nature.

Mama called me back to the real world. 'Come on, child, we don't have all day.' But she must have guessed what I'd been thinking about, for she added: 'It won't be so dreadful, asking for money to buy a candle. If you like, I'll come up to the farms with you and ask for you.'

So my heart was lighter as we set off again. We'd already covered two or three miles, but we still had a long way to go. Meanwhile our basket was slowly filling up. As she bent down to pick some dandelions by a ditch, Mama suddenly exclaimed aloud.

'Look, Geneviève!'

I scrambled down into the ditch to see what she was pointing at: a fat black cable.

'Telephone wires,' she said. 'If I really thought that the invasion everyone's talking about were coming, I'd cut that cable. Then the Germans in Sainte-Mère would be cut off from their friends in Pont-l'Abbé – I bet that would cause them no end of trouble.'

'Do you think the Allies will come?' I asked her.

She looked at me strangely for a moment, then said: 'I don't know why, Geneviève, but in my bones I feel they *will* be coming. And very soon too.'

We'd been hearing talk about an Allied invasion for so long that we didn't know whether to believe it any more. But as we moved off again Mama was speculating not about whether they would come but where. Cherbourg was her guess. It was a big port. But lots of Germans were stationed there, so if that's where the Allies chose to come, then there would be a terrible bloody fight.

We arrived at the first farm. As she had promised, Mama came with me up to the door of the farmhouse and explained why we had come. The farmer's wife was very generous; the sum she gave me was one third of the price of the biggest candle in Mademoiselle Lepresvost's shop window. And as she pressed the money into my hand she said:

'God pays special attention to the prayers of children. I have a son who's in prison in Germany. When you go to your First Communion, don't forget him in your prayers. That way he'll come home safe.'

I promised her I wouldn't forget, and as she thanked me I saw the tears in her eyes. I understood then that war was a special sorrow for mothers – mothers of all countries, who have to sit at home and wait

28

for their sons to come home . . .

The second farm my mother took me to was huge; the farmhouse itself looked much like Monsieur Leroux's house, except that it was less isolated, only a stone's throw from the road between Sainte-Mère-Eglise and Pont-l'Abbé.

The lady who answered the door had known Mama for a long time, and she invited us in for a bowl of steaming coffee and a big hunk of toasted bread from one of those huge twelve-pound loaves known as 'tourtes'. The pretty young girl who waited on us, I decided, must be the lady's granddaughter.

After one more farm, we had enough money for me to buy the largest candle in Mademoiselle Lepresvost's shop, and Mama commented, with a twinkle in her eye, that I seemed a lot bouncier as we began to make our way home. Poor Mama: she never understood how shy I was, no matter how hard I tried to overcome it.

On the return journey, Mama kept eyeing that telephone cable, which sometimes lay openly on the grass verge.

'I'll never forgive myself for not bringing the wire-cutters,' she muttered. 'It would be so easy to cut that cable. . .'

I suggested we could go to one of the nearby houses and borrow some.

'The Germans would shoot us on the spot if they caught us,' she said.

'I'm not afraid,' I declared. 'Come on, Mama – let's do it! You're always saying we should follow our impulses! Oh, do let's! I'll go and ask at that house over there. All right?'

She nodded, and off I ran. An old lady answered the door and asked what I wanted.

I blushed and stammered a bit, then said in a rush of words: 'Well, you see, I-I've broken some spokes on my bicycle wheel – and if I could cut them away it'd help me get home faster. You wouldn't have something I could cut them with, would you? A pair of wire-cutters, perhaps? I'll bring them right back – my bike's just out there on the road, not far away.'

The old lady looked at me strangely, as though she didn't know whether to believe me or not. Then she said, 'I don't know if I've got any wire-cutters. It's been so long since I've used any. Come on in; we'll go down to the cellar and have a look.'

We had to cross a wide courtyard filled with weeds, but it was slow going because the old lady was not very steady on her feet.

29

'You're not from round here, are you?' she said. 'What brings you to this part of the world?'

'I'm going to have my First Communion at Sainte-Mère-Eglise,' I told her, 'and I've been visiting some farms to ask for money so that I can buy my candle.'

'Why didn't you come and ask me?' she asked. 'I would have been glad to give you something towards your candle.'

'Thank you, Madame,' I said, 'but my mother told me only to go to the big farms.'

By now we had reached the cellar. There were all sorts of tools lying about, most of them as old as she was. Hanging on the wall I spotted a large pair of wire-cutters, the kind that farmers use when they're mending fences.

I pointed to them. 'That's just what I need – that pair of wire-cutters,' I told her.

'Then help yourself, child,' said the old lady.

'I'll bring them right back,' I promised again, and dashed off to where Mama was waiting on the road.

Even if she was curious as to why I really wanted those wire-cutters, the old lady had such trouble walking that she would never have been able to follow me. I felt a bit guilty at borrowing something under false pretences, although in fact the bicycle did have several broken spokes and I could use the wire-cutters to cut them. And besides, it wasn't really so bad cutting that telephone cable; the Germans were our enemies, after all.

Mama was sitting at the side of the road, looking down into the ditch. I flopped down beside her, panting, and showed her the wire-cutters. Mama examined them thoughtfully, then glanced down at the cable – we were sitting on it. Despite their rusty appearance, the cutters worked fine. With one quick snip, Mama had cut the cable. Then she stood up and walked a few steps down the road, motioning me to follow. Again we sat down by the ditch. Again she cut the cable, and I took the loose piece and flung it behind a hedge.

It was our first act of sabotage – but it wasn't over yet. Mama hid the wire-cutters under the dandelion leaves in the basket and we strolled innocently down the road for a hundred yards or so. Again we sat down at the edge of the ditch, and repeated the operation. Mama had decided that we should make a dozen or more cuts, every few yards, so that the Germans would not be able to repair the cable simply by pulling it and splicing it together. This way they would have to replace the entire length.

We were just preparing for our fifth cut when a handsome rabbit suddenly bolted from under our feet; we must have disturbed his afternoon nap. He gave us quite a start, and we stood watching him bound off.

'Let's move on a bit,' Mama said. 'I'm sure he's got his burrow round here somewhere, and we don't want to disturb the whole family.'

She was right. We soon spotted the rabbit hole, and there were several baby rabbits romping around it. We walked on for another few yards before attacking the telephone cable again.

When Mama thought we had done enough damage, she trimmed the spokes of the bicycle wheel, hid the wire-cutters under the dandelions again, laid the broken spokes on top of the greenery in the basket, and told me to pedal the bike back to the old lady's house to return the cutters. She meanwhile started back down the road, putting as much distance as possible between herself and the scene of the crime.

The old lady was waiting for me, sitting on the steps up to her kitchen. I made a great show of the broken spokes, laying them out on the stone steps beside her, then took the wire-cutters out of the basket and returned them to their place in the cellar. When I got back to her, the old lady handed me an envelope.

'Here, child,' she said. 'It's a little something for the day of your First Communion. Buy yourself a little treat. Go on, take it.'

I was terribly embarrassed. 'I can't, Madame – Mama would be cross with me.'

The old lady smiled. 'Take it anyway. If your mother's upset, you tell her to come and talk to me. Go on – I insist. It's all right, child,' she added, drawing me down to embrace me. 'I'm not as poor as I look. Now run along with you. It looks like rain, and if you're not quick you'll get soaked before you're home.'

I hopped on the bicycle and sped away. Mama must have been walking really fast, or maybe I'd been at the old lady's house for longer than I thought. Anyway, I didn't catch up with her till I reached the bridge over the river into La Fière. I got off the bike and gave Mama the envelope; I told her I hadn't wanted to take it but the old lady had insisted.

I could see from her expression that Mama was cross. Blushing, I

31

tried to explain.

'Honestly, Mama – I did try to refuse it, but she wouldn't take no for an answer. And she said if you didn't believe me then you ought to go and speak to her yourself.'

Mama didn't answer. She opened the envelope and let out a cry of horror.

The envelope contained a hundred-franc note, the largest note in circulation.

'What in the world will we do with this?' she exclaimed. Then suddenly she turned on me, really angry now. 'We may be poor, Geneviève, but we're not beggars. That woman must have been mad to give it to you – and you were very wrong to have accepted it.'

Then I had an idea. 'Listen, Mama – let's give it to the priest on the day of First Communion. Let's give it to Father Roulland.' For it was still the custom then for all those taking First Communion to make a small offering to the village priest. Since people round our area were so poor, it was usually only a modest amount, but Father Roulland was going to be spoiled for once.

We walked on in silence. I could see Mama was still upset.

'I don't see why you're so cross, Mama,' I said, taking her hand. 'That old lady was only trying to be kind – first she lent us the wire-cutters, then she gave me the money. She just wanted to make us happy.'

'When you're a little older you'll understand,' Mama said. 'It's a question of dignity. A question of pride.'

'I know,' I said. 'But the old lady had her pride and dignity too. When the rich give money to the poor, in a way they're making an offering to God, aren't they? She was just trying to please God.' Then, breaking into a hop, skip and jump, I added: 'Oh I wish I could see those Germans' faces when they find what we've done to their cable!'

Mama smiled. 'Me too,' she said. Then her expression became very serious. 'But listen, Geneviève, you've got to swear to me that you won't say a word about it to anyone. Not a soul must know what we've done – not even Papa, not even little Claude. You understand?'

'But Papa would be proud of us——' I began.

'No he wouldn't,' Mama said firmly. 'He'd be furious. He might even beat us – and you don't want to be beaten, do you? Promise me, Geneviève. Not a word to anyone.'

I promised.

At that very moment the heavens opened and the rain came down, just as the old lady had predicted; a fine icy rain that lashed our faces. We were still about a mile from 104. By the time we arrived home we were both shivering. As we trudged the last few yards to the house, Mama glanced out over the greenish waters of the swamp, lapping at the embankment by the level-crossing.

'If the Allies are coming,' she said, 'I hope they don't come by sea.'

The Night of June 5th

There was a fire burning in both fireplaces when we got home that afternoon, and the house was lovely and warm after our chilly excursion. Papa had lit the fires – one in the kitchen, the other in the downstairs bedroom. He had been recruited by the Germans several weeks earlier for night duty, guarding the railway bridge between Level-Crossings 103 and 104, so he slept in the mornings and spent the afternoons pottering around. He had spent most of his spare time that week scraping, cleaning and repainting his boat. Since he had started night duty, he'd had no time to hang around with his drinking companions, and we were all benefiting from the change of routine. I even had the illusion – it didn't last long – that he might be reformed; he might never drink again.

It was only about seven o'clock, yet it was already getting dark – more like autumn than early summer. For supper, Mama heated up a big bowl of milk, into which Claude and I dipped our fat 'tartines' of toasted bread. Then it was time for bed. But before I went upstairs, Mama asked me to put the chicken into the big stewpot to cook; then Papa would have something to eat if he stopped at the house during his rounds that night.

I went down to the cellar to fetch some vegetables, but a sudden gust of wind blew out my lamp and I had to grope about in the dark. The vegetables came from the Sheepfold's big garden. One of us went over to the Sheepfold every day, to check the cattle, feed the chickens and pick some vegetables. Tonight my elder brother Francis was sleeping up there; he was studying for his exams, and it was a quieter place to concentrate on his books. He also took care of milking Blanchette, our big fat cow. Blanchette was ours – at least, she had been loaned to us by the man who owned the herd. He didn't pay Mama for looking after his cattle, but he let us keep all of Blanchette's milk. And that was a considerable help in those hard times; our milk, our cream, our butter all came from Blanchette's generous output.

Papa headed off towards the bridge, to relieve the guard at nine o'clock. Each guard consisted of shifts of ten men, all of them huddled together like sardines in the sentrybox the Germans had built next to the tracks. None of them knew what they were supposed to be doing, or who they were supposed to be guarding against. The Germans had recruited them, so there they were – a motley crew of all ages, all sizes, all descriptions. The oldest of them was Monsieur Touze, who often stopped off at our house for a cup of coffee on his way home to Sainte-Mère-Eglise. Others, like Gabriel – or 'Gaby' as everyone called him – were still in their teens.

I'd been asleep for about an hour when a loud roaring noise woke me up. It had been ages since I'd been wakened by a passing train. But this wasn't a train; it was something quite different. Little Claude was awake too.

'Sounds like aeroplanes,' Claude said.

I got up and looked out of the window. Claude was right. They were planes, and they were flying very low. I could see their huge silhouettes against the clouds. It wasn't the first time planes had flown over our house; in fact they came over almost every night, and we always said a prayer for them. So, although the noise was louder than usual, I thought no more about it and climbed back into my bed. And yet . . . Why were there so many of them tonight? And why were they flying so low? Suddenly I remembered Mama's words that afternoon: 'If the Allies are coming, I hope they don't come by sea.' Could they really be coming? No, surely not; not in this awful weather. It was just some planes flying over our marshes in the usual way, only this time they happened to be a little lower.

Claude slipped into bed beside me and whispered, 'I'm afraid, Geneviève. Are you afraid?'

'Don't worry,' I told him. 'Those planes make a terrible din but they'll be gone in a minute. You go back to sleep, there's a good boy.'

Mama called up to us: 'Stop talking you two! Time you were asleep!'

I got out of bed and went to the top of the stairs. 'It's not us that's making all the noise,' I called down. 'It's the planes – and Claude's scared. Can we come downstairs?'

Neither of us was really scared any more, but it was always tempting to snuggle down into Mama's big soft bed. We were still making our way downstairs towards my parents' bedroom when the front door burst open.

It was Papa Maurice, pushing Gaby in front of him. He was obviously so excited he could scarcely get his words out straight.

'This is it, woman! They're coming! Invasion! Too damn many planes, don't you see? Has to be it! They're coming, they're coming!'

I caught Mama's eye and she smiled, putting a finger to her lips, reminding me of my promise not to tell anyone of our work that afternoon with the wire-cutters. I was absolutely dying to tell him, but a promise is a promise.

Mama glanced at Gaby and said to my father: 'Where are the others? What have you done with them?' Then she noticed something unusual and went over to have a closer look. 'And your armbands – where are they?'

Papa Maurice looked happier than I'd ever seen him. 'I'll tell you, woman, I'll tell you. Just let me get my breath. You know what I said to myself when I saw those planes flying over? I said to myself: "Maurice, get the hell out of here – fast as your legs can carry you!" So I told all the blokes in the sentrybox, "I'm going home for a bowl of soup. Want to come? How about it – a big bowl of hot soup to warm your bones!" And do you know what? Not a taker – only Gaby here. Stubborn lot of fools! "Come on," I told them, "do you good to stretch your legs." "No," they said, "too damn cold out tonight." I ask you! Anyway Gaby and I left them there – told them we'd be back soon. Soon – hah! So we wrapped our armbands round some heavy stones and dumped them in the marsh – probably under six foot of water by now!'

Papa was radiant, and I was happy for him. He had hated having to wear that armband, so he must have been delighted to throw it away.

He decided we should celebrate the occasion, and told me to set some glasses on the table while he went down to the cellar to fetch the cider.

Any excuse to open a bottle! He turned to go down the cellar, but before he had taken two steps the kitchen door was suddenly kicked open from outside, and standing framed against the darkness was a strangely dressed man carrying a machine gun, which was aimed menacingly at us.

36

Here we were expecting friends, ready to kiss and laugh and celebrate; instead of which, this fierce-looking stranger, his jaw set, his gun trained on us, had burst in on us from nowhere.

He kicked the door shut behind him, as violently as he had kicked it open. He didn't say a word. He just kept looking at us, as though waiting for someone to make a wrong move. My heart was pounding; I sensed, in that frozen moment, that if any of us did move then he would surely kill us on the spot. Yet some part of me was studying him objectively. Where had he come from? His clothes were dry, so he must have come along the railway tracks, the only dry spot in the area. And he was filthy. I remember thinking to myself: 'Goodness! He could at least have washed his face and hands!' For indeed his face and hands were black with what looked like soot.

How long was it since he had arrived? Seconds or hours? Yet I felt, despite that menacing machine gun, that we were surprised more than frightened.

Finally the stranger broke the silence. 'Friend or foe?' he asked, in perfect French.

What a silly question, I thought; as if anyone would ever answer 'Foe!' Anyway, how could he possibly think we were enemies, we who had been waiting for five long years for the Allies to come? I was assuming of course that this man was an Allied soldier. In the heavy silence, the intermittent roar of the planes contrasted strangely with the quiet, persistent ticking of our old clock. I thought for a second of those armbands: if Papa and Gaby hadn't got rid of them, this crazy soldier might have taken us for enemies and shot us at once.

It was Claude who finally answered him. 'Friends, Monsieur –we're all friends.' His high little voice echoed round the room as he walked straight up to the soldier, his hands stretching out towards the barrel of the machine gun.

'Friends,' the soldier repeated, lowering the gun at last. 'Really friends?' And he ran his grimy hand through Claude's blond hair.

We all breathed again. Following my little brother's example, I went over to the soldier and kissed him on the cheek. He looked surprised, but pleased. The whole room now relaxed, and my parents came back to life and walked over to him.

The soldier pulled a map from his pocket and laid it out on the table. He was all business now; the time for pleasantries was over. When he began to speak again, I thought I detected the trace of an accent. I knew that people in Canada spoke French, and wondered if that was where he came from.

'Show me where the Germans are,' he said, indicating his map.

It was the first time Papa Maurice had ever seen a military map but he seemed quite at ease. He leant over the table and studied it for a moment, then lifted his head and asked the soldier:

'Where is my house on the map?'

The soldier pointed to a little black square.

Then, with a little grey stub of a pencil that the soldier lent him, Papa underlined several places.

'The Germans are here, at the Château d'Amfreville,' he said, 'about a mile from here. And at Port-de-Neuville, also about a mile away. At Fresville, too – that's just over a mile from here. And they're at the Château de La Fière, too; that's also about one mile away.'

'You mean we're surrounded,' said the soldier.

Papa Maurice looked surprised. 'We?' he said. 'What do you mean – "we"? You're not alone?'

'No, of course not,' the soldier grinned. 'Hear all those planes? They're full of paratroopers who are being dropped in.'

Mama, who had gone very pale, I noticed, moved over to him. 'You mean, Monsieur, that lots of paratroopers are going to come down here tonight?'

'Not "going to come", Madame,' he said. 'They're coming down right this minute.'

'But they can't!' she cried. 'You've got to stop them – quick, before it's too late. They'll all drown!' And she seized his arm and led him out to the level-crossing gate. The marsh waters were washing against the embankment only a yard away. 'You've got to stop them,' she repeated. 'They'll all be killed if they land here.'

The soldier turned to Papa Maurice. 'How deep is that water?'

'Four or five feet,' Papa told him. 'Almost six feet in some places. But that's not the worst of it. The river Merderet flows through the swamp, and of course the water's much deeper there.'

I watched the soldier as he stood there trying to work out what to do. The roar of aeroplane engines overhead was almost deafening now. In my mind I pictured the big white canopies of silk suspended between heaven and earth. Hundreds of young men were drifting down towards a watery grave. The trap the Germans had set was going to work – and there was nothing we could do about it.

Or was there? After all, we knew the Americans were tall men, so perhaps the water wouldn't reach over their heads. And unless their

1. Aerial view of Level-Crossing 104. *Imperial War Museum Collection. Editions Robert Laffont: Service Iconographique.*

2. Level-Crossing 104. *Author's collection. Editions Robert Laffont: Service Iconographique.*

3. The Sheepfold, which has stood empty for over twenty years. *Author's collection.*

4. Château d'Amfreville. *Author's collection.*

equipment loaded them down, perhaps they could wade to safety on the railway embankment. But someone would have to let them know where the railway embankment was, steer them towards it perhaps. If they started to wade eastwards, they'd fall into the Merderet's deeper waters – over fifteen feet deep in places – and then they would be lost. There was nothing to show where the shallower marsh waters ended and the deeper river waters began. We knew, of course, but even in full daylight a stranger wouldn't know.

Papa Maurice made for the door, nodding to Gaby to follow him, and they went out to fetch Papa's boat. As they launched it Papa looked at the soldier and asked him what the equivalent was for '*Venez ici, les gars!*'

'Come here, boys,' the soldier told him.

And as Papa poled the boat out over the dark swamp waters, I could hear him repeating to himself: 'Come here, boys. Come here, boys. Come here. . .'

Meanwhile Mama had lit a paraffin lamp, which she turned up as bright as it would go. Now she went out with it, and climbed up on the level-crossing gate, waving it back and forth in the hope that the soldiers who had already landed in the marsh would see it and know where to go for firmer ground.

Suddenly I had an idea. I dashed down to the cellar and brought two large bundles of firewood back upstairs; they were very heavy and it was a bit of a struggle, but finally I made it. One bundle I dropped by the kitchen hearth, the other I stood upright in the fireplace in my parents' bedroom. The fires that Papa had lit had long since died out, so I had to relight the fire, but the wood was so dry that it caught almost immediately. Flames shot up the chimney, burning so fiercely that the soot lining the flue quickly caught fire too. Within minutes, there were bright flames shooting out of the chimneytop – flames that would be visible for miles around.

Seeing what I had done, Mama came running in. 'Well done, Geneviève!' she cried. 'Now let's light the other fire too.'

'I tried to, Mama,' I told her, 'but the bundle of wood was too thick to fit in the kitchen chimney.'

So she took the belt from my nightgown and slipped it round the bundle of firewood, pulling it tight. Now the bundle fitted easily, standing upright in the kitchen hearth. We set it alight and soon it too was merrily blazing away, sending flames roaring up the chimney.

I went outside and stood on the railway tracks to admire my

handiwork. It was a fantastic sight. The low-flying planes were still sweeping overhead, and the night sky above the marshes was filled with scores of billowing white parachutes, swaying to and fro as they gently descended. And, spewing from the two chimneys like torches held aloft by a giant, there were the bright flames that I had lit, illuminating the darkness. The trap the Germans had set was not going to work. The soldiers would see the house and head for the higher ground on which it stood; there was less chance now that they would flounder towards the river and drown. And for any who landed in deeper water, Papa Maurice would be there to rescue them in his boat. The chief danger was for those who might land near Fresville or the Château d'Amfreville, both of which were German strongholds. Still, I was sure that when they saw our house lit up, the soldiers would head towards it to regroup. And, with a sudden shudder of excitement, I realized that the Germans' plan would actually work against them now: with the marshes flooded, the only way the Germans could reach Level-Crossing 104 was via the railway tracks, either from 103 to the east or from Fresville to the west, and both routes were too exposed for them to risk an attack.

The soldier – he turned out to be American, not Canadian – went into the kitchen to talk to Mama. I couldn't hear what they were saying, but a moment later he came out to me and wrapped a warm blanket round my shoulders.

At that moment I was happier than I can say. I stood there on the railway tracks, snug in the blanket, watching the blazing flames from our chimneys soaring into the sky, and I remembered some lines of poetry that we had once read in school:

> *O you inanimate objects,*
> *Do you possess a soul?*

Yes, I thought; our house has a soul – a warm, maternal, vibrant soul. For at that moment our humble house suddenly looked very beautiful to me. The roof, still wet from the rain, gleamed beneath the dancing flames; every brick and roof tile seemed alive, inviting, as though beckoning to the soldiers out there in the marsh, offering them a refuge, promising them a welcome.

The American was pointing something out to me.

'See that parachute?' he said, indicating the white folds draped over a nearby telephone pole. 'That's the one that brought me.'

The telephone pole must have broken his fall, for the long lines reached almost to the ground.

I asked him if all the soldiers would be able to speak French like him.

'No,' he laughed. 'Not many Americans can speak French.'

So I asked him to teach me a few words of American.

'What do you want to say?'

'Well,' I said, 'I want to greet your soldiers. I want to tell them my name is Geneviève, and that I'm happy to see them, and that I've put a big pan of milk on the fire, and they're welcome to a cup if they'd like it, and they can come into the house to dry off by the fire.' Then I pointed to the flames roaring out of the chimneys, and added: 'And I want to tell them it's nice and warm in our house, and——'

'Hey! Hold on a minute,' he laughed. 'You want to tell them too much! First let me tell you how your name is pronounced in English: *Jen-e-veev*, though we spell it just like you. So why don't you greet them by saying: My name is Jen-e-veev. Go on – try it.'

'My name is Jen-e-veev.'

'Good. Now, what else do you want to say?'

I asked him what was the English for *chers amis*.

'Dear friends,' he told me. 'But why don't you greet them with "Hello boys!" Even before you tell them your name.'

I was still practising what my new friend had taught me when a scraping sound suddenly alerted me to the fact that Papa Maurice and his boat were returning. The level-crossing had been paved with stones to make it easier for carts of hay to cross the railway line, and the sound I heard now was the hull of the boat scraping against those paving stones.

Papa Maurice had rescued his first batch of paratroopers. They were jam-packed in the boat, all standing upright so that they each took up as little room as possible. If I had tossed one of Claude's marbles at them, I guessed it would never be able to trickle down to their feet – that's how tightly they were packed. Normally the boat draws very little water, but, laden as it was that night, Papa was having great trouble making it the last few yards to the house. Several soldiers jumped out and started to push the boat forward.

I stepped across to greet them, my heart pounding. 'Hello, boys! My name is Jen-e-veev. How are you?'

'Very well, Jen-e-veev!' they shouted back. 'Very well indeed!'

And then, while my teacher friend started talking to some of the new arrivals, I led several of the others into the warmth of our kitchen.

41

Our house had one peculiarity that I haven't mentioned: it was not completely level. The foundations had sagged in places, because of the swampy land, and now the floors all tended to be very uneven. In fact we had to prop up our tables and chairs to keep them horizontal. But this defect turned out to be a blessing that night. The soldiers were dripping wet and the water was pouring from them on to the floor; but, thanks to the sloping kitchen floor, the water simply drained away, back into the marshes whence it had come.

I looked around the room full of soldiers. They were shaking themselves like huge dogs that had been tossed against their will into the swamp. From that moment on I always thought of them as *our* soldiers.

Mama had filled her biggest pan with Blanchette's milk, which had slowly been heating up all this time. Never was it so much appreciated as that night! Each soldier had his own metal mug; he would come forward and hold it out, while I ladled warm milk into it from the pan. They were all carrying an incredible amount of gear with them. I remember being impressed by the knives hanging at their hips as much as by the automatic rifles slung across their chests. In fact they reminded me of the fat little Michelin man in the tyre advertisements. And they seemed to have pockets all over the place, in which they kept the strangest things, such as powdered coffee or chocolate, which they mixed into the hot milk I served them. And they had bars of chocolate too, which they offered to me. Oh it did taste good, that chocolate! I'd had it before, but not for a long time, because such luxuries were unheard of during wartime, and I had completely forgotten what it tasted like.

Despite their unexpected bath in the swamp waters, the men's faces were still black. When I first saw them, I could only think that Americans were a dirty lot. But then of course I realized that they had blackened their faces on purpose, to be less visible in the darkness.

The heat from our fires was such that the soldiers were soon drying off. One of them was turning his pockets inside out when out fell a little fish, still alive and squirming. Everyone started laughing, and one or two of them bent down to try and catch it again. Finally someone caught it, and held it up in triumph. I wanted to rescue the fish, but I hadn't a clue how to say so in English and my teacher friend was nowhere to be seen. I tugged the man's arm and said, 'Please. . .' Then I added the two words I'd heard Papa practising when he had gone off in his boat: 'Come here.'

The soldier understood. He followed me outside, and we gently returned the poor fish to the marsh waters.

Back in the kitchen, all the soldiers were now turning their pockets out to see if they'd caught a fish too – and one man discovered a tiny green frog in his cap. There was another roar of laughter and the men started to toss the poor thing from one to another. I tugged the soldier's arm again, and again he understood; the frog was soon returned to its rightful home.

Just then I heard Papa's boat returning with another batch of paratroopers, as thoroughly soaked as the first lot. I ladled out more spoonfuls of hot milk, and noted anxiously that the level of milk in the pan was rapidly going down. Blanchette was giving us about two and a half gallons a day, but already we had used up all yesterday's supply and half of the previous day's. But simmering alongside the milk was the old chicken. The broth in which it had been cooking for the past several hours would add up to about twenty-five pints, and to that Mama now added more water, up to the brim of the great stewpan. The chicken was nice and plump, so that even with extra water the broth would be delicious. Served piping hot, it would warm the next load of soldiers that Papa Maurice brought home.

I went upstairs to put on my clothes and shoes, groping about in the darkness. From the window I could see the little light bobbing where Papa Maurice had fixed it to the prow of his boat. The next batch of men were arriving.

I dashed back downstairs and out towards the boat. Suddenly overcoming all fear of my father, forgetting my usual timidity, I held out a hand to help him from the boat. Normally I'd never have dreamed of doing such a thing, but it was special that night. I led him into the kitchen, sat him down and served him a steaming hot bowl of chicken broth, topped with a spoonful of the *crème fraîche* that he loved so much.

He stared at me, astounded, obviously wondering what on earth had come over me. But I knew: something had changed. I was no longer a little girl, terrified by a big man. I was nearly an adult, and I was doing my bit to help people who needed help.

Papa Maurice was so exhausted he could hardly stand. He looked pale and drawn with fatigue, and I could well understand why. I knew from experience how hard it was to punt that boat. I'd often made the trip to the Sheepfold and back, with the boat full of vegetables from the garden, a couple of gallons of Blanchette's milk and a stack of firewood. The outward trip was always a pleasure, with the boat light and the current going with you; but the return journey was quite another matter. Papa was as strong as a horse, but even he was finding this night's work stretching his muscles and testing his stamina to breaking point.

A heavy thud, followed by the sound of something sliding down the roof, brought us all to our feet. Papa dropped his bowl and exchanged a nervous glance with my mother. Then, without a word, they both ran towards the back of the house. The paratrooper who had just landed on the roof had probably been knocked out by the shock. My parents knew, from the angle of the roof, that the man would probably have fallen into the deep waters at the back of the house. They would have barely seconds to find him; if he had been knocked senseless he would drown before he recovered consciousness.

They returned a few minutes later, carrying the inert man between them. The other men moved aside to let them pass. They sat him down in front of the fire, and Mama removed his boots and some of his dripping clothes so that she could rub him down with her mixture of Calvados and cologne. He had lost his helmet in his fall, but he did not seem to have broken any bones. Yet nothing Mama did seemed to have any effect on him.

I handed Papa another bowl of broth, to replace the one he had dropped, but he just shook his head and headed back out into the night to find more drowning paratroopers.

Some men were arriving under their own steam, one by one or in groups of two or three, some from the Big Swamp, others from along the railway line. Those lucky enough to have landed on dry land remained outside, letting those who were drenched take advantage of our warm kitchen to dry off. I offered soup to all of them, and they all accepted.

By now the kitchen was so crammed with men that I had to squeeze my way between them. Papa was bringing back more. The milk pan had long since been emptied, and the broth was nearly finished, too. But the newcomers would need something warm inside them, to keep the chill from their drenched bones. Mama put on more pans to heat, and the soldiers mixed their powdered coffee and chocolate as fast as she could boil the water. Despite the hour and the situation, the men all seemed to be in excellent spirits, laughing and joking, and offering me everything they had – especially chocolate. They also tried to give me little tablets that were marked *Chewing Gum*, which they explained was for chewing, not swallowing, but I found it a strange idea and politely refused.

My teacher friend arrived in the kitchen to address his men. They would be launching their attack at six o'clock in the morning, he said.

Suddenly I had a thought, a very important thought. The man had already left the kitchen and was striding away down the railway tracks. I dashed after him, calling to him to stop.

At last he heard me and turned. 'What is it?' he asked.

'My parents forgot to tell you something – and I think it's important,' I panted. 'You see, there's a *mirador* at the entrance to the Big Swamp.'

He didn't know what a *mirador* was.

'Well, there's a platform up a tall tree,' I explained, 'and there's always a German up there on guard.'

'Ah. An observation post,' he said.

'Yes, and if you don't hide your soldiers before dawn, he'll see you. But there isn't anywhere you could hide – there's nothing but water out there. So if you want to take the Château d'Amfreville, you ought to do it now – tonight. I can help you. There's a way through the marshes that's never more than a foot or two deep; I can lead you there if you like.'

'I'm not sure. . .'

'Better be careful,' I told him earnestly. 'The Germans are a really nasty lot.'

He grinned at that. Then he said, 'Tell me, Geneviève . . . It's true, isn't it, that the only way out of here is along the railway line?'

'Yes,' I told him, 'but not in any direction. You mustn't go towards Fresville – there's as many Germans there as at Amfreville. You should head for La Fière.'

We both turned and gazed along the railway tracks, the long metal lines gleaming in the fiery glow that still rose from our chimneys. I suddenly realized there hadn't been a train along for ages. And there probably wouldn't be another one that night. Someone was doubtless making sure of that.

The American now turned to me and asked what was my father's name.

'Papa Maurice,' I told him, puzzled.

Without explaining, he took me by the hand and led me to the level-crossing gate. He cupped his hands round his mouth and shouted: 'Papa Maurice! Papa Maurice! Come here, Papa Maurice!'

45

'I'm coming, I'm coming,' responded a voice from out in the marshes.

The big American stood behind me, his arms round my shoulders. We leaned against the gate and watched the astonishing spectacle that continued to unfold before our eyes. Paratroopers were still floating down through the night sky, but further off now, nearer the Sheepfold. The planes made one or two low passes over our house, and I could hear a loud voice coming from one of the planes – I learnt later that the man was using a megaphone – directing the soldiers towards our house and to other areas of higher ground.

The drone of the aeroplane engines excited me. I envied the men who were flying them, and said as much to my American friend. He grinned and ran a hand through my hair, drawing me close again. I was savouring every wonderful moment of that night, conscious of everything that was happening around me, anxious only to experience the full intensity of the present. To think I had at first taken this nice man for an enemy! He was our friend; they were all our friends, these soldiers – *our* soldiers – and I suddenly had the strong feeling that they would all be all right; that none of them would drown in the marshes round our house. I was so deliciously happy that I burst out singing.

'That's a pretty song, Geneviève,' said the American with a smile, pronouncing my name the American way. It sounded strange to me, but I liked the way he said it.

By the light of the flames still rising from both chimneys, we could see Papa Maurice's boat slowly making its way towards us. It was not crowded with soldiers this time; either Papa Maurice had hurried to come to us, or else there were not many more soldiers to be rescued in the Little Swamp.

The American asked Papa Maurice if he could show him the nearest observation post.

'I can do better than that,' Papa Maurice told him. 'I can take you there myself.'

He climbed out of the boat, obviously weary but still eager to help. 'I think I've fished them all out,' he said. 'You're lucky – they had a swim they hadn't expected, but otherwise they're all right.'

Both men crossed to the gate on the Big Swamp side and were leaning on it to talk.

'The closest *mirador* is just over a mile from here,' Papa Maurice said, pointing in the direction of the Château d'Amfreville. 'Takes about forty minutes to get there. And there's another one at the château at La Fière – but it'll be easy enough to take that one. We can go along the tracks, and there's only the single guard on duty there. What's the plan, then?'

'We're leaving sooner than I'd planned,' the American said. 'Your daughter tells me there's nowhere to hide round here once it's daylight. La Fière sounds like the place to make for. What do you think?'

Papa Maurice nodded. 'Yes, it's true, you are very exposed round here and you would stand a better chance at La Fière. Want me to show you the way?'

'Thanks,' said the American, 'but you've done enough for one night. If I were you I'd go and get some rest.'

But Papa Maurice wasn't done yet. 'You know, Monsieur, I have a bone to pick with those Germans. I'd be glad to come with you, and if I could be useful——'

The American gave Papa a friendly slap on the back.

'Oh – but listen,' Papa went on, 'I've just remembered something. The Germans got us to build machine-gun posts at various places. We really dragged our feet over it, though, and they never got round to installing the guns. But the shelters could be useful to you, couldn't they? A good joke to play on the Boches, eh?'

'Okay,' grinned the American. 'We'll take you along with us, Papa Maurice.'

He turned and went back into the house to round up his men. Within minutes they were all filing out of the kitchen and lining up on the railway tracks. Only one of them was missing: the paratrooper who had crashlanded on our roof.

My friend – it was clear by this time that he was the commanding officer – went back into the kitchen to fetch the missing man.

'Not him!' protested Mama. 'He's in no shape to go anywhere. Leave him here; as soon as he's better we'll send him after you. He can't even stand yet.'

But my officer friend was determined. 'Sorry, but he'll have to come with us,' he announced firmly.

'Be reasonable, Monsieur!' argued Mama. 'He can't even hold a rifle – how do you expect him to defend himself? Leave him with us for a day or two. Otherwise you're as good as sending him to his death.'

The officer made no reply; he simply signed to two of his men, and they took the unfortunate soldier by the arms and trundled him off to

47

where the others were all lined up.

Mama ran after them and jammed a woolly hat on the young man's head. 'We couldn't find his helmet,' she explained, 'but at least this will keep him warm.'

The soldiers were lined up in two rows on both sides of the railway tracks, facing each other. I wandered along between the two rows, and as I passed I noticed some of them grinning to themselves in the darkness, obviously amused at the presence of a little girl in their midst. At the end of the line Mama was waiting for me. Together we stood and watched as the men turned and marched away. I'm sure her heart was as heavy as mine. I couldn't take my eyes off the receding column of men. Our soldiers. Would we ever see them again? Soon the night had swallowed them.

The house seemed horribly empty now. Claude, whose eyes were drooping, slid into bed beside Gaby while I helped Mama clear up. The paratroopers had left us a hoard of chocolate, sweets and cigarettes; they were everywhere – on the table and the mantelpiece, on shelves and windowsills. But I felt desperately miserable. The war had only just begun for our soldiers. I knew very little about war. I'd never seen so many soldiers as tonight, so many planes and parachutes and troopers. To me the Allies had been nothing more than an idea, a far-off hope – until tonight.

In fact, I had met one Allied soldier before that long night – just the one, though, and he wasn't even in uniform.

It was an autumn evening in 1943, when we were living at the Sheepfold. I was coming home from Sainte-Mère-Eglise, where I'd been running some errands for Mama. It was just after eight o'clock, when the curfew came into force, and as I didn't have an *Ausweiss* (a pass that permitted me to be out after dark), I was taking a shortcut through the fields, hoping to avoid a German patrol.

As I approached a farm called La Couture, which means 'Sewing' or 'Fashion' – strange name for a farm, I used to think – I saw a man beside the ditch that ran alongside the road. He was stooping down, his back to me. Dressed in a grey jacket, a pair of ragged trousers and wooden clogs, he seemed totally preoccupied with whatever he was doing. My first thought was: a poacher, setting his trap.

Silently I crept up behind him and whispered in his ear: 'You're making too much noise! The people in the farm will hear you.'

He spun round, pointing a gun straight at me. Then, seeing I was only a child, he lowered the gun.

'What are you doing out at this hour?' he asked, speaking in French.

I told him I was taking a shortcut home because I was so late. 'Don't worry,' I said, pointing to his gun, 'I won't tell anyone.'

He smiled and pocketed his gun. Then he said: 'Come and help me.'

He had been burying something, and I knelt down to help him cover it over with earth and dead leaves. I was dying to ask him what he had been burying, but I was too shy; besides, it seemed wrong for a little girl to ask an adult what he was up to.

There was a strange sort of hat lying on the ground beside him, made of wool and leather. I asked him if he'd let me have it as a souvenir.

The man hesitated. Then he said: 'If they ever catch you with it, you'll be in dead trouble. And your family too.'

I could tell what he meant from his grim tone, but I still wanted the hat. Finally he agreed to let me have it, making me promise not to say a word to anyone, not even my mother.

Then he asked me how to get to Saint-Sauveur-le-Vicomte. I pointed him in the right direction, then walked part of the way with him.

The night smelled good. I had tucked the peculiar hat inside my blouse. Anyone who saw us – him in his clogs, me in my boots – would have thought we were just another peasant boy and girl on their way home. But, although his French was perfect, I knew from his accent that he didn't come from our region. I thought he looked terribly handsome, though he seemed very old to me; he must have been at least twenty. I was naturally curious as to where he had come from and what he was doing here in Normandy. But I didn't dare ask him – and he wouldn't have answered me anyway.

We parted company at a place called La Patte d'Oie de Cauquigny, not far from the marshes. Saint-Sauveur was twelve miles in that direction: he couldn't miss it, I told him.

He took both my hands in his and squeezed them. 'Thank you,' he said. 'You're a brave little girl.'

'Not little,' I said. *'Big.'*

'Right,' he grinned, teeth gleaming in the darkness. 'A brave *big* girl.'

He was already a few steps away from me when a sudden thought came to me.

'How will you manage without an *Ausweiss?*' I yelled after him.

He turned and smiled. 'My papers are all in order.' And with that he was gone.

When I got home that evening, I raced straight upstairs to my bedroom and slipped the strange hat into my mattress, tucking the straw around it until I was sure no one could possibly find it. And I went to sleep thinking of the man who was walking so purposefully through the darkness.

I kept my promise: I never mentioned him to anyone. But two days later my curiosity got the better of me, and I retraced my steps across the fields to the spot where he had been burying something. I scraped away the dead leaves and earth – and uncovered a parachute. My friend with the gun had arrived like an angel from heaven. Now he had disappeared who knows where into the Normandy countryside.

What would become of them, all those cheerful, gum-chewing soldiers who had landed in the marshes round our house, and filled our kitchen with their powdered coffee and chocolate?

I couldn't get to sleep when they had gone. Mama heard me crying and she tiptoed upstairs to comfort me.

'You were marvellous tonight,' she told me. 'And the soldiers will never forget their little Jen-e-veev.'

'Are they all going to die?' I asked her between sobs.

'Don't be silly,' she said. 'The war is nearly over. Lots and lots of Allied soldiers are coming to France now – our soldiers were just an advance team, to prepare the way for the rest. They won't be alone for long, don't you worry. Now, off to sleep with you. Tomorrow's going to be a long day.'

But try as I might I found it impossible to get to sleep that night. I was too worried. True, Papa Maurice was with them, and he knew every inch of the way; he also knew exactly where the Germans were.

For the first time in my life, I was anxious for Papa to come home. He would tell us what had happened and reassure us that our soldiers were still safe. Besides, I saw him in a new light now. He had acted like a real hero. Oh, I had no illusions; he would still drink, he would still beat me up from time to time. But now I had a reason to admire him, and I resolved to try to love him more.

I tossed and turned in bed. It was no good; I knew I'd never get to sleep. No matter what Mama said, I had to get up.

Down in the kitchen, I found Mama asleep in a chair, her head against the mantelpiece. The soot was still burning in the flue, though less brightly than before. They had certainly done their share, those two chimneys.

Tiptoeing around so as not to wake Mama, I took a chocolate bar from the table. Heaven only knows how much I had eaten that night – more than I'd ever had in my whole life, I should think. For me the taste spelled happiness. I bit off a piece, but the magic had gone; it didn't taste the same now that the soldiers had left.

I went outside and pumped a bucket of water, trying to keep the worrying thoughts at bay. Mama would be pleased to find the coffee ready when she woke up. Gaby and Claude were still fast asleep in bed. The house was peaceful.

But what about our soldiers? The thought kept coming back to me. Maybe Papa would never return. Maybe the Germans were waiting for them, laying an ambush for them . . .

In the midst of my anguish I suddenly remembered the telephone wires that Mama and I had cut that afternoon. Only that afternoon! So much had happened since then; it seemed a world away in time.

Tuesday, June 6th, 1944

Six in the morning. Day was just beginning to break, and the sky was as gloomy and overcast as ever. On the calm waters of the marshes, the multicoloured parachutes still floated, the only bright note in that dark damp morning.

I was in the kitchen when I heard the sound of footsteps. I dashed outside: it was Papa Maurice, walking up the railway tracks. He was alone, his cap pulled down over his eyes, and he was wearing his tall rubber wading boots.

Tremulously I called out to him, asking how things had gone at La Fière.

'Everything's fine, child,' he said, a note of excitement in his voice. 'Where's your mother?'

'Asleep in the kitchen,' I told him. 'I've made the coffee – do you want some?'

'You bet I do,' he said.

So we went into the kitchen and he sat down at the table. Mama immediately woke up, and her first words were:

'Where did you take our boys, Maurice?'

'They're at Emile's farm,' Papa said. I knew that this meant they were near Level-Crossing 103. 'They've had a good start. I led a few of them to the Château de La Fière – the Boche in the lookout tower didn't get a chance to fire; probably didn't even know what hit him. And the Americans took the château. Maurice Salmon is over the moon about it; we celebrated with a round or two of his best cider. Apparently some general has parachuted in near the Leroux farm – General Gavin, I think his name was. And there's another general over at 103 – General Ridgway, they told me. And our boys have taken all the bridges: the one over the river, the railway bridge and the one at La Fière. Oh – but there's bad news too, I'm afraid. All the blokes in our guardhouse have been killed. Bloody fools! Old Touze, Garcia the Spaniard, the district officer's son – I saw their bodies. There may have been more. If only they'd listened to me! As soon as the Americans saw the swastikas on their armbands – bang! It was all over. Couldn't find Emile and his family; must have scarpered. Can't say I blame them. Anyway, several gliders have landed around La Fière, one of them right in front of the Sheepfold – not a scratch on it. Oh, and I saw Francis. He's fine. Told him not to budge while there's still a German alive in the neighbourhood.'

Papa Maurice's eyes were shining, and his words came tumbling out so fast it was sometimes hard to catch what he was saying. He paused to take a gulp of coffee, then went on.

'Not all the gliders made it down in one piece. Two of them hit some trees, and most of the blokes in them were killed. Poor lads, they didn't stand a chance.'

'What's a glider, Papa?' I asked timidly, refilling his bowl of coffee.

'An aeroplane without an engine,' he told me. 'What they do is hook it up to a plane somewhere over in England; the plane tows it to wherever it's going, they cut the tow-line, and the glider floats down and lands as best it can.'

'Can't they steer it?' I asked. 'What do they do if they find they're heading for a tree?'

'They can steer it a bit,' Papa said, 'but it's not like a plane. And in the dark . . . Anyway, that's what happened to one of them – smack into the big oak, killing everyone.'

Then Mama had a question; she wanted to know when the reinforcements would be arriving – the ones our soldiers had told us were coming across the sea.

'Today,' Papa said. 'Around midday, or this afternoon at the latest. They're supposed to be meeting up with our paratroopers – it's their job to take Sainte-Mère-Eglise and hold it till the reinforcements arrive.'

Mama shook her head sadly. 'The sea must be terribly rough in this weather,' she said.

'Worst weather I've seen in years,' Papa agreed. 'But the people who've been organizing this invasion must know what they're doing. Maybe they even wanted the weather to be bad, we don't know. Anyway, I've got work to do. There's three men missing, and I've got

53

to find them – alive or dead.'

Little Claude had just woken up and he came into the kitchen rubbing his eyes. The first thing he saw was Papa's new armband, the one the Americans had given him.

'What's that?' Claude asked. 'What does MP mean, Papa?'

Papa Maurice didn't know, but he felt about in his pockets till he found a small book, which he handed to me.

'Here, Geneviève,' he said. 'It's a dictionary. Everything you want to know is in there. Take a look.'

I flipped through the pages, not sure how to use the dictionary, but finally I found what I wanted.

'MP – Military Police,' I read out.

Papa's chest puffed out with pride. Only now did he appreciate the honour the Americans had bestowed on him by giving him that armband.

He looked at me across the kitchen table, his eyes moist. 'You're a lucky girl, you know, to be able to read like that. . .'

Eagerly I offered to teach him, but he shook his head impatiently.

'Not now, not now. I've got things to do,' he said. 'Go and wake Gaby, tell him he's coming with me. If those missing men are wounded, I'll need his help to get them back.'

I watched them leaving in the boat. They kept close to the railway tracks, so as to be less visible to the Germans stationed at Port-de-Neuville. Papa made Gaby lie down in the bottom of the boat, in case the Germans did see them and opened fire. They were heading in that direction because it was the one area that Papa hadn't explored the night before.

I stood there daydreaming as the dawn broke over the marshes, hoping and praying that Papa Maurice would find the three missing men, and wondering what the next few hours would bring.

Boom! A sudden explosion echoed across the swamp, startling me, nearly toppling me off my perch on the level-crossing gate and into the marsh waters. I had the impression that it had come from Amfreville.

I was starting along the railway line in that direction when there came a second explosion – and a house went up in flames right on the edge of the Big Swamp. Poor Jeanette, I thought. For months she'd been preparing her trousseau, piece by piece, ready for her wedding in a few weeks' time. Now it would all be lost in the fire. But maybe she and her family had had the sense to move out . . .

A third explosion. This one came from the far end of the Big

Swamp, and I saw the flames leaping from the little farmhouse that belonged to Martha and Manuel. We used to see Manuel every day; after the Germans had flooded the marshes, Manuel used to come round daily to count the cattle, and he would always stop off at our house for coffee. And now perhaps he was dead . . .

Again the cannon roared, and this time it was the upper floor of the Château de La Fière that literally exploded. Mama, who had come out onto the railway tracks where I was standing, said she had seen the château's windows flying out. We could see for miles around from our vantage point up there on the railway line.

Maurice Salmon had lived in the château for several years, and he had been a family friend for as long as I could remember. He was thirty years old, very tall and extremely handsome. He also made the most wonderful cakes. Two years ago, he'd made a huge cream cake for my brother Francis's First Communion, and he had promised to bake the same sort of cake for my First Communion too. Just thinking about that cake was enough to make my mouth water. And what was even more delicious was the notion of eating such a sumptuous cake under the very noses of the Germans. Papa Maurice had gone all the way to Bacilly, without a proper pass, where his uncle owned a flour mill, and he had brought back a bulging sackful of fresh bread and several pounds of fine flour. Now Maurice might be dead too . . .

Bullets were starting to fly around our heads, so Mama herded me back indoors. I was fascinated by the singing noise the bullets made as they sped past us and lodged harmlessly in the marshes or sometimes in the log pile in our back yard.

Despite the danger Mama decided to go over to the Sheepfold; she wanted to milk Blanchette, she said. She didn't need the boat – it was too heavy for her to use, anyway; she always walked along the railway tracks to 103, where there was a path leading up to the farm. Before she set off, she made me promise not to let Claude outdoors under any circumstances.

I nodded, but I could see in her eyes that Blanchette was just an excuse; the real reason she wanted to visit the Sheepfold was to see how 'our' soldiers were managing.

I watched her slight figure disappear in the distance, her step as firm and energetic as ever; she seemed oblivious to the battle that was raging around her.

Time passed very slowly. The whine of bullets and boom of cannons continued unabated. I busied myself by cleaning up the house, knowing that Mama would be pleased to come home and find that I had relieved her of some of her chores.

'Woman! Come out and give me a hand!'

It was Papa's voice. I ran out and saw him arriving at the level-crossing gate on the Little Swamp side. His boat was carrying a strange cargo: the wooden ladder from the Sheepfold was lying lengthways along the boat, from bow to stern, with a parachute folded on top of it to serve as a mattress. And on this improvised stretcher lay an injured paratrooper, who smiled at me as I ran to meet the boat.

'Where's your mother?' Papa demanded.

'Gone to the Sheepfold to milk Blanchette – she'll be back soon.' Then I suddenly realized that Gaby was not in the boat. 'What's happened to Gaby?' I asked.

'He's back there with another soldier who's hurt, though not as badly as this one. As soon as we've got this bloke into bed, I'll go back and fetch them.'

As Papa Maurice was tying up the boat, I could hear him muttering to himself:

'Too heavy . . . kid's too small . . . we won't be able to shift him. . .'

'I'm stronger than you think, Papa,' I told him.

'Well, all right, let's give it a try,' he said. 'You take that end of the ladder, and when I say "lift", help me raise it so we can get it over the edge of the boat. He's heavy, mind, and he's badly hurt, so don't you dare drop him.'

'Course I won't drop him!'

I was talking big, but in fact I was terrified. I was small and skinny; and, after four years without enough to eat, none of us was very strong. But if faith could move mountains . . .

We managed the first bit all right, lifting the ladder out of the boat. Then, step by step, we made our way slowly towards the house. It was an uphill climb to the courtyard, though, and I could feel the ladder bending in the middle. What if it broke? No, Papa had made it himself; it was good and strong.

Little Claude opened the door to us as we arrived, and carefully, one step after another, I crossed the threshold. Behind me Papa was issuing instructions.

'Put the ladder down on the floor, but only when I say "now". Watch you don't pinch your fingers. There . . . Careful . . . *Now!*

Good. You see child, when you set your mind to it, you can do all sorts
of things.'

I bit my tongue. 'If only you asked me nicely,' I wanted to say,
'you'd see what I could really do!' Wasted breath. The fact was that
Papa Maurice was in a good mood; or at least, he had other things on
his mind that kept him from picking on me. Be thankful for small
mercies, I reminded myself.

I turned round to take my first good look at our patient. He smiled
at me, and like so many of the other American soldiers, I saw that he
had beautiful gleaming white teeth. But perhaps his smile was hiding
a grimace of pain, for I soon realized that his leg was very badly
broken, not once but in several places. The bones were even
protruding through his boot.

Fortunately Mama appeared right at that moment, for I wouldn't
have had any idea what to do. I heaved a sigh of relief. I noticed that
her milk pail was empty; but Blanchette was the least of our worries
now.

Mama sized up the situation immediately. Without exchanging a
word, she and Papa bent over the man's broken leg. Papa took the
soldier's knife and, with Mama's help, cut away the boot, inch by
inch, careful not to touch the protruding bone. When they had
managed that, they started to cut his trouser leg, from the knee down.
Finally the leg was bare – if you could call it a leg; it was an enormous
mass of swollen flesh, covered with cuts and bruises and patches of
dried blood. The bones had broken through in three different places.

Up till then we had lived for years with little or nothing, and we had
grown used to it. But suddenly I understood, for the first time, what it
was to lack not only material things but also knowledge. We had no
bandages or disinfectant. Worse, we hadn't the slightest medical
knowledge to cope with such an injury. How should the fracture be
set? *Could* it be set? It came to me then that ignorance was a deeper
form of poverty. And it was here, to our house, that God had sent one
of his poor wounded creatures. I had to admit, I was having more and
more trouble understanding this God.

But Mama kept a cool head. She found an old sheet in a cupboard
and tore it into long strips about four inches wide. Then she started
rolling them into bandages, and asked me to help. I did my best,
trying to work out what she was going to do with them.

Meanwhile Papa Maurice had put the water on to boil. As it started
to bubble and steam I went to take the kettle off the fire, but Mama

told me to leave it.

'I want it to boil for several minutes,' she said.

'But why?' I asked.

'Haven't you learnt about germs at school?' she said. I nodded. 'Well, boiling water destroys them.'

'But there aren't any germs in the country,' I said. 'I thought there were only germs in the cities.'

'Then you thought wrong, Geneviève. There are germs everywhere – even in that kettle of water. It's rainwater, you see; it ran down the roof, which is dirty from the passing trains, then ran along the gutters, which are also dirty. The filter at the top of the pump cleans the water but it doesn't kill the germs. That's why I want the water to boil for several minutes.'

Finally Papa removed the kettle from the stove. I watched his every move: I had so much to learn, I realized. He poured a little of the boiling water into a salad bowl, then added several drops of chlorine bleach. He swished it around the bowl, making sure that it cleaned every square inch.

'Just in case any stray germs are hiding in the bowl,' Mama explained.

I nodded. 'But I still don't see how you're going to mend his poor leg.'

'Watch,' she said.

Kneeling down on the stone floor, Mama now began to wash the soldier's cuts and scratches, gently, slowly, a little patch at a time. She had added a half-glass of Calvados to the water, and I smiled to myself; for once, the Calvados was going to serve a useful purpose – if only she could have used up Papa's whole supply . . .

Papa had gone outside, and when he came back into the kitchen a few minutes later he was carrying a plank of wood about ten inches wide and roughly as long as the soldier's leg. It was the first time I had ever seen a splint being applied. When Mama had finished washing the soldier's leg, and all the wounds were clean, she asked Papa Maurice to lift the leg as carefully as he could. Then together they slid the plank underneath it. And finally, using the home-made rolls of bandages, Mama fastened the splint to the man's leg.

That was all they could do for the time being. Now we had to get him into bed. Between them my parents lifted the ladder again and carried it into their bedroom, resting the ladder on the edge of their bed. Then, with amazing gentleness, Papa managed to remove the folded parachute from beneath the injured man, and he was edged slowly onto the bed. I was astonished at the gentleness Papa was displaying; I'd never thought him capable of it.

The poor soldier must have been in terrible pain throughout the whole procedure, but he never once cried out from the time when we lifted him out of the boat. Now, to dull the pain, Papa brought him a large glass of Calvados. He meant well, but that didn't stop the soldier grimacing as he took his first swallow – and he refused the rest of the glass. Papa didn't insist; presumably he concluded that the American just did not share his passion for liquor.

Then Papa and Mama went back out to the kitchen, leaving me alone with the soldier in their bedroom. I tried to remember the few words my American friend had taught me the night before.

'My name is Jen-e-veev,' I announced, careful to use the American pronunciation. 'Your name, please?'

'George,' he said. 'Lieutenant George Wingate.'

I dashed into the kitchen to tell my parents this piece of news. They were busy burning the dirty bandages and cleaning the floor.

'Papa! Mama! The wounded paratrooper is a lieutenant. His name is George Wingate,' I announced excitedly.

'I know,' said Papa. 'He told me on the way back in the boat.'

Mama asked Papa Maurice where he had found the man.

'In Bernard's fields,' Papa said. 'He looked pleased to see me. Odd, though – the first thing he asked me was not to turn him over to the Germans.'

'What a funny thing to say!' said little Claude, who had been following every step of the operation since we had brought Lieutenant Wingate into the house.

'You're right, boy,' Papa said. 'I'm for the Allies, but it's not written on my face, you know.'

'Papa,' went on Claude, who hadn't missed a trick, 'why did you break the middle rungs of your ladder?'

'Oh, you noticed that, did you?' Papa snorted. 'Well, it made it easier to carry him, that's all. It was a long way from Bernard's fields to where I had left the boat, near the bridge.'

'Why did you go over there?' Claude asked. 'I mean, to Bernard's?'

'Better to find the living than the dead, I decided,' said Papa grimly. 'If he had landed in the water, he'd have been drowned long before. So I went to look round the fields first. And as you see, I was right, wasn't I?'

'Clever Papa! Clever Papa!' Claude laughed and clapped his hands with delight.

Obviously pleased, Papa lifted Claude into the air and planted two fat kisses on his cheeks.

Before he went back to fetch Gaby and the other injured soldier, Papa took another look at 'his' paratrooper in the bedroom. We crept in behind him, and gazed down at the now sleeping lieutenant. He was a big man, with light brown hair, and his eyes, I had noted earlier, were very dark, nearly black. We spoke in whispers so as not to wake him.

'How did you find him?' Mama wanted to know.

'Same way I found them all last night,' Papa Maurice said. 'I called out "Come here boys! Come here!" And he heard me and shouted back. Simple as that.'

My parents' bed was the big old-fashioned sort, standing high off the floor, a sturdy box-spring, and a thick mattress stuffed with goose down; the quilt was also stuffed with down.

I caught the tender expression on my father's face as he gazed down at the sleeping lieutenant. 'You're a lot better off here,' it seemed to say, 'than out in that field where I found you.'

There was practically nothing left to eat in the house, apart from all the chocolate the soldiers had left behind. But I had long ago learned that there's nothing like a good cup of coffee to calm a hungry stomach, so I warmed some up for Papa before he went out again. He didn't even take the time to sit down; he simply drank it standing up, then headed straight out for his boat, but I quickly filled a flask with the rest of the hot coffee and ran out and placed it in the prow of the boat.

Before he went, Papa turned to Mama and mentioned that I'd said she had gone to the Sheepfold that morning.

'Yes,' Mama told him. 'I went to milk Blanchette as usual. But I have to confess I didn't bring any home. I gave it to all the soldiers who're hiding up there in the bushes and hedges. Poor young men, they haven't had a thing to eat or drink except for that chicken broth Geneviève and I gave them last night. You don't mind, do you?'

'Of course I don't mind,' Papa said. 'You know where their food is? At the bottom of the marshes, that's where. And half their munitions too. So I've decided. As soon as I've brought this other bloke home and found the third one, I'll go back and try to fish their stuff out of the swamps.'

'You'll never do it,' exclaimed Mama. 'There must be tons and tons of it.'

'So?' shrugged Papa. 'I'll just make as many trips as it needs.' And, to Mama's obvious disbelief, he added: 'It'll be easy.'

There was no point arguing; his mind was made up. He asked Mama to fetch him the long-handled broom and a woollen scarf. I could tell that Mama was dying to ask him what he wanted them for, but she went and got them and gave them to him without a word. And once again the boat started off across the marsh waters.

The next paratrooper Papa brought back was even bigger than the first. He was a giant, a lovely big blond giant, who laughed at everything anyone said. He managed to limp ashore using the broom as a crutch, the scarf wrapped around the bristles.

He was well over six foot tall, and his blue eyes sparkled with humour. His jaw was constantly busy with the inevitable chewing gum. As he entered our house, the thought crossed my mind that he was the sunshine coming in, after a long absence. My parents helped him across the kitchen and settled him in a chair by the fire. He had a terrible sprain; his ankle was so badly swollen that it had cracked his boot.

Gently, carefully, Mama cut away the leather boot, with me looking on and marvelling at her ability and patience.

The giant had not come empty-handed. He had wanted to recover one of the lost boxes that had landed in the water, and he and Papa had managed to fish it out and bring it back with them. He asked us to open it: it was full of army rations. So, for the time being at least, our food problem was solved.

'My name is Jen-e-veev,' I told him, again using the American pronunciation.

'And I'm Kerry Hogey,' he smiled.

Claude sat down in front of him and asked if he wanted to play a game of cards.

'Give the poor man a chance to get comfortable,' Mama protested.

But Kerry was already making himself at home, and with a roar of laughter he accepted the challenge. So there they were, the giant and the child, engaged in a heated game of cards, half in French and half in English. Thank heavens for the pocket dictionary that Papa had brought home with him.

Again Papa set out, this time in the direction of Fresville. He returned early in the afternoon, his boat laden with wooden crates of food rations and metal ammunition boxes. But no paratrooper.

Mama and I watched him approaching the level-crossing gate to moor his boat. His face was sombre.

'You didn't find the third one. . .' she began timidly.

'There's a parachute floating in the Merderet, at the point where Three Rivers joins it.'

That was the only explanation Papa made.

Even assuming the parachute had belonged to a man who was drowned, it was remarkable that only one man had been lost. But it was possible that even he had made it safely to the shore in some other direction. We would never know.

Papa began unloading the boat. Where would we store all those cases? The soldiers were camped along at Level-Crossing 103, about a mile away, and probably would not be returning our way. That meant we would have to take the food and ammunition to them, otherwise they would die of starvation. The gunfire from the direction of Sainte-Mère-Eglise had not intensified, which probably meant that the reinforcements had not yet arrived. But how could we get their boxes to them?

Papa had a sudden brainwave. He fetched the old wheelbarrow from the cellar and piled several of the cases into it. Then he set off down the tracks with it in the direction of 103.

He was soon back, his barrow now empty. The soldiers had been very grateful. They had told him that if he could find any other cases that had fallen into the marshes, he should take them back to our house and stack them in the courtyard; then they would come and collect them as needed.

Papa also brought back some terrible news. Madame Brisset, who was the governess at the Château de La Fière, had been killed by the bombs. She had a daughter of my age – Bernadette. What, I thought, was going to become of poor Bernadette?

Papa seemed to be tireless. It was all Mama could do to persuade him to sit down for five minutes and drink a cup of coffee or eat a few biscuits. He was soon off again in search of the missing boxes and crates.

The Germans stationed in the Château d'Amfreville had continued to fire in our direction, but we were beyond their range. Still, Kerry pried open one of the metal boxes, and quickly assembled a machine gun. Then he hobbled out to the gate and kept Papa covered as he punted his way off across the marshes. Even if the Germans at Amfreville could not reach Papa, there might have been others lurking around Port-de-Neuville.

Mama carried a bucket of boiling hot water out to the yard; she had put a handful of rock salt into it, and she gestured to Kerry that he should soak his foot in it. He protested, but she wouldn't take no for an answer. So, with his usual laugh, he gave in; he lowered his foot into the bucket and kept it there while he trained his sights on Papa's boat.

I stood beside him, my heart pounding, terrified that I might see Papa being shot at; he was totally exposed out there on the water. But nothing happened. Perhaps the Germans had abandoned Port-de-Neuville. Anyway, now Papa could fish for his boxes in peace.

Mama insisted that Kerry should come indoors and get some rest, and she led him into her bedroom, where Lieutenant Wingate was now awake. The two men immediately took to each other, and I listened to them chatting away. I guessed, from their smiles and gestures in our direction, that they were talking about our part in rescuing them. Gaby joined them, but the language barrier prevented him from sharing their conversation.

Meanwhile Mama and I started to prepare lunch, using the duck eggs that I'd gathered during my egg-hunt yesterday morning. Despite his obvious pain, Lieutenant Wingate managed to eat his omelette, and I realized that he hadn't eaten since leaving England the night before. We washed it down with the sweet cider that Papa had never had a chance to drink last night. The two Americans seemed to like it; they even asked for a second glass.

Mama had insisted that Kerry should eat his lunch in bed. Again he had protested, but she shot such a menacing look at him when he started to get up that he quickly subsided, laughing that huge laugh of his. It was such an infectious laugh that we all joined in, laughing so loudly that it almost drowned out the gunfire outside.

Outside the battle was still raging. But it would never come in here. We were drinking American coffee out of Mama's best porcelain cups, which her father – a sailor – had brought home after one of his voyages. Our house was like a haven of peace and harmony. And, as though we all realized this at the same instant, there was a sudden moment of silence.

It was abruptly shattered when Gaby burst into tears.

Mama took him in her arms, soothing his sobs and asking why he was crying.

Between sobs he managed to make us understand that he was so happy to be here, that he felt good with us, but that he didn't know where his parents were or what had happened to them.

'I've got to go and find them,' he announced tearfully.

'Don't be so silly,' Mama said. 'You're a good son, and of course you're worried about your parents. But just think: if you hadn't listened to Papa Maurice and left the sentrybox with him, where would you be now? You'd be dead. And what would happen if you tried to get to the village? It's six miles from here, right in the middle of the battle zone. You'd never get there, Gaby – and your parents would never see you again. So you take my advice, stay here till things have settled down.'

Claude climbed onto Gaby's lap and looked up into his face coaxingly. 'C'mon, let's play cards – you an' me an' Kerry.'

Gaby ran his fingers through Claude's hair, clearly trying to make up his mind what to do. Distress was etched on his face; I wanted to hug him and tell him I understood, because we too were separated from a member of our family: Denise, my elder sister, who worked on a farm a long way away. Beautiful Denise, who filled our lives with laughter and sunshine – when would we see her again?

Papa made dozens of trips in his boat that afternoon; our courtyard was beginning to look like an army depot. If the reinforcements arrived soon, the soldiers probably wouldn't need either the food or the ammunition. But if there was a delay, those boxes could spell the difference between life and death to our soldiers.

Between La Fière and Amfreville the fighting grew more intense. We learned later that La Fière had been the first village in France to be liberated. Our soldiers had occupied it last night, and they had no intention of giving it up. But the Germans were equally determined to dislodge them. House after house that I used to pass every day was pounded to rubble – like Lawyer Jean's, and Monsieur and Madame Cuquemelle's.

The booming of gunfire was also growing louder; it seemed to be coming from Saint-Hubert and Saint-Germain, from the direction of the sea. It sounded as if things were not going too well on the beaches. And, if that were true, how long could our paratroopers hold out by themselves?

As I listened to the gunfire, it suddenly occurred to me that something was missing: birdsong. My friends the ducks and wildfowl of the marshes must have been huddling in their nests wondering what all the noise was about.

Kerry had had a few hours' nap after lunch, but when he awoke he immediately resumed his watch by the level-crossing gate, covering Papa on his continuous mission to and fro across the marsh waters. Papa himself hadn't slept at all the night before, and I couldn't understand how he managed to keep going. As for Lieutenant Wingate, he was obviously very ill; he was in constant pain and running a high fever.

Mama was very worried about the lieutenant. She announced that she would not be going back to the Sheepfold that day. Francis could look after Blanchette and the chickens, she said. Her place was here, with her patient.

Through the half-open door I watched her tending the injured American, applying fresh cold compresses to his brow every few minutes in an effort to reduce his fever. She had barred Claude and me from the room; she was afraid that we would disturb him. So I peeked through the door at him, watching him fight the pain and marvelling at his courage. I remembered that dreadful winter when I'd been confined to bed, after the boiling soup had scalded me, and I really felt for him.

It seemed there was nothing I could do for him. I felt useless, frustrated. Then I had an idea. That morning Claude had taught the lieutenant a few words of French, and we'd had a lot of fun when he repeated them in his delightful American accent. Now I decided to use the pocket dictionary and write out some English sentences for him to correct when he felt better. This kept me happily occupied for an hour or two.

Later Mama came and asked me if I knew where Gaby was.

I told her that I'd seen him going out, maybe to the outside lavatory or maybe to join Papa in the boat.

'He's not in the lavatory,' Mama said, 'and I know Papa doesn't want him in the boat. He said it was too dangerous, he didn't want the responsibility.'

In fact, Gaby had decided to leave. Mama eventually found a little note he'd left on the railway tracks, thanking her for her kindness and explaining that he felt he had to go and find his parents.

Night was falling. Mama brought in several bundles of hay, normally

65

used in the rabbit hutches, and spread them out on the kitchen floor. Tonight they would serve as her mattress. She rigged up a hook to hold the bedroom door open – the sloping floors caused it to swing shut by itself – so that she and Papa could keep an eye on the patient during the night.

Reluctantly, Mama let Claude and me into the bedroom to kiss the lieutenant goodnight. We tiptoed in, but he was awake, his face flushed and shiny with perspiration.

I bent down and whispered in his ear, in English: 'I love you, George.'

He didn't answer; he just stared at me intently. Then I saw the tears glistening in his eyes. He raised a hand, as if to lay it on my head, but he didn't have the strength; his arm flopped down on the sheet.

I begged Mama to let me sleep downstairs with her, so that I could keep watch over the injured lieutenant too, but she wouldn't hear of it. I even tried my 'doe-eyed' look, which generally melted even the hardest heart, but even this tactic failed. She chased me off to bed.

Upstairs she asked me to make sure Claude said his prayers because she didn't have time to stay with us tonight. So Claude and I knelt down together and prayed. Then we crawled into bed. Claude fell asleep almost at once, but I couldn't get to sleep at first. I had been up for forty-eight hours. Yet I didn't feel tired; in fact, I felt as if I could go on even longer. But even as I thought this I was already falling asleep.

Wednesday, June 7th, 1944

It was barely daylight when I awoke, roused by the scraping of the boat against the railway embankment. Quietly, so as not to disturb Claude, I slipped out of bed and went to the window. Just as I'd thought: Papa was already hard at it, his boat filled with boxes. How long had he been up? I threw on some clothes and, holding my shoes in my hand, tiptoed downstairs, making sure the steps didn't creak. The staircase led to my parents' bedroom and I didn't want to wake our guests.

Mama was in the kitchen. The coffee pot was on the stove and she was busy gathering up the hay that she had slept on.

Keeping my voice low, I asked her how our patients were.

'They're both awake,' she told me. 'You can go in and kiss them if you like. Just be sure you don't wear them out with your chattering.'

I ran into the bedroom. Lieutenant Wingate – George, as I now thought of him – was looking much better. Rested, more relaxed; he seemed to be in less pain, too. I took his head in my hands and looked at him intently. Neither of us said a word; it wasn't necessary, for our eyes said everything that had to be said.

Mama came in, bearing a tray with two bowls of hot coffee and biscuits from their K-rations. Kerry greeted her with a big smile. He helped me raise George to a sitting position, and Mama slipped an extra pillow behind his back. He drank the coffee but refused the biscuits. Mama offered him another bowl of coffee.

'No thank you, little mother,' he said in English – which sent me running to the pocket dictionary.

The problem was that I didn't know how to spell 'mother' so I couldn't find it in the dictionary. Kerry came to my aid, guessing what

I was looking for. As he took the dictionary from my hands, a slip of paper on which I'd scribbled some English phrases fell out. Kerry picked it up and read it, then showed it to the lieutenant.

George smiled at me. '*Bravo, Geneviève! C'est très beau!*' he said in French in his marvellous accent.

'Not *très beau*,' I told him, '*très bon.*'

Delighted to be corrected, George smiled again, repeating '*Très bon . . . très bon . . .* '

I was so pleased to see him feeling better that I danced around the room, laughing and clapping my hands.

'I thought I told you not to bother our patients,' Mama exclaimed as she returned to the bedroom. She grabbed me by the hair and led me out of the room, but not before I'd managed to blow a kiss back to George. He was laughing at Mama's mock-serious scolding.

To atone for my sins, I decided to sneak out and pick a big bunch of yellow flags, which grew in abundance alongside the railway tracks, in the marsh waters. The trouble was that to pick them I'd have to wade into the water up to my waist.

Fifteen minutes later I was back in the kitchen with my flowers, soaked to the skin, shivering with cold, and well aware of the risk I'd taken. In fact, I had probably come within an inch of my life, for the bullets had been whizzing around my ears, but I'd been too intent on my task to feel really frightened. Mama didn't know whether to kiss me or spank me – I didn't tell her that I'd had to crawl back to the house on all fours. Anyway, she undressed me, dried me off, rubbed me down with her special concoction, and gave me a set of dry clothes, scolding me all the while.

When I was dressed again, I asked Mama if I could take a bowl of coffee out to Papa, to warm him up, for it was another wretchedly cold day.

'Absolutely not!' Mama cried. 'You're not leaving this house again. Go upstairs and call him from the attic window.'

So I went up the the attic and opened the window. 'Come here, Papa Maurice! Come here!' I called in English.

Papa had been unloading another cargo from the boat. He looked up at me and yelled: 'What d'you want, you little pest?'

'I've heated up some coffee. Come and drink it while it's still hot.'

'I'll be in in a jiffy.'

When Papa came in, Mama got him to help her change the lieutenant's dressings. Then Papa came back into the kitchen to drink

68

his coffee; he seemed reluctant to sit down while he drank it, as though half-expecting that he wouldn't be able to get up again.

'How long have you been out on the marshes?' I asked.

'Damned if I know,' he said, scratching his head. 'Since about Monday night at eleven, I should say.'

I gasped. 'You mean you didn't go to bed last night either? But why?'

He waved a weary arm out at the marshes. 'See how choppy the water is out there today? Well, just imagine what it's like out at sea. That means the invasion will probably be delayed until there's calmer weather. And that means there won't be any reinforcements yet, or any food or ammunition for our boys. So they'll be desperate for every case I can recover from the marshes.'

'But Papa,' I reasoned, 'you're too tired! You'll die of exhaustion – or else you'll get a bullet in the head.'

'So what?' he said. 'That wouldn't bother you too much, now would it? No one to punish you then, eh? You're lucky I've been so busy these past couple of days, or I might have found time to give you a good thrashing.'

'I don't think I'd mind dying,' I said idly.

'Don't be so stupid,' he retorted. He got to his feet and went to the door, pausing on the threshold. I followed him, and pointed to the mounting pile of boxes and crates that filled the courtyard.

'You really think they're going to need all that?' I asked.

''Fraid so.'

'And . . . is it going to be terribly hard for them?'

He nodded, then shrugged his shoulders in a gesture of helplessness and headed back out to his boat. I watched him go, marvelling at his strength and tenacity. For the first time in my life I felt real admiration for this hard-hearted man.

Mama decided she had to make another trip to the Sheepfold. She wanted to make sure Francis was all right, and she also wanted to milk the cows – not just Blanchette, but all the cows from the surrounding farms, many of which had been abandoned. This way she would be able to provide all our soldiers with fresh milk to drink.

The poor cows, Mama told me later, were so swollen with milk that as soon as they saw her arriving with her bucket, they headed towards her in a stampede. By the end of her marathon milking session Mama found herself with about forty-four gallons of milk.

The commanding officer at the headquarters that the soldiers had set up at one of the nearby farms apparently couldn't believe his eyes when Mama arrived, her slight figure pushing a barrow on which were several large churns, each containing four or five gallons of milk. When she made him understand that the milk was for his soldiers, he called to one of his men and had him transfer the churns into a jeep. Then off they went, my mother and the soldier, stopping by every bush and hedge where the Americans were concealed to dispense her fresh milk. The paratroopers were ecstatic, especially the ones she recognized as 'hers'; they greeted her so warmly that she was to remember that day for the rest of her life. From what they told her, we were virtually the only civilians left in the area. Most of the farmers had fled, as had the people who lived at Level-Crossing 103.

When she found someone who understood French, Mama explained about the plight of Lieutenant Wingate and asked if a doctor could be sent to help him. Impossible, they told her; no medical team had been parachuted in with them on Monday night. But their commanding officer, a major, promised that as soon as he found someone with any medical knowledge at all, he would send him over with whatever medicines they had at their disposal.

It was six o'clock by the time Mama arrived home. I noticed that the tip of one of her wooden clogs was missing, and her big toe was protruding through the hole.

'I'll have to mend it,' she laughed. 'I just can't be seen walking around in such awful footwear.'

'What happened?' I asked.

'A piece of shrapnel.'

'Mama! Were you hurt?'

'Not a scratch, child. It was my lucky day,' she smiled. Then she told me about the piece of flying shrapnel that had clipped the tip of her clog right off, and how she just kept on walking, thanking God for protecting her and asking him to keep up the good work.

I asked her how Francis was.

'Fine. He goes outside only when he absolutely has to. The Sheepfold is as solid as a rock.' Then Mama wanted to hear about her patients.

'The lieutenant's asleep,' I told her. 'But I think his fever's up again.'

'And Kerry?'

'Out by the gate, covering Papa again. I made him sit down and put

70

5. The River Merderet. X marks the spot where Geneviève fed pike near the bridge on the railway line. *Author's collection.*

6. June 5th, 1944: American planes dropping paratroopers over Sainte-Mère-Eglise. *Editions Robert Laffont: Service Iconographique.*

7. D-Day casualty. *Editions Robert Laffont: Service Iconographique.*

his foot in a pail of hot water – and do you know what, Mama? He's learnt to imitate your expression when you're cross! Oh he does make me laugh!'

Then Mama told me the rest of the story, how she had milked the cows and taken it to the soldiers and how she had asked them to send a doctor.

'I'm worried about the lieutenant,' she said. 'I'd feel a lot better if only a doctor could see him. Still, the major said he'd send try to find someone who can help.'

Mama had brought some of the milk home, and now she used it to prepare hot drinks with the paratroopers' chocolate powder, and gave it to our two patients.

Kerry's ankle was clearly on the mend, but George seemed worse than ever. He drank his chocolate in silence, evidently suffering.

When Mama changed his bandages and washed his wounds again, I saw his poor swollen leg. It looked terrible. Mama was worrying about gangrene; I didn't know anything about it, except that it was something we couldn't possibly deal with.

Then I happened to glance out of the window. Someone was heading in our direction, crossing the distant bridge over the river.

I went out and called Papa, who was busy unloading more boxes from his boat. He turned and squinted in the direction I was pointing. Then he went into the house and borrowed the lieutenant's binoculars, and focused them on the approaching figures.

'There's three of them, walking along the railway line . . . They're going very slowly . . . I think they're wounded.' He turned to Mama. 'Now listen, woman. I'm not going to interfere if you think it's your duty to look after them, but don't expect any help from me.'

'That's no way to talk, Maurice——' began Mama.

'Those three soldiers are Boches,' he said.

Apparently disbelieving, Mama took the binoculars and looked for herself. Then, wordlessly, she handed them back to Papa.

I wondered what was going through her mind. Her expression was calm, but she must have been asking herself all sorts of questions. What was she going to do? We knew the Americans had orders not to take any prisoners, at least not for the next few days. So what would happen when our two guests met these three Germans?

'Can I look through the binoculars?' I asked timidly.

'You'll see them soon enough,' Papa told me coldly. And with that he tossed the binoculars to my mother again and returned to his boat.

71

Evidently he was going to leave us to our own devices while he went off on yet another trip across the marshes.

We stood there in silence for a moment, Mama and Kerry and me, watching him go – and watching, too, as the three Germans made their way slowly towards us. There was no doubt about it; they were clearly heading for our house. Where else would they go? There was no one else for miles around.

Suddenly Mama made up her mind. She chased Kerry indoors and, despite his heated protests, sent him back to bed.

'What are you going to do?' I asked her anxiously.

'We'll see how things develop.'

Kerry's rifle was leaning against the wall. Mama picked it up and took it into the bedroom. George was fast asleep, but Kerry was watching her intently. She put one finger to her lips and pointed to the rifle, then pointed out towards the railway line. She slipped the rifle under the eiderdown, where Kerry could easily reach it. Kerry nodded to show he understood. He would cover us if necessary, but he wouldn't start anything. Then Mama went out, closing the door between the bedroom and kitchen.

The three Germans were almost at our house now, two of them supporting the third. The man in the middle seemed to be in pretty bad shape. When they reached the front yard, they paused, but Mama made a sign to them to come in. They didn't seem to be armed, and their uniforms were torn and spattered with mud.

Where had they come from, I wondered. The railway lines had been in American hands since yesterday morning.

One of the Germans addressed Mama, speaking impeccable French but in a voice that was toneless and weary.

'This lad's lost a lot of blood, Madame. He'll die unless you help him.'

The injured man was very young, about twenty perhaps. He had taken a bullet through the thigh; his leg was bleeding badly and he was obviously in great pain. The third man, considerably older, had been shot in the heel, though his wound was far less serious.

Mama made them all sit down, then she turned to me and asked me to fetch a bundle of hay from the cellar.

The first German came with me, and helped me carry a great bale of hay upstairs, where we then spread it across the kitchen floor. Then Mama told me to find the parachute that still lay on the ladder; she wanted it as a sheet.

The German brought the parachute over and spread it out on the hay as she directed. Meanwhile she was cutting away the trouser leg of the injured young man. Now she got him to lie down on the improvised bed, while she washed and bandaged his wound, then found a pair of pyjama trousers that belonged to Francis and slipped them on her new patient. As usual she had cleaned the wound with her mixture of water and Calvados, and now she gave him some to drink. His reaction, I noted, was much the same as George's had been the day before.

'Drink it up,' she admonished the young man. 'It's all we've got to ease your pain.'

The first German, the one who spoke French, was tall and handsome. He was about forty years old, and everything about him indicated good breeding. He was undoubtedly an officer, I thought, though he had removed his stripes from his uniform. I also noticed that the other soldiers had removed their buttons, and I wondered what this meant.

Strange times. Here we were, harbouring two Americans and three Germans, and the common bond between them was that they were all miserable, wounded and in pain. I asked Mama if I could offer the first German a cup of coffee, and she said of course I could. He accepted it with a sad little smile, gazing down at his two companions now stretched out on an American parachute on the floor of a French peasant's kitchen.

Just then Kerry hobbled into the room. Unarmed. There was a look of wary curiosity in his eyes; he later told me that this was the first time he ever saw a German. No one said a word. Then, spontaneously, the German offered Kerry his hand. Kerry hesitated for a fraction of a second; he glanced over at Mama, who nodded almost imperceptibly. Then the blond giant took the German's proffered hand, and both men studied each other amicably.

Inside 104, on this seventh day of June, 1944, there were no enemies: there were only men, joined together by their mutual bond of suffering.

It was clear that they immediately took a liking to each other. I watched with disbelieving eyes as they sat down beside the fireplace, drinking together, sharing a cup of American coffee, trying to communicate. According to the rules of war, they should have been out on the battlefield, trying to kill each other. But it seemed that 104 was a very special place, where the rules no longer applied.

The two other Germans had fallen asleep on their bed of hay. The younger one was fast asleep, I was sure of that – but I wasn't so sure about the other one. There was something about the third man that disturbed me. I don't know if it came as a result of my loneliness as a child, or whether it was a God-given thing, but I have always had an ability to sense what's in a person's mind, a sixth sense that enables me to foresee trouble. Mama said it was a gift God had given me to keep me from being too proud; and, since I could read only unpleasant thoughts, it was indeed humbling to see how ugly and base some people were.

I could tell that this German was thinking evil thoughts. I knew that his presence under our roof was somehow a threat to our lives. I couldn't precisely say how, or why, but I was sure that it was he alone who posed the threat.

The first German, the one who I thought of as an officer, took out his wallet and showed us several snapshots of his family. His mother, an elderly lady with snow-white hair, had the same air of rectitude and decency that he had. In fact, he looked very much like his mother. In another snapshot, a beautiful young woman was holding two children by the hand, both about my age. The fine stone house and its manicured lawns behind the young woman seemed to conjure up a life of ease and comfort, as far removed as was possible from the fire and blood that had brought us all together today.

Then Kerry too brought out some photographs, first one of his parents – a good-looking couple who seemed far too young to have a son of his age – then one of his fiancée, and a third of a scraggly dog.

Though they spoke no common language, Kerry and this German officer had established this immediate though tenuous bond; it was almost tangible. Yet there was a basic difference in their moods. Despite his wound, Kerry seemed to emanate happiness and conviction; I could sense that he belonged among the victorious. The German, on the other hand, was full of anguish; his eyes, his face, his carriage all betrayed his inner feelings. For these two, at least, the outcome of the war was no longer in doubt.

Mama concocted a delicious meal for us all, using vegetables from the Sheepfold mixed with meat taken from the American K-rations. It was a strange assortment around the table that evening: Mama and little Claude and I; Kerry and the German officer. Only Papa was conspicuous by his absence. After the meal, the German woke his two companions and forced them to take some nourishment. Kerry and

Mama went in to see George; but Claude and I were not allowed in, which I knew meant that he was worse.

In the distance, we could still hear the boom of artillery fire over in the direction of the sea. I wondered what it meant. Could it be that the Allies, because of the bad weather or because of stiff German resistance, had called off the invasion; decided to sacrifice their paratroopers who had jumped into Normandy to prepare the way – *our* paratroopers? No, I decided; that was impossible. They would never abandon their own soldiers; and they surely wouldn't let us down, we who had waited for them for so long.

I went out to the pump to fetch some water. Mama would have been furious if she knew, but I couldn't stay indoors. As I glanced down the railway tracks, I couldn't believe my eyes. There was a sort of car bouncing along between the tracks. Several soldiers were seated in the car, but I didn't know how they managed to stay in their seats because the car was bucking up and down as it hit each sleeper. I dropped my pail and ran back into the house, calling out to Mama.

Mama appeared at the doorway, and looked in the direction I was pointing. She broke into a broad smile. 'That's a jeep,' she told me. 'It's a special sort of American army car that can go anywhere, even in water I think.'

'How do you know that?'

'Because,' she said with a sly smile, 'I've driven in one of them.'

The jeep pulled up at the level-crossing. I ran up to it, greeting the Americans with a smile and my stock phrase in English:

'Hello, boys! How are you?'

One of the soldiers replied in perfect French: '*Très bien, Mademoiselle, ça va.*'

Mama took him into the house and led him into the bedroom to see Lieutenant Wingate. He emerged a few minutes later.

Still speaking in French, he said: 'Don't worry, Madame. I'll see to it that you have what you need right away.' Then, turning to the German officer, he added: 'I'll be back shortly. Then I'm afraid I'll have to take you with me. I'll need you to point out your unit's present position.'

And with that he went back out to his jeep and sped away down the railway line again.

I gave Mama a quizzical look.

'He's gone to fetch some medicine for the lieutenant,' she told me. 'His fever's gone up. But I'm sure the medicine will help to bring his temperature down.' And she repeated the words to herself, as if trying to reassure herself: 'I'm sure the medicine will help. . .'

As she moved past the German officer, he touched her arm. 'I wonder, Madame, if you could let me have a sheet of paper and an envelope,' he said, his face sad beyond description. 'I should like to write a note to my family. I know that I'm going to die today, and I'll never see them again.'

'Don't be silly! Don't talk like that!' Mama admonished him. 'You're not injured, and the war is surely over for you. So why do you talk about dying? Your wife would be angry if she could hear you.'

The German officer looked at her steadily. 'In a little while the Americans are going to take me with them while they reconnoitre our positions. And I know what that will mean for me.'

'Don't be so silly,' Mama retorted. 'The Americans are men of honour. They wouldn't shoot an unarmed man.'

Mama sounded very convincing, but the German interrupted her.

'You don't understand, Madame. It's not the Americans who are going to kill me.'

Suddenly Mama understood the full implication of his words, and she buried her face in her hands. Then she looked up at him again. 'You don't mean . . . You don't mean to say. . .'

'Yes,' said the German softly. 'That is exactly what I mean.'

He knew that the Germans would see him in the jeep with the Americans and would assume that he had betrayed them. They would either shoot him, or maybe even decide to wipe out the jeep and everyone in it. Either way, he wouldn't stand a chance.

'So I just want to write one final letter to my family,' he finished.

Mama laid her hand on his shoulder, fighting back the tears. 'My poor boy,' she said. 'My poor poor boy. How stupid war is! How unbelievably *stupid!*'

I saw, then, that they were both crying. I quickly cleared the tabletop and wiped it, then ran to find a notepad and some envelopes.

Kerry and the other American soldiers who'd arrived in the jeep were sitting on the courtyard steps outside. After he had finished writing, the German slipped his letter into an envelope along with the snapshots he'd shown us earlier. Then he opened his wallet and removed some money from it, which he handed to Mama.

'For all the trouble we've caused you,' he said. 'And for them,' he added, gesturing to the other two German soldiers lying on the makeshift bed on the floor.

He didn't know my mother.

Drawing herself up to her full height, Mama addressed him in a voice I hardly recognized. 'Keep your money, Monsieur. If I took you and your comrades in and did my best to care for you, it was out of Christian love. Your money means nothing to me. I wouldn't touch it.'

The German officer looked completely stunned. Coming from a woman whose poverty was so obvious, this categorical refusal to accept his money surprised and upset him.

'I didn't mean to offend you, Madame,' he said. 'Please excuse me. And please, promise me you'll send this letter to my wife and children.'

Mama's face immediately softened. 'Don't worry,' she said. 'I promise.' And she took the letter and slipped it in between the sheets in the linen cupboard.

The jeep was already making its crazy way back down the railway tracks towards us. As soon as it arrived, the American officer leapt out and ran into the house, making for the bedroom. He gave George two greyish tablets, which he said ought to relieve the pain, then handed Mama several small boxes containing more of the pills, having written the dosage on one of them.

'And you can give the pills to them, too,' he added, pointing to the two injured Germans on the kitchen floor. 'It won't cure them but it will help ease the pain.'

His words were followed by a heavy silence. This American soldier, who seemed to exude such confidence and calm, was about to commit an act of utter lunacy. He was venturing out on a mission that would risk not only his own life, but the lives of his men and of the German as well. We had heard what he'd said to the German officer earlier, so we knew that he considered it an important mission. But everyone knew that Amfreville, where they would be going, was swarming with Germans – or everyone, it seemed, except this American.

'Let's get going,' he said.

Mama stepped in front of him. She begged him not to go. It was crazy, she said. Weren't there enough dead men already? Why take unnecessary risks? 'I tell you, as sure as I'm standing here, the whole of Amfreville is full of Germans,' she told him. 'If that's what you want to know.'

I chimed in too, saying that Mama was absolutely right. We had lived here for years and knew exactly where the Germans were

77

stationed. He'd been here less than two days – why couldn't he listen to us?

His point was that he needed specific information; he wanted to find out precisely where every German machine-gun emplacement was situated, and the only way to find that out was at close range.

I still wasn't convinced, but who were we to argue with military men?

He seemed slightly taken aback by our determination to prevent his mission. But eventually he swept all argument aside with one simple sentence:

'We're here to win the war,' he announced firmly. Then he turned to his men. 'All right, boys, let's get going.'

I watched them all pile into the jeep, the German officer seated in front between two of the Americans. He turned round for one last look back at our house. His face was a mask of sorrow. I suspected that if he wanted to save his own skin, he had only to tell the Americans everything they wanted to know; he probably knew where every soldier and every gun emplacement was in Amfreville. But he was a German, and he had no intention of betraying his comrades. Despite what Mama had said to him a little while back, the war was not yet over for him.

The engine spluttered into life, and the jeep careered off along the tracks in a spray of gravel. Then, to our astonishment, it turned off the railway line, down the embankment and headed out across the marsh waters. Mama had been right: this peculiar car could also drive on water.

The jeep had gone less than a hundred yards when the Germans opened fire. Stray bullets whizzed around our ears, hitting the house, while we scuttled back in doors and kept our heads well down. But when Mama had turned her back for a moment, I made for the stairs, and crawled up to the attic where I peeked out of the window to see what had happened to the jeep.

The Germans were still raking the area with fire, but the amphibious jeep continued towards the château, a double spray of white water flying in its wake. At the bridge to the island, where a tributary stream flows into the river Merderet, the jeep's driver must have realized he had gone too close to the German installations. He tried to stop. The next thing I saw was all five men diving from the jeep into the marsh waters.

Kerry had been following their progress with me. He was furious to

78

see his mates in trouble like that – even though it was their own fault –
and he was powerless to help them. He stomped around the attic room
in a frenzy of rage. Why hadn't they listened to us, I thought. What on
earth had possessed them to go off on that suicidal mission?

'For God's sake! They're all going to be slaughtered!'

I looked round. It was Papa Maurice, back from his latest fishing
expedition, who had joined me at the attic window.

'You should have stopped them!' he told me, his face livid with
anger. 'You should never have let them set off for Amfreville in the
first place!'

'We tried – but they wouldn't listen to us,' I said.

He stood at the window for a moment, watching the men's progress
through George's binoculars. Suddenly he handed them to me.

'Here, look for yourself, child,' he said.

I asked him to show me how to adjust the binoculars, and for a
moment his fingers were in front of my eyes. I couldn't believe what I
saw. His hands were raw. The skin had been rubbed away during the
past thirty-six hours that he'd spent endlessly punting his boat
through the marshes.

My desire to watch the battle vanished. I grabbed Papa's wrist and
dragged him downstairs to the kitchen. He didn't know what I was up
to, but he offered no resistance. I made him sit down and started
preparing bandages for his hands. Both thumbs and little fingers had
been literally worn away to the bone; there was no flesh on them. I
could only imagine how he was suffering. He kept protesting that I
was making a fuss about nothing, but at last I had managed to clean
and bandage his hands. Then I set about persuading him that his job
was done: he had retrieved all the boxes that had fallen into the
marshes; our yard was piled high with them. And I discovered now
that I could be as pig-headed as he was himself – a chip off the old
block, in fact. I glanced up at the bull whip hanging on the wall; it no
longer sent a shiver down my back. I decided that from now on I
would obey Papa only if I wanted to.

Somewhat against my better judgement, but thinking that under
the circumstances it would please Papa, I poured him a big glass of
Calvados. A fatal mistake. Hardened drinker though he was, he
hadn't touched a drop since midday on Monday – and in that same
period he had neither slept nor had a bite to eat. The result was almost
immediate: as soon as he had drunk the Calvados, he passed out,
slumped across the table.

Mama and I weren't strong enough to carry him. I quickly spread some straw on the floor of the bedroom next door, then we dragged him through and heaved him on to it. We didn't even take his boots off.

I stood there, gazing down at him, this man whom I had always feared and hated – only now I felt a new mixture of love and admiration for him. He hadn't stopped once since Monday night when the first paratroopers had arrived; he had used up every last ounce of energy in his body, until finally he had collapsed.

I bent down and whispered in his ear: 'Papa, you're a hero . . . I love you.'

It was a good thing he couldn't hear me; he would have been furious at the mere thought of being called a hero – in fact, he'd probably have hit me.

Above him on the bed, George was sleeping fitfully, his fever still high despite the grey pills. When he and Papa awoke, I knew they'd be glad to see each other. George thought of Papa as his saviour; he had repeatedly told us how much he admired him. And Papa felt just as strongly about the man whose life he had saved. It was strange, I thought; what could this foreigner from across the sea possibly have in common with the coarse, illiterate peasant who now lay beside him? And who would have thought that gruff, tough old Papa Maurice could feel so strongly and tenderly about another human being?

It was touching to watch them together. Between trips to the marshes, Papa had kept popping into the bedroom to see 'his patient' and find out how he was doing. If George seemed better, Papa's face lit up with pleasure; if worse, his expression would be clouded and sombre. It was Papa, too, who had insisted on taking George his cups of coffee, and waiting there while he sipped it. And as for the lieutenant, whenever he saw Papa he would seize his hands and hold them, and they would stay like that, just looking at each other, not saying a word.

Now, though, Papa was out for the count, and Mama and I were in charge. For him the war no longer existed; his worries about the food and munitions boxes were over, and his anger at our failure to prevent the Americans from going to Amfreville was calmed by his deep sleep. And so, a short while later, Papa did not see the jeep bouncing back along the railway line towards us, with only four men in it. We couldn't tell if they were wounded. And their German prisoner: what had become of him?

Suddenly the steady sound of gunfire ceased. Only the ruins of the Leroux farmhouse and the Cuquemelles' house reminded us of how close the battle had been.

Mama was dividing her time equally between her American and her German patients, dispensing medicine, changing dressings, applying compresses. Suddenly she paused by the window, staring out at the railway line.

'What is it, Mama?' I asked, going over to her side.

'I don't know. . .' she said. 'But I could have sworn I saw a head bobbing in the water down beside the tracks, about three hundred yards away.'

For several minutes we both stared out over the marsh waters lapping at the foot of the railway embankment, but we saw nothing more. She must have been mistaken. To make sure, I went upstairs for another look from our bedroom window.

Suddenly I saw it – not a head, but a hand and then an arm reaching up out of the water. My heart started pounding. I knew it was our German officer.

'You're right! You're right, Mama!' I shrieked, bounding back downstairs.

Mama was looking through the binoculars. 'The poor man must be drowning,' she exclaimed. Then she dropped the binoculars and dashed out of the house, making for the railway tracks. The moment they saw her, the Germans opened fire, but they were too far away and the bullets splashed into the water, several hundred yards short.

I saw her kneel at the water's edge, reaching out to the injured man. His body was in the water, and his head kept slumping under the surface, then jerking back up again. Mama tried to help him to his feet, but he couldn't stand. She somehow managed to drag him a few hundred yards towards the house but he was too heavy for her, and she had to keep stopping.

I couldn't bear it any longer. I dashed along the tracks to meet her.

'Go back!' Mama screamed at me. 'For God's sake, go back! You'll be killed!'

I jumped down into the water at the foot of the embankment – it came up to my waist – and waded on towards her. It was hard trying to move fast through the water, and I was out of breath by the time I reached them.

I had been right: it *was* the German officer who had gone off in the jeep with the Americans a few hours ago. He was in a terrible state.

81

He'd been shot in the chest, and bubbles of blood were rising to the surface and bursting with a dry little plop. You didn't have to be doctor to see that he was in a critical condition. But maybe we could save him . . .

'The first thing we must do is stop the bleeding,' Mama said. 'I'm going back to the house to fetch a towel. You stay here with him. Keep his head above water – he's not strong enough to do it himself.'

She made me sit down in the water, my back against the embankment, holding the German's head in my lap.

'If we hold the towel tight against his wound,' she went on, 'it might stop the bleeding. I'll be back soon. I don't think there's any danger of the Germans shooting at you now. I'm sure they've been watching through their binoculars and seen that we're trying to save one of their men.'

So, as Mama ran off to the house, I sat in the water with the man's head on my lap, stroking his forehead. He must have been hit at the moment we'd seen all five occupants of the jeep diving into the water. That was three hours ago. For three hours, then, he must have paddled and crawled and pulled himself towards us, one painful move after another, knowing that he would be taken in and cared for if only he could reach our house. It was a miracle he had made it this far.

Mama arrived back with the biggest towel she'd been able to find. Carefully we removed his blood-soaked shirt and pressed the towel against the gaping wound in his chest. The German, who had been growing paler by the minute, revived and opened his eyes.

'I'm thirsty,' he whispered. 'Very thirsty. . .'

My first thought was: how could he possibly be thirsty when his body was immersed in water? Mama sat down and took his head on her lap, while I raced back to the house and made a pot of very strong coffee. Within a few minutes I was back, and Mama was feeding the coffee to him in little sips. Then an idea struck her.

'Maybe those grey pills would help him,' she said.

Again I raced back to the house and found the pills. It was like a hospital ward in there, with my little brother Claude acting as the charge nurse. He was sitting beside the bed where Kerry and George were lying, leaning over them every few minutes to change the cold compresses on George's forehead. How he had changed in the past two days: serious and silent where he had once been laughing and happy-go-lucky. Pain and suffering had matured him almost over-night. Before heading back to Mama and the German, I paused to give him a big hug.

Mama was shaking her head. The towel was by now as red as the shirt had been. There was no chance of saving the poor man. Even if the bullet itself, which had pierced his lung, had not proved fatal, his monumental effort in making his way back here undoubtedly would. But Mama refused to give up.

'Remember how Papa brought George back?' she said. 'Maybe we can use the ladder to get him back to the house.'

This time it was she who went while I sat in the water with the German's head on my lap. In a few moments she was back with the ladder. But it was no use: he was far too heavy for us to lift. We tried to slip the ladder under him in the water, but that didn't work, so we set it on the bank and tried to pull him on to it. All in vain. I was furious with myself for being so small and weak.

But at least the grey pills were working: he seemed to be in less pain now.

'Stay here,' Mama told me. 'I'm going to take the boat and see if I can find someone to come and help us.'

She took the heavy ladder and went back to the house again.

I knelt down in the water and held the German's head against me. Just then the sun, which we hadn't seen for days, broke through the clouds and bathed the German's face in its glow. But only for a moment; soon it was gone again. At least I knew it still existed.

The German's breathing was easier now, and that awful whistling sound as he breathed in and out had stopped. He opened his eyes and stared at me.

'I feel better now,' he said, his voice so faint I could barely hear it. 'Doesn't hurt any more. . .' There was silence for a minute or two, then he said: 'Tell me, child, why are you staying here with me? Your mother takes care of the wounded out of Christian love – she told me so herself. But what about you? You're far too young to know what Christian love is. So why are you here?'

'Shh, shh,' I kept saying. 'Don't try to speak. You'll wear yourself out.'

'No, I'm all right,' he said, 'thanks to the pills your mother gave me . . . Do you know how good it feels not to suffer – even for a few minutes? No, of course you don't. Anyway, I want an answer to my question: why are you here?'

'I'll tell you,' I said, 'but on one condition: that you don't talk any more and wait quietly till Mama comes back with help. All right? Well then – I'm here because Mama couldn't manage by herself,' I told him. 'She tried to carry you back to the house, but she couldn't manage it alone, so I thought that together we might . . . Actually, there's another reason too. I owe God a debt, you see, and being here is my way of repaying Him.'

'You owe God a debt?' he smiled. 'Now you must tell me about that.'

I scowled at him and told him not to talk; I even raised my hand to threaten him if he didn't obey. His smile grew broader. I couldn't help thinking how crazy this was: me, a little girl, raising her hand as if to strike him, frowning at him, this man whose life was slowly ebbing away – and he found it funny.

I still had a lot to learn about grown-ups, but at that moment I felt closer to this man, my enemy, than I'd felt to anyone else in my life.

'All right,' I said, smiling back at him. 'I'll tell you about it.' Even if he thought it was a silly story, I decided, it might help to pass the time, help him forget his pain for a moment or two. 'But no interruptions, remember.'

He blinked his eyes by way of assent.

So I began my story. 'One evening when I was leaving school, I was terribly hungry. Actually, I'm always hungry; sometimes I wonder how a girl as skinny as me can eat so much and still be hungry. Anyway, this particular day, I saw a German soldier standing in front of Monsieur Deloeuvre's house, munching a piece of bread and butter. I stopped and stared at him, and I'm sure he could tell I felt envious of him eating that bit of bread and butter. Well, he beckoned me into the garage beside Monsieur Deloeuvre's house, which the Germans had turned into a kitchen. Ooh, it did smell good in that kitchen! The soldier made me sit down and he gave me a huge plate of food, and I gobbled it all down, and when I left he shook my hand like I was a grown-up. I felt terribly pleased with myself, because I'd been so hungry, and also because he had been so nice to me. And every afternoon after that, the soldier stood by the gate and watched for me, and if he was alone he would invite me in. He made special snacks for me. But we never said a word to each other – he couldn't speak French. He seemed happy just sitting across the table from me and watching me eat. Perhaps he had a little sister like me in Germany . . .

'Well, it went on like that for a long time. But one evening when I was sitting in the kitchen eating my snack, we heard footsteps coming towards us across the courtyard. The soldier looked terrified, and he gestured that I should go and hide in a cupboard – the top part was where they kept bread, and underneath was a space for sacks of flour. He made me kneel down between two sacks of flour, and pulled an empty sack over my head, to make me look like another bag of flour. It was one of those cupboards with double doors – you know, the upper doors opened separately from the ones below.

'The officer who'd come into the kitchen walked straight across to the cupboard where I was, and he opened the upper doors. I huddled in there while he inspected the shelves above me. I was trying not to breathe in case he heard me, and I closed my eyes and prayed. I told God that if only the officer didn't find me, I'd make it up to Him one day. And the officer didn't find me, he just shut the upper doors and went away.

'But my soldier friend – I think he was the cook – was too frightened to let me into his kitchen after that. Instead, he used to slip a piece of bread or a biscuit or bit of cake into my schoolbag as I walked past on my way home. He used to stand just inside the fence, and as I walked by I would turn my back to the fence, and he'd slip whatever he had into my bag. He went on doing it for weeks, but then one day he was gone. I went past the house every day, but I never saw him again.

'Well, that's the story. One of your soldiers was kind to me when I was hungry, so today I'm glad to be here to help you. And repay my debt to God.'

The German smiled. Every once in a while I had to wipe the blood from his lips. I asked him how he felt, and in a voice that was almost normal he said:

'Those pills your mother gave me have practically erased the pain.'

'Erased the pain' – it was the first time I'd ever heard that expression, and I remember it to this day. The German spoke perfect French, not only without an accent but with an elegance I wasn't used to. He seemed calm, serene; yet I was sure he knew he was going to die. It was as if he was thoroughly resigned to his fate.

'Tell me another story,' he said.

'All right,' I agreed, 'I'll tell you about the time I committed a dreadful sin.'

'A dreadful sin,' he repeated, smiling. 'I find that hard to believe.'

He closed his eyes. I hoped I wasn't boring him with my silly little stories, but it seemed that they amused him.

'It was just before Christmas. I was having lunch at this lady's house

– she was a dear old lady and she lived next door to the school. She had a German officer lodging with her, a tall handsome man who didn't speak a word of French. As a Christmas present, his family had sent him an enormous box of sweeties. I remember the lid was decorated with a beautiful Christmas tree. Well, on an impulse the officer gave the box to me. I'd never seen such a lovely box of sweets, filled with chocolates and all sorts of delicious things that we hadn't seen in France for years. It was like a dream come true.

'That night, as I made my way home, I hugged the box to my heart. I promised myself that I wouldn't open it, that I'd share it with my family. But it was a long way home and it was a miserable cold night. So I said to myself: "Just one little sweet won't hurt. . ." Then, before I knew it, I had eaten two, then three, then four – till there were hardly any sweets left in the box. And when I got home, Mama was furious with me. She made me go to confession. Father Roulland told me that I'd sinned, and that I might go to Hell. I believed him then, but now I think he was wrong. In fact, I'm sure he was wrong.'

'What makes you so sure?' the German asked, opening his eyes again.

'Because,' I told him, 'I believe that we're in Hell already.'

That led us into a discussion about Heaven and Hell, God, faith, hopes and fears . . . We talked about everything and anything under the grey sky, both of us completely oblivious to our surroundings – the cold water chilling our bones, the distant boom of artillery fire, the stray bullets that occasionally whined across the marshes. I even forgot my anxiety that Mama had been gone for so long. I confided in him, I told him all my doubts and dreams, and it was he who consoled and encouraged me, his head on my lap, his eyes closed most of the time, but his voice calm and normal. Every few minutes I would wipe away the blood from his lips. I felt as though I had known him all my life.

Suddenly his body was racked by a deep shudder. I asked him a stupid question. Here he had been immersed in the icy water for nearly seven hours, and all I could think of to say was:

'Are you sure you aren't cold?'

'It doesn't matter any more,' he said. 'Don't you worry about me, child.' Then there was a worried note in his voice as he added: 'Will your mother be back soon?'

'Of course she will,' I said firmly. 'She went off in the boat to find someone who can help carry you to the house. She isn't used to punting the boat, you see, and it'll take her a while to get to the nearest village and back. But she'll be here soon.'

'She's going to a great deal of trouble,' he said. 'But she'll never find anyone willing to help an enemy soldier.'

I protested at this; they were good people, the Normans, and if someone was hurt it didn't matter what uniform he wore, I told him.

'You've both done more than you should,' he said. 'You've risked your lives for me. But the truth is you can't do any more for me now. I'm very grateful for all you've both done already.'

I realized when he kept referring to 'you both' that he meant Mama and me, that he didn't know I had a father who could have come and helped if he'd been fit and sober. For their paths had never crossed, Papa's and this German officer's: when the Germans had arrived that morning, Papa had just left in his boat. Just as well, I thought, for I would have found it hard to explain to my German officer that Papa would never have lifted a finger to help him. Papa didn't understand the meaning of Christian charity – and neither did the Germans who were only a few hundred yards away in Amfreville; it would have taken them less than an hour to come across the marsh in their boat to fetch their wounded comrade. Without running any risk, either: there were no paratroopers anywhere near. And yet they didn't come.

I gazed down at my German, and tried to smile at him, but my heart wasn't in it. Nothing I could do or say could help him any more. And besides, I was getting very worried about Mama by now. She had been gone such a long time: where was she? Was she all right?

The German seemed to fall asleep. His head lay heavier on my arm and knees. Then he started up, opened his eyes, and shouted:

'Your mother! Your mother!'

'She's coming, Monsieur,' I told him. 'She's coming.'

I just said it to soothe him. But as I glanced over my shoulder, there she was – running down the railway line towards us. And if she was running, that meant she wasn't hurt.

'Tell her . . . tell her not to forget that letter,' said my German officer.

'She won't forget,' I promised him. 'Now, save your strength, she'll be here in a second.'

But Mama arrived too late. He gave one last shudder and died in my arms. His suffering was over. Almost at the same instant, the sun broke through again; the droplets of water on his face sparkled, and for several seconds he seemed bathed in a strange bright sort of beauty.

Mama had been gone for two hours; the German officer and I had been talking for two hours. From the first moment Mama had spotted him struggling back towards our house, over five hours had passed.

Those two hours had seemed like a lifetime. A man had lived, then he had died. Death in our part of the world was a natural thing; simple and logical, a part of life. That's what had made it easier for me to stay in the water all that time, talking almost normally, without embarrassment or anxiety, while the man's life ebbed slowly away. He had helped, of course; at no time did I sense that he'd been afraid.

Mama realized that he was dead the moment she saw him. She slipped her two hands under his head and gently raised him from my lap, moving him away from the embankment. His body slid beneath the water. I tried to get up but I couldn't move; I was too stiff. Mama had to lift me out of the water, and then half-carried me back to the house. We were both soaked to the skin, and our clothes were stained with blood. We had to wash ourselves and change into dry clothes and above all warm our chilled bones. After that long vigil with death, our warm silent house seeemed like a haven of peace.

I felt drained and desperately sad. Mama took me in her arms and held me tight.

'We did our best,' she told me softly. 'That's what matters, Geneviève – we tried. But his wound was too bad. There was nothing we could do to save him. When the war's over, we'll see that his family gets his letter.'

Yes, we would send that letter; it was all we could do for him now, poor man – the man who now lay beneath the marsh waters, the man who for a few short hours had been closer to me than anyone else in the world.

As soon as we got back to the house, Claude had run across to hug Mama.

'Do you have to go to the Sheepfold this evening?' he begged. 'I've been alone in the house almost all day.'

Mama cuddled him and soothed him. It was true, he'd been alone all afternoon, playing the gallant little doctor without help from anyone. Mama reassured him that she wouldn't be going to the Sheepfold; Francis could milk Blanchette, and besides, we had enough in the house to prepare the evening meal. We still had plenty of bread and milk, and the Americans' K-rations would make up for what we lacked.

The lieutenant – George – called softly from the bedroom, and Mama went in to see what he wanted. I didn't dare go in, for fear of waking Papa Maurice, but she beckoned me to join her at the bedside.

George was looking much better. The grey pills had obviously done their work. But both Mama and I remembered what the American officer had told us: 'They won't cure him but they'll make him feel better.'

Mama undid the bandages on his broken leg, and as the wound became visible, it was all I could do to stop myself from screaming out in horror. The leg was so swollen it looked as though it would burst. It was all blue and green, and it smelled horrible. Mama sent me to fetch the bottle of Calvados, and she bathed the open wounds. George said nothing; he gritted his teeth and closed his eyes.

We had no more bandages. The sheet that we'd cut up yesterday was completely used up. Mama stepped over the sleeping shape of Papa Maurice and silently handed me another pair of sheets. Remembering what we'd done before, I began to cut them into narrow strips. Then Mama changed the dressings on George's leg, handing me the dirty bandages to throw away. At the rate we were going, we'd soon be out of sheets, and then what would we do for bandages?

I decided to take matters into my own hands. I put a kettle on to boil over the hot fire, and then took it down to the cellar, which also served as our laundry room. I poured some strong soap into the water and one by one slipped the dirty bandages into it. The revolting smell and the sight of those filthy strips covered with blood and pus was almost more than I could bear, but somehow I managed it. I used a wooden stick to beat them as hard as I could, then removed them from the pan and rinsed them thoroughly. Finally I put them into another pan of fresh water and boiled them again over the hot fire.

Mama came out of the bedroom carrying a paraffin lamp, and asked what I was doing. Half-expecting her to be angry, I explained. She simply examined the results then knelt down and washed the bandages all over again, using a stiff brush. Later that evening, I rinsed them and wrung them out and hung them in the attic to dry. They would be ready to use again the next day. It would be a lot of work, but at least we could now be sure of enough bandages.

Mama prepared dinner for everyone. She asked me to feed the young German who had been shot in the thigh. Tomorrow, she said, I should go to the marsh to pick some flag irises, because they were known to have curative properties when applied to cuts. I tried to explain this to the young man while I fed him his supper, but he didn't understand a word of French. He probably thought me a real chatterbox. But at least I got a smile out of him when I approached him after dinner with a flannel soaked in eau-de-cologne and scrubbed his face so briskly that he ended up looking like the town drunk. Then I handed him a mirror, and he looked at himself with astonishment, no doubt amazed to find he was still alive.

The old German ate with us at the kitchen table. I don't know why, but he still frightened me, and I couldn't wait for him to finish his meal and go back to his corner. Papa was still asleep, but we weren't worried about him; it would do him good. Mama and I organized a regular watch, as we sometimes did in winter. In fact, it was so cold it reminded us of winter. Claude and Kerry were playing cards; Mama was sitting by the fire sewing. I took out my school books and tried to read – even though I had no idea when I might go back to school – but I couldn't concentrate.

Before I went to bed, I brought in a good supply of firewood for both fireplaces, so that Mama wouldn't have to go outside again that night. She noticed that I seemed unusually quiet, and asked if anything was wrong. I shook my head. But the fact was that I couldn't stop thinking about the man who had died in my arms that afternoon. And about George: for I knew that although he looked better, he was still terribly ill. And about 'our boys' out on the battlefield, some of whom might be injured, or even dying, with nobody to help them.

Somehow I knew that I was no longer a child, that this day had marked the end of my childhood: June 7th, 1944.

I had a dream that night. I dreamed that the German officer who had died in my arms was climbing up a beautiful staircase. He was holding a ray of sunshine in his left hand. In his right hand he held a handsome soldier's cape. He turned round and made a sign to me, far below. I was pleased to see that his uniform was clean and dry and well pressed, and that it not only had all its buttons on it again, but also its officer's stripes.

Thursday, June 8th, 1944

Dawn was barely breaking when sounds from downstairs disturbed me. I crept out of bed, careful not to disturb Claude. The two days we had just lived through had left their mark on him; his sweet little face seemed filled with a deep sadness. I tucked the blanket round him and bent down to kiss his cheek – but checked myself just in time; it would be kinder to let him sleep.

Picking up my shoes, I tiptoed towards the stairs, glancing automatically out at the marshes. It was still as grim and grey as ever. A fine biting rain was whipping at the window and, in the waters below, the waves were even choppier than in the past few days. I thought how rough it must be at sea, and wondered whether the Allies had really landed, or whether perhaps they had been delayed by the bad weather. If reinforcements didn't arrive soon, the Germans would have a chance to regroup, and then our paratroopers wouldn't stand a chance.

Mama was already up, preparing coffee in the kitchen, but her good-morning kiss was perfunctory, as though she was thinking of something else. I asked her what was wrong.

She was worried about the lieutenant, she told me; he had had a bad night, and his fever was getting worse.

'Can I go in and kiss him?' I asked.

'Yes,' she said, 'but be as quiet as you can. I think Kerry's still sleeping.'

As I tiptoed into the room, George gave me a faint smile, but I could see he was in a bad way. He was drenched in sweat, the fat beads of perspiration rolling down his cheeks, and his face was chalky-white and drawn. I knelt down beside the bed and took his hand in mine. It was burning hot. Silently I began to pray.

Mama's hand raised me to my feet, and she wiped the tears from my face. Taking me aside, she told me she was going to Sainte-Mère-Eglise to try and find a doctor.

'We can't wait any longer,' she whispered. 'I'm afraid George might die. There must be someone in the village who can come and give him proper care. I haven't any money, but I can promise to pay them when I get my next wages.'

'Why don't you take the money that the old lady gave me for my communion candle?' I asked, then went on: 'But Mama – do you really think it will help? You've done everything you can for George, the only thing left is to cut off his leg, and the doctor won't do that here. You'll be risking your life for nothing. Please don't go – think of Claude and me! If you were to die. . .'

'Don't worry, Geneviève,' Mama told me, calming my sobs. 'Nothing will happen to me. I'll pray to God as I'm walking. Whenever He's needed me, I've always done what He wanted. Now that I need Him, He'll know what to do.'

'When will you go?' I asked.

'As soon as I've finished my coffee,' she said. 'I'll have to go and milk the cows first, but I'll let the soldiers distribute it alone today while I sneak into Sainte-Mère-Eglise.' She gave a deep sigh. 'Those poor boys! They must be in a terrible state after three days and nights without sleep. And in this awful weather too. Oh – war is so *stupid!*'

I asked her what I should do while she was away.

Look after the patients, she said. 'Don't worry,' she went on, 'I've changed George's bandages already. Papa gave me a hand earlier. And keep an eye on Claude – make sure he doesn't go outside. I don't want either of you going outside at all, not even for a minute.'

I told her that I'd planned to go and collect some water avens to put on the German's wounds.

'No,' she said firmly. 'Promise me, Geneviève. You mustn't go outside under any circumstances. He's a healthy young man and as soon as he recoups all the blood he's lost, he'll be fine. The only thing I want you to remember is to give all the patients plenty to drink.'

'Where's Papa?' I asked. 'Has he gone to the Sheepfold already?'

'He's down in the cellar,' Mama said. 'He's decided to make a sort of portable chamberpot for the lieutenant. Call him and tell him coffee's ready.'

92

'But you told me not to go outside!'

'Keep to the wall and you'll be all right.'

Although the Germans entrenched in the Château d'Amfreville could have used our west-facing wall for target practice, the south-facing wall was safe enough. If you bent double and took advantage of the raised level of the railway, you could make it from kitchen to cellar in relative safety, despite the occasional bullet that whined past.

I was just opening the door to go outside when Mama called me back.

'Geneviève! Listen, I don't want you to say a word to Papa about me going to Sainte-Mère-Eglise. He might not let me go.'

I promised not to tell him. Then a sudden thought struck me, and I hesitated. 'Mama,' I said, 'there's something I want to tell you. You'll probably think I'm just being silly, but. . .'

'What is it?'

Then I told her about the old German soldier, the one who frightened me, the one I had a funny feeling about.

'No, I don't think you're silly,' Mama said thoughtfully. 'I'm glad you told me. I've seen enough of your funny feelings to know that you seem to have a sixth sense about some things. If you think there's something odd about him, I'm sure you're right. But for the time being I don't think you need worry. He's wounded, and he can't hurt anyone. As soon as he's better we'll turn him over to the Americans. Still, keep an eye on him, and if you see anything suspicious, call Kerry.'

I nodded. 'I just wish he was the one who'd died yesterday, not our nice German officer.'

'Yes,' Mama said, 'he did seem a very decent and loyal person. But remember, Geneviève, he was a German. He seemed nice to us yesterday, when he was hurt and miserable, but think what he might have been like if he'd arrived at the head of a German battalion and found us helping the paratroopers. Try to remember that, child. Never judge people by first impressions. Now, off with you – fetch your father for coffee. And not a word to anyone about me going to find a doctor.'

Down in the cellar, Papa showed me the fruits of his labour. I almost burst out laughing at the silly-looking thing he'd made, like a chair on stilts. He had cut out the wicker seat and fastened a makeshift chamberpot in its place. But silly as it looked, I realized that it was really quite practical. My parents' big old-fashioned bed stood several feet off the floor, and Papa had so designed this commode that it should be exactly the same height as the bed; now it could be moved right next to George and we could edge him across the bed and on to the pot without moving his broken leg.

Back in the kitchen Mama gave us our coffee, which we drank in silence. My mind was filled with all sorts of questions that I didn't dare ask. Why, for instance, was the roar of artillery so much louder today? Did Papa know, I wondered. I glanced over at him. He seemed more upset and depressed today, though I couldn't tell why. He seldom shared his feelings with us.

Then, suddenly, quite out of the blue, and as though he was speaking to himself, he said:

'He's had it. It's gangrene – I'm sure of it.'

Mama sighed. 'I'm afraid you're right.'

I just stared at Papa in disbelief. He really did have a heart; he was worried about the lieutenant. But then I'd learnt a lot about my father during the past three days.

Kerry emerged from the bedroom and sat down between my parents. He seemed to sense what was troubling them. He put an arm round them both and drew them close in a gesture of warm affection. Tears were rolling down Mama's cheeks. Kerry started talking, and though we couldn't understand the English words, we knew he was trying to comfort us.

It still wasn't daylight, but Mama rose to her feet; evidently she had decided to set out already. My heart pounding, I watched as she made her preparations, putting on her woollen work clothes. Was I right to let her go? Six miles was a long way to go through all that fighting. What would happen to Claude and me if she were killed? How would we be able to look after all our wounded soldiers if she didn't come back?

All of a sudden I noticed that Mama seemed to have got very fat. Then I understood. She had put on her working clothes on top of her town clothes, so that when she had finished milking the cows she would be able to go straight from the Sheepfold to the village, without having to come home to change. She could leave her working clothes at the Sheepfold and collect them on her way back from Sainte-Mère-Eglise. That way, Papa need never know what she was doing. (Mama would never have gone into the village in her rough working clothes. She liked to look neat and clean at all times, and the same went for us. It didn't matter that we were poor, she always made sure that Claude and I had fresh clean clothes to wear when we went anywhere.)

I felt a rush of pride. There she was, preparing to set out across a battlefield, risking her life at every step even though she didn't dare risk her husband's wrath. Then I found myself thinking that maybe there wasn't so much to choose between those two evils – the dangers of war or Papa's anger.

I stood at the window, watching as Mama set off along the railway tracks. When I could no longer see her, I turned from the window and took several deep breaths to try and calm my pounding heart. Now –to work.

I cleared the kitchen table and washed up the coffee cups, then prepared breakfast for our four patients. Papa and Kerry were both busy with the lieutenant. When I came to the old German and gave him his black coffee and biscuits, I could hardly control my trembling hands.

The blond German thanked me for the coffee and told me how good it was. It should have been: it was real coffee for a change, thanks to the American rations. After breakfast I changed his bandages. I had been right; his wound was healing fast, and there was no bleeding now. True, he wouldn't be able to walk for a few days yet, but we would soon be able to get him into a sitting position. The older German moved to a seat by the hearth, and I took advantage of this to fluff up the straw they'd been lying on. The blond one gave me a broad smile, but it quickly changed to a grimace when he saw me approaching with a bucket of steaming hot water and a flannel and soap.

I washed him as gently as I could, and when I'd finished I scrubbed out the bucket; it was the only one we had. Then I refilled it with hot water and offered it to the older German. He shook his head and resumed his meditative pose by the fireplace, his head resting against the mantelpiece. He hadn't washed himself once since he'd arrived. I wondered whether he was feeling so low that he just didn't care what he looked like; yet Mama had always taught us that the way you look affects the way you feel, and I was sure a wash would help him. So I tried again, offering him the bucket of hot water and soap. He shook his head even more vigorously. I gave up.

I knocked quietly at the bedroom door, and my father's gruff voice told me to come in.

'What do you want?'

95

I could tell he was in a foul mood. Timidly I said: 'I just wondered whether you wanted me to help you wash the lieutenant.'

'I'll tell you when I need you,' he snapped. 'Close the door when you go out. And leave the bucket.'

I knew better than to argue, so I turned and made a swift exit – so swift, in fact, that I stumbled and knocked my head on the door frame. Almost immediately, a bump the size of a goose egg sprouted on my forehead.

Claude was coming downstairs as I emerged from the bedroom and I met him on the bottom step and hugged him tightly. He saw my bump and his eyes widened.

'Did he hit you again?'

I told him about hitting my head on the door frame, but he seemed unconvinced. I sat him down and gave him some breakfast, but he only picked at it. He seemed silent and pensive, and I asked him what was wrong.

'Where's Mama?'

'She's gone to the Sheepfold,' I said. 'She'll be back late, though, because she'll have to track down all the cows that have strayed before she can milk them. Then she'll have to deliver the milk to all the soldiers, who're hidden all over the place, so it will take her a long time.' I was a bad liar.

Claude came over and nestled in my arms. 'Will the war be over today?' he asked.

'I'm afraid not,' I said. 'The weather's still so bad that the soldiers who are coming by boat have probably had trouble getting ashore.'

'What if they never come?'

'Never? Don't be silly!' I scoffed. 'The generals who planned the invasion won't give up now, after they've sent their paratroopers in already.'

'I wish the war would end,' he said sadly.

'*Geneviève!*' It was Papa calling. 'Come here!'

I ran into the bedroom, and Papa gave me the bucket. He had washed and shaved the lieutenant, who managed a weak smile when he saw me. But I could see the suffering in his eyes. My heart went out to him; he was so brave. Since last night the wounds on his broken leg had become even more infected and the room was filled with a terrible smell. Poor George, I thought; if only Mama could find a doctor in time . . .

After fluffing up the pillows, Kerry settled his friend back on the bed and then followed me out to the kitchen. He made me understand that he wanted to wash and shave, so I scrubbed out the bucket again and refilled it with hot water. He stripped down to the waist and began to wash himself.

I pottered around trying to find things to do, to make the time pass more quickly. But no matter what I did, I couldn't stop thinking about Mama, wondering where she was and whether she was all right. The time seemed to go so slowly. The steady tick-tock of the old clock only seemed to make it worse. Finally I couldn't bear the sound of it any longer: I went over to it and Kerry watched me, a quizzical expression on his face, as I stopped the pendulum.

At least, I decided, I could give Mama a pleasant surprise when she came home: I could make sure all the chores were done. She'd find the house as neat as a pin. I scrubbed the floor till the tiles shone, washed the windows, and even cleaned the tiles round the fireplace, which Mama generally cleaned only once a week, on Sunday mornings. The old German sat watching me curiously as I bustled around, tidying and polishing and poking the fire to make it burn better.

Kerry limped out to the courtyard and came back with a stack of canned rations for our lunch. I had trouble making him understand that we didn't need them today, because Mama had already cut up a rabbit for me to cook. I wasn't a very good cook yet, but I knew enough from Mama to be able to take over when she was gone. I mentioned to Papa that we had run out of vegetables, and that we'd soon need a fresh supply from the Sheepfold. He said he'd take the boat over to collect them.

As he was getting ready to leave, Papa said to me: 'Take good care of the lieutenant. I'm afraid he's not got very long.'

His voice was so choked with emotion that for a moment I couldn't find an answer.

Then I said: 'Don't be gone too long, Papa. The lieutenant needs you. It's easier to die when you've got someone you love beside you.'

'How would you know anything about that?'

I told him about the German officer who had died in my arms yesterday afternoon.

'How long did it take him to die?'

'I don't know exactly,' I said. 'Mama and I spent about four hours with him, but he'd already been in the swamp for hours before Mama spotted him.'

'How badly wounded was he?'

'A bullet in the chest,' I said, shaking my head. 'There's not much you can do about that.'

Now it was Papa's turn to shake his head. 'Bloody war!' he muttered. 'I'm sick of it.'

And with that he headed out to his boat. I think that he almost hoped a bullet would catch him as he crossed the marshes, that's how distressed he was about having to watch the lieutenant die.

Claude and I were left alone for several hours to care for our wounded soldiers. At lunchtime I took some food through to George, scarcely believing he would touch it, but to my great astonishment he ate every last morsel. Seeing the look of amazement on my face, he reached for his French phrase book and said, in French:

'*Je ne souffre plus.*'

He wasn't in pain any more. What did that mean, I thought. I knew that Papa hadn't given him any painkillers today; the boxes of pills were up on the mantelpiece, and no one had touched them.

I called to Kerry to come and witness this minor miracle: George's plate was empty, clean as a whistle, and he was even asking for a second glass of cider. I couldn't contain myself. I ran back into the kitchen and grabbed Claude by the arms and swung him round and round. If George was hungry again, I told myself, that meant that his body must have overcome the terrible injury to his leg. 'He's going to be all right!' The phrase was resounding in my head, over and over again. 'He's going to be all right! He's going to be all right!'

All of a sudden my anxiety vanished. Happiness breeds happiness: now I was almost sure that Mama would get home safely. Automatically my feelings of delight translated themselves into song.

'Geneviève!' Claude cautioned me. 'You'll wake everyone up!'

I smiled at him. He was right, of course – after lunch our patients all took a nap. Outside I could still hear the sporadic bursts of gunfire; inside, all was peace and quiet. No matter was what was happening beyond the walls of 104, I felt that hope had been reborn in the house.

I washed and dried the dishes, then put them carefully away. Time still lay heavy upon us, and to amuse ourselves Claude and I began to play cards. We had barely finished our second game when I saw through the window that Mama was coming back.

She was striding along the railway tracks, her step brisk, but she was alone. She did not have a doctor with her. But when she came into the kitchen I noticed a flush in her cheek and a gleam in her eye, and I guessed that her trip had been worthwhile. Claude rushed up and buried his face against her. She picked him up and hugged him, then turned to me.

'How's everything here?' she asked.

'Better than you know,' I said.

'What does that mean?'

'George. You'll never believe it – he ate like a horse! He says he feels better, and I think he's telling the truth.'

'I know,' Mama said.

For a moment I was puzzled. How could she know that he was better? Then I saw the mysterious little smile on her lips and I thought I understood what had happened.

'You didn't find a doctor,' I said, 'so you made your own special arrangement with God.'

Mama's smile was almost mischievous. 'Not with God,' she said. 'With the Virgin Mary.'

Perhaps I should explain that faith was just a part and parcel of our daily lives. God, the Virgin Mary, Jesus and all the saints were as familiar to us as our flesh-and-blood neighbours and friends. That my mother had made a 'deal' with the Virgin Mary struck me as perfectly natural.

So, while I reheated her lunch, Mama sat down by the fire and told me the story.

'I never got to Sainte-Mère-Eglise,' she began. 'The fighting is still going on there. Some American soldiers stopped me on the road that leads to the Couture farm, and they took me to an officer who spoke French. He asked me why I was trying to get to the village, and I explained that we needed a doctor for Lieutenant Wingate. He said it was out of the question. The area is still swarming with Germans, he said. He admitted that he didn't really know what the situation was in Sainte-Mère-Eglise because they had lost contact with the para-troopers who'd landed there, and he didn't even know whether they were still alive. In fact, he said he feared the worst, he thought the Germans had probably shot them all even before they reached the ground. Anyway, he told me that the Americans were hoping to set up a field hospital, and as soon as they had he would send someone over to help George and Kerry and pick up the two Germans. But there was nothing he could do for the moment.'

'And——?' I prompted.

'That's all,' Mama smiled.

But Claude and I screamed at her not to keep us in suspense. It was a long way back from the Couture farm. 'How did you get back?' we asked her.

'Well, the American officer got two soldiers to see me safely back as far as 103. If I'd been by myself I'd have been back long before now, but it took ages with those two young lads with me. Every time they heard a burst of gunfire, no matter how far away, they pushed me into the hedge or the ditch to hide until everything went quiet again. It took me twice as long to get back from the farm as it took me to get there. Oh yes, the officer also told me that when he sends the medics over he'll try and come with them. He's the one who gave me the idea of going to the Virgin Mary. Just as I was leaving, he said to me: "Keep up the good work Madame. And pray to the patron saint of your village for help." He kissed both my hands and added: "Thank you for all you've done for our wounded boys. May God bless you, Madame." He was terribly moved – I could even see tears in his eyes.

'Anyway, on my way home, I started thinking, and the more I thought about what he'd said, the more I understood that he was right. I should say a special prayer to the Virgin Mary, and She would help us.'

'What special prayer?' I asked.

'Curious as a cat, aren't you?' Mama laughed. 'Well, since you've worked so hard and done such a good job with our patients, I'll tell you. I promised the Virgin Mary that if She would save George's life, I'd make an offering of the ribbon of the poor at the next feast day.'

'Saint Marguerite's Day?'

'Exactly.'

'But what if the war isn't over?'

'Don't be silly,' Mama said confidently. 'It will be over long before then.'

The ribbon of the poor. It was the humblest and yet the most sincere offering that anyone could make. In our parish of Neuville-au-Plain, just over a mile from La Fière, the patron saint is Saint Marguerite, who was in her earthly life the poorest of the poor. Each year we pay her homage with a high mass and a feast that lasts long into the night. During the mass, the parishioners make an offering of a ribbon, usually blue or white, about four foot long and two to four inches wide. The parish priest blesses the ribbon, and the family then lays the ribbon on the statue of Saint Marguerite. The ribbon stays there till the wind and rain tear it to shreds. I've never heard of a

100

request made to the Virgin Mary in our part of the world, involving the ribbon of the poor, that was not immediately granted.

Mama had turned in her hour of need to the Virgin Mary. So she had known, even before I'd said a word, that George was already on the road to recovery. It is said that faith can move mountains – so why can't it cure gangrene?

We tiptoed into the bedroom, where both the Americans were asleep. George's face was relaxed and peaceful; his face was no longer bathed in sweat, the way it had been that morning, and he was less pale and his breathing was more regular. But most striking of all was the fact that the awful smell that had filled the room that morning had now completely gone.

Mama and I exchanged happy, conspiratorial smiles. I was convinced George was indeed going to pull through. Somehow I just knew that he'd passed the worst; from now on he would gradually get better.

Suddenly, whether because of our presence or simply because he'd slept long enough, George stretched and opened his eyes. He looked astonished to see us both there, standing motionless at the side of the bed. Taking our hands in his – a gesture he would have been too weak to make that morning – he smiled faintly.

'Mama . . . Geneviève. . .' he murmured.

Claude joined us in the bedroom, and I lifted him up so that he could see George. He leaned over and gave him a noisy kiss on the cheek. Kerry awoke, and slipped wordlessly from the bed; he grabbed his broom-crutch and hobbled off to the kitchen – and returned a moment later with a tall glass of cider which he gave to George. George downed it with obvious pleasure.

Outside the muffled roar of distant gunfire echoed across the marshes from the direction of Amfreville and Fresville. But we didn't care; the only thing that mattered now was that George was going to get better.

I asked Mama if I could go outside to wait for Papa at the level-crossing gate.

'I want to be the first to tell him that George is better,' I explained. 'Papa was so upset about George. I'm sure he only went over to the Sheepfold because he couldn't stand the thought of being here and watching George die.'

But Mama wouldn't hear of it. She repeated that I was not to go outside for any reason whatsoever. If I disobeyed, Papa would be furious.

'Besides,' she added, 'he may have been drinking.'

I knew what she meant. In the cellar at the Sheepfold there were two enormous barrels, each of them containing nearly four hundred gallons of cider. One was what we called 'pure juice' – strong stuff, with a high alcoholic content – and the other, diluted with water, served as our everyday drink. A few snorts of the former was enough to send Papa into a state of aggressive semi-drunkenness.

Late that afternoon I heard Papa's voice calling me. He sounded as though he was in a foul temper.

'*Geneviève!* Come and help me unload the boat!'

Normally he would have been perfectly capable of unloading the boat himself, but since his long stint in the marshes, his hands were swathed in bandages.

I went outside, remembering to hug the wall in case the Germans felt like using me for target practice.

Papa's boat was laden down with food. He had picked masses of vegetables, collected a basketful of eggs, an old chicken, a couple of rabbits, plus a pail of milk. The prow of the boat was virtually hidden by two huge bales of hay, which I guessed he had brought back for Mama and himself to sleep on. He had also brought back an ample supply of firewood, for our woodpile at 104 had been rapidly dwindling.

Silently I helped Papa unload the boat. I was bursting to tell him the good news, but I didn't dare say a word.

Then, as he watched me struggling to lift one of the great bales of hay, he said: 'That's too much for a skinny little thing like you.'

This unusual display of thoughtfulness gave me the courage to blurt out the news:

'We've got a surprise for you, Papa.'

'What surprise?' he asked gruffly, but I could see that his curiosity was aroused.

'George is better,' I told him, the words tumbling out. 'You'll see. He ate everything on his plate at lunch.'

Without pausing in his labours, he said tonelessly: 'The remission before death.'

I had heard the expression before. Often, before they die, people have a period of several hours – or even days – when they seem to make a miraculous recovery, as though their body has suddenly pulled itself

8. A drowned American paratrooper. *Special Collection.*
Editions Robert Laffont: Service Iconographique.

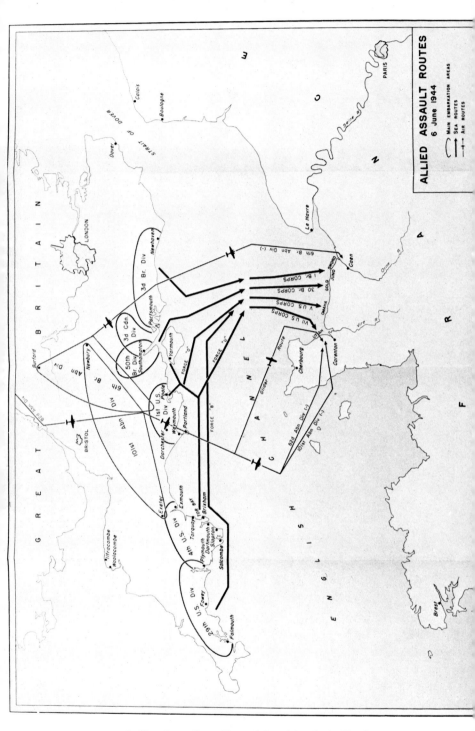

9. Map from *Cross Channel Attack* by G. A. Harrison.
Editions Robert Laffont: Service Iconographique.

10. Soldiers in combat, June 1944. *Editions Robert Laffont: Service Iconographique.*

11. The battle of Sainte-Mère-Eglise. *Editions Robert Laffont: Service Iconographique.*

together. I was positive that this was not the case with George.

'You're wrong,' I told Papa. 'Mama tried to go to Sainte-Mère-Eglise to find a doctor, but she was turned back, so on her way home she made a vow, and her prayers were answered. It's as simple as that.'

Papa set down the pail of milk on the ground, looking at me strangely, as though he hadn't really absorbed what I'd been saying. He stared at me fiercely, and I quaked before his angry look.

'If you're lying. . .' There was no need for him to finish the sentence.

'Go and see for yourself,' I told him, trying to hide my nervousness. 'I can finish unloading the boat. Anyway, with your hands like that, you shouldn't be carrying things.'

But he just stood there, still staring at me.

'Go on, go and see,' I said. 'What are you waiting for?'

Then he ran, faster than I'd ever seen him move before, towards the kitchen. Later Mama told me what happened when Papa had entered the bedroom. George was awake, and Papa dashed over to the bed, grasped the lieutenant's hands in his big peasant paws, dropped to his knees and started to sob, his head buried in the pillow. George gently withdrew one of his hands and stroked Papa on the head, like you would do to a small child.

'Papa Maurice. . .' he kept saying. 'Papa Maurice. . .'

Papa finally regained his composure and pulled up a chair so that he could sit beside the bed. He was still sitting there, in silence, clutching the lieutenant's hand, long after night had fallen. He couldn't believe the miracle had really occurred. And yet there it was, right before his eyes.

If further proof were needed, Mama made a big pot of cabbage soup topped with *crème fraîche* for supper that night, and Papa himself took the steaming bowl in to the lieutenant, who devoured every last drop.

Mama let us stay up later than usual that night, but Papa didn't even seem to notice. When Claude and I finally headed up the stairs to our room, Mama accompanied us, and as we crossed the kitchen she noticed that the younger German had tossed his blankets off. With the same gentle and maternal gesture that she would have used to us, she gently pulled both the parachute that served as a sheet and the coarse woollen blanket back over him.

She must have noticed the loving look I gave her as she turned round again. 'Yes, my child,' she said, smiling sadly, 'war is for men.

103

We women are made to love.' And then, so softly that I could hardly catch her words, she added: 'And to suffer, too.'

Friday, June 9th, 1944

Yesterday the birds weren't singing. Would it be the same today? I looked out of the attic window at the endless expanse of water that surrounded us. Another miserable grey morning. What had happened to the sun, I wondered, which at this time of year usually turned our marshes into a sparkling wonderland. The minute there's a bit of sunshine over Noires Terres, the waters are full of shining iridescence, all tender colours, and the marshes are a hive of activity as ducks and geese and a myriad other waterfowl strike up a chorus that lasts half the day. Later the sparrows join in, and the other tuneful creatures of the swamp. Papa used to say it was unusual to hear such a swelling chorus from the birds; it was only because guns had been banned and there had been no hunters for so long that the birds had acquired a new sense of security. But the hunters were back now, looking not for game but for other men. The result was the same: the birds had stilled their voices, scared into silence by the constant gunfire echoing day and night across the marshes.

What will today bring, I wondered. Will we live to see the end of it? Will the invasion really come today, will the reinforcements arrive to help the paratroopers who've had to cope by themselves during the past four days? These were the thoughts running through my head as I pulled on my clothes that morning.

But there was something else in the air: I sensed danger, closer than before. I cocked my ears for some unusual sound either in the house or outside, trying to detect what had prompted my suspicions.

I went downstairs with a sick feeling in the pit of my stomach, a knot of fear that I couldn't ignore. Four big cups of steaming coffee were lined up on the kitchen table and their aroma filled the kitchen with a delicious smell. But I knew I wouldn't be able to eat my breakfast or even drink the coffee. I was too worried.

Mama was buttering some slices of bread, and I went up to her and asked, as casually as I could: 'How are our patients this morning?' Then, before she could answer, I spotted the big mound of what looked like freshly made butter and I asked her: 'Did you make that this morning? I didn't hear you using the churn.' For we had our own churn, which made marvellous butter but which also made a terrible grating noise as the blades turned and meshed. It was a noise that was loud enough to waken the dead – but I hadn't heard it that morning.

'Yes,' Mama said. 'Francis had taken the cream off the milk that we haven't used these past couple of days and Papa very thoughtfully brought it back with him last night. I churned it down in the cellar, so as not to wake anyone up. As for our patients, George, Kerry and the blond German all slept like logs, but the older German spent most of the night coughing.'

'So that's why you made the butter.'

'Well, yes and no,' she told me. 'We'll all benefit from it.'

I knew that butter was a wonderful remedy for a cough. Drink a hot mugful of hot milk in which a spoonful of butter has been melted, and your coughing will have stopped within ten minutes. And the cough will go away completely if you repeat the remedy once a day. Despite the cold and dampness of the marshes in winter, and even despite frequent dips in the icy water itself, we never suffered from coughs or colds simply because of this buttery drink. In our family, with lots of sailors on both sides, we called it 'spreading oil on the water', the analogy being the maritime habit of using oil to calm stormy waters at sea. In any case, it was a remedy that always worked for us.

The Germans must have had to wade through the swamp waters on their way to our house, and the older one had caught a bad cold. But tomorrow, thanks to Mama's home-made medicine, he'd be as good as new.

'Did he take it without grumbling?' I asked her.

'Yes, as a matter of fact he even smiled,' she said.

She asked me to help serve breakfast to our patients. If she had prepared breakfast, I thought, that meant she had already changed all their dressings.

'By the way,' she said, 'yesterday you bandaged the young German too tightly.' A bandage shouldn't be too loose, she told me, in case it slipped off; but neither should it be too tight, because then it can prevent the blood circulating properly. She said she'd show me the right way to do it next time she changed his bandage. 'That way you'll remember,' she smiled.

'By the time the next war comes along,' I said, 'I ought to be a good nurse, don't you think, Mama?'

'There won't be any "next war",' she said. 'This will be the last one.'

I shook my head. How could she be so naive? The whole history of France is one long succession of wars, each more murderous than the one before. And if you go back and study early history, it's exactly the same. The Old Testament was full of wars; I knew that from reading my Bible. Maybe Hitler was the devil, but he hadn't invented anything; Joshua had wiped out the city of Jericho thousands of years ago.

I was only eleven, but already I'd read and seen enough to make me doubt those rosy stories about the glorious future of the world. I think adults are wrong to treat children as though they were stupid little creatures with nothing to do all day long except eat and sleep and play. Children have minds, too, and they can see through adults who're lying to them.

'You seem very thoughtful this morning,' Mama said, breaking into my daydream.

I asked her if I could take George and Kerry their breakfast.

'You like those two a lot, don't you?' she said.

'Yes – and so does Claude,' I replied.

'And what about those two——' She nodded at the two Germans lying on their bed of straw on the floor. 'Do you like them too?'

I wasn't so sure about the Germans. I didn't wish them any harm, I told her, and I was happy enough to look after them, nurse them back to health, but . . .

'You ought to like them,' Mama said.

'But they're *Germans!*'

'Well, some day you'll have to forgive them in your heart,' Mama said. 'So why not start forgiving them now?'

'After all the awful things they've done to us? All the deaths they've caused? You want me to forget all that? Can Bernadette forget that she has no mother now because of them?'

'Who's talking about forgetting?' Mama said. 'We shouldn't try to forget, but we can and must forgive. Ah, but perhaps you need to be older to understand a thing like that.'

'I've thought about all that,' I told her. 'The only thing that matters is that nothing happens to you or little Claude.'

'Are you afraid?'

Caught off guard by her question, I blushed to the roots of my hair. Then I said shyly: 'Yes . . . I've got one of those bad feelings. I can sense danger, Mama.'

She gave me a long hard look, but she said nothing.

When I took the coffee through to the bedroom, I found that Kerry was already awake. But he shook his head, and made me understand that he wanted to get up and have his breakfast with us at the table. George was not only looking better than yesterday, he was obviously feeling much better, I thought, as I examined his face and his eyes – his expression seemed alive again – and I offered up a silent prayer of thanks to God for this miracle.

Mama announced that she was going over to milk the cows again, leaving me in charge as usual. Despite the enormity of the events taking place all around us, there was a comfort in maintaining the regular routine of tasks and chores.

Claude finally woke up and came downstairs, and I gave him his breakfast, thinking at the same time that I should invite Papa in for a cup of coffee too. I found him down in the cellar, hard at work on another strange contraption.

'It's for the lieutenant,' he explained. 'I'll give it to him as soon as he's ready to start walking.'

When I looked more closely I saw that he was making a pair of crutches. Partly to please him, I suggested that when he finished the crossbar, I'd be glad to pad it with soft cloth so that it would be more comfortable to rest on.

'You mean to tell me you know how to sew?' Papa scoffed.

'Of course I do,' I retorted. 'Mama teaches me all sorts of things. Though, to tell the truth, I'd much rather do carpentry work with you.'

'Carpentry?' he laughed. 'You're crazy! That's not a girl's work.'

'I'd still like to learn it.'

'All right, then.' He handed me his plane. 'Here – see if you can smoothe down that piece of wood.'

A bit clumsily, I tightened the plank of wood in the vice and . . . Papa burst out laughing: I was too short to reach the top of the plank.

'Better start eating more,' he teased.

I wasn't beaten yet. Over in one corner of the cellar stood a wooden crate that had contained hand grenades. I pulled it across to the vice, adjusted the lid so that it was steady, and climbed on top.

'You see? I *am* tall enough!'

Papa let me make several strokes with the plane, then he put his hand out and raised my elbow an inch or two.

'More supple,' he said. 'You need to be more supple with your arm – and your wrist too. It makes the work much easier. There, that's the way to do it. . . . Not bad! You do have some talent, child.' He ran his fingers over the surface I had just planed down. 'Not bad, not bad at all.'

'I like wood, Papa,' I announced.

'You do?' he said, looking surprised. 'I like wood too. That's what I like best in the world. Wood.'

'Will you teach me how to make things?'

'We'll see,' he said. 'Perhaps one summer holiday – if I have time. But first you've to learn to read and write, that's much more important than anything else.' I could tell by his tone of voice that he was thinking sadly about how he had never learnt to read or write, and I quickly changed the subject.

'Claude wants you to come up and have breakfast with him,' I told Papa. 'He's been complaining he never sees you any more.'

He smiled and put down the plane. He always responded when his son wanted him. But evidently he had gone on thinking about that little episode in the cellar. He stared at me thoughtfully over the rim of his coffee cup.

'What do you want to be when you grow up, Geneviève?'

It was the first time he ever asked me such a thing. But without hesitation I told him: 'An aeroplane pilot.'

'Don't be so daft. That's not a woman's job either.'

'But there are lots of women pilots,' I told him. 'There's Maryse Bastie, Maryse Hilze, Helene Boucher——'

'How do you know?'

'I've read about them in books.'

'Well, I couldn't afford to pay for your studies,' he said, 'so you'll have to forget that idea.'

I didn't dare tell him that I wouldn't have expected him to pay for anything. There are certain truths that are better left unsaid, if you want to keep peace in the family.

So I simply said: 'Don't worry about me, Papa. I'll manage all right.

109

I'm just as stubborn as you are.'

This apparently amused him. The fact was that we were alike in many different ways: I have his eyes, his violent temper, his emotionalism, his love of solitude and the outdoors. But what I wanted to avoid at all costs was to resemble him morally. So I fought against it, as hard as I could. Yet I had to admit that during the past few days he had shown me another side of himself, a less harsh side. I had watched him devote himself wholeheartedly to helping others, saving their lives even at the risk of his own. He had acted really heroically. And I had discovered that he was capable of caring about the suffering of other people; I had even seen him cry over someone he cared for.

My parents – heroes? It didn't surprise me about my mother. Self-denial and sacrifice were so much a part of any peasant woman's role, especially when it came to bringing up children. Heroism seems to become a habit. But Papa, the 'Old Man', the drunk whom I had hated so much and so misjudged? As Mama said, beware of first impressions.

I watched this man, this hero, playing with my little brother, and suddenly I was overcome with emotion. I got up and kissed him.

'I really love you, Papa,' I said.

He reddened and turned his head away. My unexpected declaration must have affected him more deeply than I'd expected, or than he wanted to show.

Mama came back, carrying the big pail full of milk. It was almost midday, and I had already set the table and prepared lunch. Mama complimented me, something she rarely did, apparently for fear of spoiling me and because she thought I'd never be able to tell sincere compliments from mere flattery if I received them too often.

We took turns at looking after the patients, but Papa reserved for himself the task of serving and caring for George, who was without question our spoilt child. Mama helped me hoist the younger German into a sitting position on his bed of straw, and we propped him up with a thick eiderdown so that he could eat in a comfortable position. His colour was better and he too seemed well on the way to recovery. Kerry and the older German ate their lunch at the table. I noticed that they barely exchanged a word. Clearly Kerry didn't like him any more than we did. His sour face was enough to put off even the big amiable American.

110

After lunch, Mama helped Kerry back into the bedroom, despite his protests that he wanted to stay in the kitchen with us. But according to Mama's hospital routine, patients had to take a nap after their meals, and on that she was intractable. When Kerry was slow to obey, she scowled at him ferociously – and he burst out laughing. He seized her and gave her a big kiss on the neck, as though she were his own mother, then disappeared into the bedroom trailing laughter in his wake.

With our four patients safely asleep, we sipped our coffee quietly. Except for the distant rumble of big guns, it seemed a perfectly normal, peaceful day. But suddenly my feeling of apprehension returned. The knot in my stomach seemed even tighter. Papa had spotted someone approaching along the railway tracks, from the direction of Crossing 103.

Papa went into the bedroom and found George's binoculars, returned to the kitchen and stood at the window, following the visitor's progress down the line towards us. Still not saying a word, but his face mirroring his doubt, he came back to the table and sat down again, sipping his coffee.

'What is it, Maurice?' Mama asked anxiously.

'A Boche,' was the terse response.

'Is he armed?'

'Not that I can see – but you never know.'

'But he can't do us much harm,' Mama said, as if trying to reassure herself. 'Even if his intentions aren't the best, he'll see right away that we're good, decent people who don't pose a threat to anyone.' Then, pointing to the two sleeping Germans, she added: 'Besides, he wouldn't dare harm us. Who'd look after his comrades?'

Despite her words I felt the knot tightening in my stomach. I took a deep breath to calm myself.

'Should I go and wake Kerry?' I asked. 'He's got a rifle.'

'You keep out of this,' Papa said abruptly. 'I'll take care of this.'

More to keep my hands busy and my mind occupied than for any other reason, I poured some more coffee for both my parents. As I poured Mama another cupful, her eyes met mine, and in them I could read both indecision and anxiety. She was afraid, too, I thought – yet she was smiling.

Our house was the only one in the area. There was no likelihood that our visitor was simply passing by. Papa opened the door and stood there waiting for the man, while the rest of us huddled behind

111

him. Papa was right. It was a German soldier. He entered our courtyard, and his face reddened with anger as he saw the stockpile of American food and munitions crates. He walked around, touching first one box then another.

'You there!' Papa called out. 'Come over here!'

The soldier stared at him insolently, but Papa refused to be intimidated.

'Leave those cases alone and come over here,' he ordered, his voice full of authority.

The German seemed to understand French. He hesitated a moment at the entrance to the little courtyard, but Mama gestured behind her at the two German soldiers fast asleep on the kitchen floor, and put her finger to her lips. He probably didn't know what she was pointing at, but finally he did come into the kitchen, and seemed amazed to find two of his comrades peacefully asleep on their straw bed.

I offered to make the man a cup of coffee, but he brushed me aside and strode across to the older German, shaking him roughly by the shoulder. The German abruptly woke up and jumped to his feet, whereupon they started a rapid conversation in their own language. They walked over to the door and looked out at the pile of ammunition, their discussion growing more and more animated. Then the new arrival turned back to us and addressed us in French, his voice filled with anger and hate:

'You will tell me immediately which villages are in the hands of the American paratroopers.'

He was looking at Papa as he said this, but Papa didn't bat an eyelid.

'If you think I'm going to tell you where the Americans are, then you must be mad.'

'I demand that you tell me without delay.'

The German soldier didn't know who he was ordering about. I knew there were going to be fireworks. As the German opened his mouth to repeat his demand, Papa suddenly leapt at him. He grabbed him with his big peasant hands, twisting the man's arms behind his back.

'In this house,' he said, 'it's Papa Maurice who gives the orders. You will obey like all our other guests. And if you don't obey, I'll shut you up for good. See?'

The German soldier collapsed on to a chair. 'Please understand, Monsieur,' he began, his voice now softer and more conciliatory, 'I'm a soldier and all I want to do is rejoin my regiment.'

Papa released his hold on the man. 'I don't give a damn what you want, lad. Your war is finished. You're staying right here.'

'No, Monsieur,' protested the German, 'the war is not over yet. I can still serve my country. Please – let me go.'

'Ah-ha!' Papa snorted. 'You're not so superior now, are you, lad? You're not ordering, you're asking, eh? Well, at least that's a step in the right direction.' He paused, looking down at his captive. 'You think we should let you go, do you? Why should we do that? So that you can tell your mates to shoot at us? What do you take me for – an idiot? Haven't you done enough mischief already? You must be even stupider than I thought, you and the rest of the German army!'

The newcomer pointed to the cup of coffee I had offered him a few minutes before. 'Do you mind . . . ?' he said.

Mama nodded. He drank the coffee in silence. Then he went across to the older German and helped him back on to his makeshift bed. I remember thinking as I watched them that it was odd how warmly they clasped each other's hands: there was no warmth in either of their hearts, I was sure of that.

Before we knew it, the newcomer had made a dash for the door. He started running as fast as his legs would carry him down the tracks in the direction of Fresville. Taken by surprise, Papa hesitated. Then he turned and ran into the bedroom, grabbed Kerry's rifle, and raced out onto the railway line after the German. But the German was already a long way off. Papa tried to fire a shot after him, but the rifle wasn't loaded. So Papa put it down and raced down to the cellar, emerging a moment later with a hand grenade. He raised his arm as if to lob it after the retreating figure of the German, but then he lowered it and walked sadly back to the house.

'I've never killed anyone,' he said, 'not even a Boche. I just can't bring myself to throw this grenade at him while his back's turned.'

'You're right,' Mama said, in an effort to comfort him. 'Just because they act like bastards doesn't mean we should too.' And then she added under her breath: 'God willing.'

By nightfall we had put the man out of our minds. We were gathered round the fire making small talk; Mama was doing some sewing, Kerry and Claude were playing an endless game of cards. Suddenly Papa hissed at us to be quiet.

We all fell silent, and I could see in the bedroom that George had propped himself up on one elbow. In the distance we heard the dull

113

roar of a plane passing overhead. That was all: just an aeroplane. Mama went back to her sewing, I continued rolling up the strips of bandages that would serve as bandages tomorrow, Papa returned to his post next to George's bed.

The roar of the plane grew louder. Mama and Papa exchanged glances, then, without saying a word, they both got up. Mama turned out the paraffin lamp on the table. Kerry and Claude protested that they couldn't see to play cards now, but Mama silenced them.

Papa snuffed out the lamp in the kitchen, then he went out and closed all the shutters. Mama took a piece of old blanket and covered the door window, which didn't have shutters. Papa came back in, and returned to his place beside George.

'Smells a bit fishy to me,' he said. 'That plane coming in so low . . . It's as if it's looking for something specific – and I've got a feeling that something is us.'

Just then the older German started up in his bed and shouted at us triumphantly.

'*Kaput!*' he shouted. '*Vous kaput!*'

So that was it: the plane was coming to search us out, and he knew. Papa jumped up, strode over to the man and slapped him hard across the face. The blond German suddenly awoke, saw what Papa was doing, and demanded to know why Papa was assaulting his comrade. The older German started talking to him in their own language, then the blond one began to sob.

Papa came back to George's bed. 'It's those boxes of ammunition in the yard,' he said. 'That's what they're after. But there's no moon out tonight – with any luck they'll miss us. Still, we can't rely on luck alone. No noise, anyone – and no light. Keep an eye on the fires in the hearths,' he told Mama. 'They're all right as they are – I looked when I was outside and you can't see any smoke. Just make sure that you add the right sort of wood to keep it from smoking.'

That meant small logs, neither too thick nor too damp; Mama knew how to make a perfect fire. But even so, I thought, the plane could hardly miss us. The house was painted ochre, a colour that must stand out like a bright spot in the dark.

The seconds ticked slowly by, each as long as an hour. The blond German was still sobbing, knowing that death was stalking him, stalking all of us; and the irony of it was that it was his own people trying to kill us.

A sharp whistle broke the silence, then a heavy explosion shook the house. The first bomb. It had fallen in the marshes, but it hadn't missed by all that much.

'One down,' Papa muttered between clenched teeth.

'What's happening?' Claude asked him.

'There's a Boche plane up there,' Papa said, 'and it's trying to blow us all up. But don't you worry, boy. All your mother has to do is pray to her God and then everything will be all right.'

I couldn't tell whether he was joking or being serious. Was it possible that since George's miraculous recovery, Papa was beginning to believe in God?

We all fell silent again. The only sounds were the menacing throb of the plane overhead and the sniffling from the German in the corner. Finally, as if to lend courage to his cowardly comrade, the older German stood up, thrusting his right arm up in the air.

'*Heil Hitler!*' he shouted.

The savage cry rang through the house. That was too much for Papa. Turning purple with fury, he crossed the room and seized the German, lifted him up and then threw him back down on his bed of straw.

'One more remark like that out of you and I'll break your skull!' he roared.

The older German lay there rubbing his ankle; it had been on the mend up till then, but he must have hurt it again when Papa threw him down.

A second bomb, then a third, fell in close succession. I took little Claude on my lap. Every time another bomb exploded he buried his head against my chest. Then several minutes went by without an explosion, and Claude raised his big blue eyes to mine.

'Are we all going to die, Geneviève?'

I lowered my head and whispered in his ear, so that no one else could hear: 'I think so, poppet. He may miss us once or twice, but in the end I expect he'll get us.'

'Are you afraid?' he whispered back.

'A little bit,' I admitted. 'But it's not as bad as it might be – after all, we're all together.'

'Hold me tight, Geneviève,' he murmured. 'I want you to be holding me when I die.'

I cuddled him to me, wrapping my arms around him as tightly as I could. Then another bomb landed on the tracks nearby, and the whole house seemed to lift from its foundations, trembling, just as we were.

'Geneviève,' Claude whispered again, 'do you think God's going to take both of us? Together?'

'Of course He will,' I said. 'He knows how much we love each other, so He wouldn't want to separate us.'

'And Mama too?' Claude persisted. 'And the wounded soldiers? Even poor George, just as he's getting better? Oh Geneviève, that's horrid!'

I tried to soothe him, and told him to go to sleep, not to think about what was happening, but that was impossible.

'Geneviève. . .'

'Yes, Claude?'

'Please will you tell me what you were going to give me for my birthday?'

'Claude!' I rebuked him gently. 'You know that's a secret. It's not your birthday till September 30th. You'll have to wait till then.'

Claude knew that I'd been making numerous secret trips to the cellar, and whenever he asked to come with me I told him that he couldn't, because I was making him a present for his sixth birthday. Birthdays were sacred, and presents were only ever opened on the day itself. But under the circumstances I couldn't find it in me to deny him this one last pleasure.

'All right,' I said at last. 'I found this big thick fir branch that fell off a goods train, and I've been making you a hobby horse out of it. Carving it myself! When it's finished you can ride it either with or without wheels on it.'

I'd done all the carving with my own two hands. I got the idea from the branch itself: someone had drawn a beautiful horse on it, and all I'd had to do was follow the drawing.

The roar of the plane warned us that it was coming back, and the whistle of another falling bomb told us that he wasn't far from the mark. Another bomb exploded on the railway line, quite close by, and again the house trembled on its foundations. I hugged Claude even tighter. By the fireplace, Mama was sitting with her head buried in her hands, and I guessed she was praying. Papa was sitting by the bed, holding one of George's hands in his.

The minutes passed, and the plane seemed to have disappeared. Perhaps it had run out of bombs, I thought. How many bombs did such planes carry? The supply surely wasn't inexhaustible.

'Geneviève,' began Claude again, 'what would happen if a bomb hit

116

those boxes of ammunition in the yard?'

'There'd be an enormous explosion,' I said, 'and all of us would be blown straight to Heaven – and the house too. Where we are now, there'd be nothing but a huge hole.'

'Would the people in Sainte-Mère-Eglise hear the explosion?'

'Of course they would. Everyone for miles around would hear it. But don't worry,' I added, 'I think the plane has run out of bombs.'

I was wrong. A burst of lightning tore through the air, but it was further away this time, well down the line towards Level-Crossing 103. Then another, quickly followed by a third, made me think that the pilot had given up, that he was now letting his bombs drop more or less at random along the railway line.

Suddenly I saw that Mama was trembling. She'd been a model of calm up till now, and at first I couldn't think why she should have lost her composure. Then I realized she was worried about Francis at the Sheepfold, which wasn't far from 103.

Little by little the roaring engines faded away, till at last we could hear nothing more. But no one dared go to bed. The plane might come back . . . So we stayed there, as if frozen in some strange tableau, throughout the night, until the first light of dawn convinced us that our nightmare was truly over.

117

Saturday, June 10th, 1944

We had had our share of surprises over the past five days, but looking out of the window that Saturday morning we could hardly believe our eyes. The bombs had knocked over telephone poles like matchsticks; the railway tracks, both in the direction of 103 and Fresville, were twisted and broken, rising from the scooped-out craters like crippled arms. And in the marshes the bombs had traced a necklace of huge holes, and the water – normally so placid – made strange and ever changing whirlpools. The astonishing thing was that all the bombs had fallen within a radius of about a hundred yards from the house, forming an almost perfect chain around us. How did we manage to escape? It seemed miraculous. Papa, Kerry, Mama, Claude and I gazed out at the pattern of bomb craters in utter silence. Claude and I exchanged glances. Then Papa turned to Mama, shaking his head in undisguised awe.

'You can tell your God that I take my hat off to Him.'

'Why don't you tell Him yourself?' Mama replied gently.

Papa shrugged and turned away.

The older German, for obvious reasons, now kept even more to himself, and we made no further efforts to help him. And after what had happened last night, Papa had made up his mind to ask the American headquarters to send us an armed guard. He hopped on his bicycle and set off along the railway tracks, zigzagging as he went in order to avoid the craters and to confuse the constant sniping from German guns around the Château d'Amfreville. We watched him go with our hearts in our mouths, expecting to see him topple off his bike at any moment. But somehow he managed to weave his way through the hail of machine-gun fire until we could see him no more.

When he returned several hours later, he brought some bad news. The paratroopers were virtually out of ammunition, and in some places they had resorted to hand-to-hand combat. The fiercest fighting was going on at the Patte d'Oie de Cauquigny. General Gavin and General Ridgway had set up headquarters near there, but they and their men knew they were done for unless help arrived very soon –within a matter of hours, in fact.

Papa had asked about the American officer who'd stopped in at our house and who knew about all the boxes of rations and munitions that he'd fished out of the swamp.

But apparently the officer had never reached them. He'd been killed before he made it to their headquarters. The Americans could hardly believe it when Papa told them about all those boxes he'd recovered: ten tons of munitions and five tons of rations! But even if Papa were exaggerating, the results of his salvage operations would give them more food and materials than they needed.

'And so they're coming to collect the crates,' Papa finished. 'In fact, they'll be here any minute.'

And, indeed, it was only minutes later that the increase in firing from the Germans announced that the Americans had arrived.

The soldiers gazed around in wonder as they stood in our courtyard piled high with crates and boxes, and saw the ring of bomb craters around the house. They spent most of the rest of the day manhandling the crates away.

It was painful for us to watch them, those tall, smiling, cheerful soldiers – 'our' soldiers – who had first set foot in our house only five days before. Their eyes were circled with dark rings of fatigue, their faces had become pale and sallow, and their jaws dark with several-day-old stubble. The laughter had been drained out of them by the terrible hours and days they had since lived through. And what was more, although they were determined to fight to the finish, they must have felt that they'd been abandoned, that the long-promised reinforcements would never arrive.

For the first time in my life, I resented the fact that I was still young – too young to help them. I wanted to go with them, to care for them and nurse them; if necessary to hold their hands when they were wounded or dying. But there was nothing that any of us at 104 could do to help them now.

It was about five o'clock that afternoon. I was up in my bedroom,

119

peering out of the window through George's binoculars. Suddenly I saw them in the distance, a line of soldiers walking in single file alongside the high hedge that borders the Big Swamp, all bent low, moving with deliberate caution. Who were they? Where were they going? I strained my eyes and tried to focus the binoculars on them. Then one man at the end of the line suddenly straightened up for a moment, and I realized who the men were.

'*Germans!*' I shrieked in alarm.

They were almost certainly from the Château d'Amfreville, and it looked as though they were making for Cauquigny. I knew that the American soldiers who'd come to collect the ammunition would not yet have got back to Cauquigny, because they had told us they'd be stopping off at a farm near Level-Crossing 103. The Americans occupying the Cauquigny chapel were an isolated outpost, and the Germans were heading towards them. Unless the Americans could be warned, they would all be massacred, for they had nothing but their knives and bayonets to hold off the German column.

Suddenly I had an idea. If Papa Maurice could take his bicycle, he might – by using the maze of little lanes – manage to reach the chapel before the Germans. Then he could warn the Americans, so that they could at least take some sort of measures to defend themselves, or perhaps abandon the chapel and retreat to safer quarters.

But I hesitated for a moment. If I called Papa, I'd have to confess that I'd borrowed George's binoculars without first asking his permission. That would probably earn me at least a slap in the face. Too bad. I turned and leapt down the stairs, two at a time.

'Mama! Mama!' I yelled. 'Where's Papa?'

Even before she had a chance to reply I was already making my way down to the cellar. I grabbed Papa by the sleeve and dragged him up to my bedroom without saying a word. When I'd got my breath back at last, I pointed out over the Big Swamp.

'Hurry!' I panted urgently. 'Hurry!'

Papa grabbed the binoculars from me and peered out in the direction I was pointing.

'Bastards! Filthy bastards!' he roared. 'They're going to attack our boys!'

'Are you going to go and warn them, Papa? Are you taking the bicycle?'

'Of course,' he said. 'It's my only chance. I may not make it to the chapel, but I'll try. And on my way I can alert the soldiers stationed at the farm near 103 – the ammunition is stocked in the barn there.'

'Let me go with you, Papa,' I pleaded. 'There's going to be a battle and the boys will need a nurse. I've learned a lot and I'll take all the bandages I can find, only please let me go with you!'

He looked at me curiously for a moment. Then he said: 'All right, girl. I'm pushing off now. But you'd better ask your mother first.'

'What if she says no?'

'Let your conscience be your guide.' Then, as he crossed the room to the head of the stairs, he suddenly stopped and turned back to me. 'And you can try praying to your God,' he added. 'You're going to need all the help you can get – and so are those soldiers over there. Good luck, girl.'

'Good luck, Papa.' I hugged him for the first time in my life with real pleasure.

Papa collected his bicycle and started off towards 103, pedalling furiously. I went to find Mama, hoping against hope that I'd be able to make her let me go with Papa. I knew it wasn't going to be easy.

I found her in the kitchen. 'Mama! Mama! Papa's gone off to Cauquigny, and I'm going too! Quick, help me get all our bandages together – there's bound to be lots of soldiers wounded when the battle starts!'

'What are you talking about?' she demanded.

Impatiently I explained about the Germans I'd seen heading for the chapel where the Americans were. 'And they haven't got any ammunition left, and it's going to be a terrible slaughter! Oh, please hurry Mama!'

Firmly, calmly, Mama said: 'You're not setting foot outside this house, Geneviève.'

'Oh yes I am!' I cried. 'Papa said I could!'

'A battlefield is no place for children,' Mama retorted. 'War is for grown-ups.'

'You think I'll get killed? Is that it? Well, so what if I am? I don't care! I'd rather die over there with our soldiers than go on living in this house where I'm treated like a dog!'

I don't lose my temper very often, but when I do I lose control completely. Before Mama could recover from my outburst, I dashed into the bedroom. George asked what we'd been arguing about, but I just flung open the cupboard and pulled out some sheets, then turned to dash out again.

Too late. Mama, who had followed me into the bedroom, had shut

121

the door and was leaning hard against it; I couldn't budge it.

'Geneviève,' she began calmly. 'Listen to me, Geneviève. Calm down and listen——'

'I haven't got time,' I shrieked.

'Please, Geneviève——'

'Mama, do you want me to get *really* angry?'

Mama knew that my temper tantrums, although infrequent, were totally uncontrollable. And when I wanted to I could summon up enough strength even to push her aside.

I made one last attempt to persuade her. 'Mama, what's the point of saving all those men from drowning if we're just going to let them die now? We've got to help them! And don't go telling me I'm too young. I'm as old as you are! Oh don't look so surprised – you think about it: what do you ever do when Papa attacks me? You just sit and cry in a corner!'

I'd gone further than I meant, and Mama's tears were flowing down her cheeks. But I couldn't stop myself. I was so angry that even her tears didn't affect me. All I could think of was how our boys were going to die, and my heart felt as though it was breaking.

'Geneviève, listen to me. I've got a very good reason for not letting you go over there. Let me tell you what it is. Then, if you're still determined to go, I'll give you my permission.'

Her words had a calming effect, and as I stood there with my arms full of sheets, I nodded to show that I was willing to hear her out.

'When you go out walking with your little brother,' Mama began, 'you have to keep an eye on him all the time, to make sure he doesn't go too near the water. That's true, isn't it? Now, have you stopped to think how those soldiers feel about you? They probably feel they have to keep an eye on you. Instead of concentrating on defending themselves they'll be worrying about whether you're all right. It could cost them their lives, Geneviève. Is that what you want?'

My anger was evaporating. Mama was right. I hadn't thought about that.

'I'm sorry,' I mumbled. 'I'm sorry I said those horrible things to you, Mama.'

'That's all right,' she said soothingly, 'I know what you were feeling.'

'But surely there's *something* we can do for those soldiers?' I cried desperately.

'Pray, child. Pray to God.'

I went upstairs to my room, feeling that I had all the weight of the world on my shoulders. I sat on the edge of the bed, then spotted the binoculars where Papa had dropped them on the windowsill.

I leapt up and grabbed them, focusing them with trembling hands.

The Germans had surrounded the chapel at Cauquigny. The Americans were filing out, one by one, their hands over their heads. With no ammunition left and only their knives to defend themselves, it had been an unequal fight. The Germans lined them up in a double column, and they started marching off. I guessed they would be heading for the German headquarters at the Château d'Amfreville. There must have been about thirty Germans, and the same number of American prisoners.

They had gone some three or four hundred yards when two German soldiers grabbed one of the prisoners and pulled him from the American ranks. They forced him to undress at gunpoint, then tied a rope around his ankles and threw the other end of the rope over the branch of a nearby tree, and hoisted him up so that he was hanging head-down a couple of feet above the ground. I remembered what my parents had told me: in wartime, they'd said, prisoners and wounded soldiers were relatively well treated by their captors. So what was going on here?

Suddenly one of the Germans pulled out a knife and started slashing at the man who was dangling from the tree. He twisted and turned at the end of his rope in an effort to protect himself, but in vain. The German went about his business almost methodically, as though he had all the time in the world.

I put down the binoculars and burst into tears. That poor American! I'd got to do something to save him – but what? I was about a mile away from them. Maybe I could take the boat? No, it was on the wrong side of the railway line. Maybe Mama could help me carry it across the tracks to the right side? No, it was hopeless. It would take me hours to get there in the boat, and by that time all the poor paratroopers would have been killed. Even if I did make it in time, why would the Germans pay any attention to me?

I wiped away my tears and picked up the binoculars again, torn between the desire to avert my eyes from the horrifying scene and the need to know what was going on.

The other American prisoners were watching, helplessly, as their comrade dangled at the end of his rope, the German still slashing at his helpless body. Suddenly a bunch of them – eight or ten, perhaps –

rushed their captors, whose attention had evidently been focused on the twitching victim. They must have been unarmed, those Americans. There was a brief skirmish, followed by a burst of gunfire. The Americans fell to the ground. I got the impression that the Germans had aimed for their legs, but I wasn't sure.

The Americans who hadn't attacked the Germans were now made to come forward and drag their comrades back against the hedges that bordered the marsh. Then they were ordered back into line. The Germans advanced on the wounded paratroopers and began to take their revenge, repeating the vicious torture with their knives. I watched in rising horror as the Germans stabbed at the fallen men, now shrinking into the hedge and vainly trying to protect themselves from the flashing blades.

I seemed to share their dying agonies, as though I too were being stabbed and slashed by those knives. I felt sharp pains all over my body. I felt sick. I couldn't bear to watch. I fell to my knees and started to pray.

I have no idea how long that scene of vicious butchery continued. Half an hour? An hour? I don't know. The last image I had was of two Germans cutting the rope from which the American paratrooper had dangled, then dragging him along and heaving him into the swamp. Then, apparently pleased with their afternoon's work, the Germans marched off in the direction of Amfreville. As far as I could see, they had no prisoners with them.

Dusk was already shrouding the murder scene in a merciful blanket. I began to shake from head to foot. Thirty or more American soldiers, unarmed prisoners, had been massacred. I felt a wave of shame suffusing my whole body, shame at being alive in a world where such atrocities could occur. And I knew at last, with total conviction, that this was Hell; Hell wasn't a place where people went after death, Hell was right here on earth.

I went downstairs. Kerry, Claude and the American guard that had been dispatched to stay with us that morning were all deep in a game of cards. They merely glanced at me as I entered the room, and if they noticed my expression and my tears they presumably thought it was because Mama had punished me. They had no idea what I had witnessed from my room upstairs.

I tiptoed into the bedroom to return George's binoculars without waking him up. But he was already awake, and he looked at me closely.

'*Oh Geneviève!*' he said in French. '*Vous beaucoup pleurez!*'

I nodded. I didn't trust myself to speak, because I knew that if I did I would burst into tears. I picked up the notebook that lay on the table beside him, and in it I wrote, as legibly as I could:

'Germans are very bad men.'

I wished my limited vocabulary included an English word that was stronger than 'bad', but it didn't.

George read my message then looked up and asked: 'Why, Geneviève?'

I took the notebook back and wrote: 'Germans have killed thirty American soldiers.'

George sat up suddenly, propping himself on one elbow and staring me at me. 'Where?' he asked.

'A mile away,' I whispered.

'Are they all dead?'

I nodded.

George took the binoculars from me and set them down on the table. Then he picked up the damp flannel Mama always kept beside him to cool his brow, and gently he wiped away my tears.

'My little Geneviève. . .' he murmured. 'My little Geneviève. . .'

I felt old and tired, so tired I wanted to die. I kissed George then straightened up. Tonight Mama could take care of the patients without me. Kerry and our American guard would be only too glad to help. I would go up to bed.

I crossed the kitchen where Mama was setting the table for supper. As I passed her I said: 'Don't ever talk to me again about God. I don't believe in Him any more.'

Mama didn't know what I had seen from my window upstairs; she probably thought I was referring to our emotional scene that afternoon.

'You're just saying that because you didn't get your way today ' she said. 'Maybe some men had to die this afternoon but you don't know how many God's going to save. So don't judge what you don't know.'

I shrugged my shoulders. I felt too sad to say goodnight to anyone; even Claude would have to go without his usual goodnight kiss. How could I wish anyone a 'good night' after what I had seen.

I couldn't go to sleep. Every time I closed my eyes I saw again the torture and suffering that I'd witnessed a few hours before, and again my body would be racked with pain and my soul filled with sorrow. No prayers tonight. You're not my friend any more, God.

125

Later that night Papa came home with the news that he had never made it to Cauquigny. By the time he reached the American lines, the fighting had already started. But the Americans had been warned that a German column was advancing towards the Cauquigny chapel, and they had withdrawn some eight hundred yards, back into the ruins of the Leroux farm near the bridge over the Merderet, leaving only sixteen men behind to cover their retreat.

My only consolation, hearing Papa's story, was that only sixteen Americans had been captured, not the thirty I had supposed. Of those sixteen, none had survived.

Sunday, June 11th, 1944

My first glance out of the attic window told me something strange had happened. First of all, I realized that it was full daylight: this was the first time since the paratroopers had landed that I hadn't woken up at the first faint light of dawn. That wasn't so surprising, though, for last night I hadn't been able to get to sleep for hours; haunted by the events of that day, my weary body had refused to respond to its normal clock. But as I stared out over the marsh waters – as choppy as ever beneath the grey sky – at first I could not define what was so strange.

I slipped into my clothes and ran downstairs, taking the steps two at a time, so that I burst through the partially closed door at the bottom of the stairs and fell into the arms of the American guard in the kitchen. He laughed at my abrupt arrival, and said something in English that I couldn't understand. Mama and Papa were also in the kitchen, and they seemed to find my arrival equally comic, for they too were laughing. They were oddly relaxed, their faces beaming for the first time in ages. Something had definitely happened – but what?

'What's going on?' I asked Mama.

'Curiosity killed the cat!' she smiled. 'First say good morning to everyone. Then I'll tell you, not before.'

I did the rounds as fast as possible, giving everyone a swift peck on the cheek, including Kerry and George. When I came to Papa, I hesitated for a moment, then took my courage in both hands and gave him a kiss too. The guard pointed to his cheek, smiling, so I obliged and gave him a polite peck as well, then turned to Mama impatiently.

'Tell me now!'

Without saying a word, Papa handed me the binoculars and led me outside, where he pointed in the direction of Amfreville.

Then I realized what was so strange about that morning. Here we were, outside, standing on the railway tracks in a direct line with the Château d'Amfreville, and no one was shooting at us. Silence reigned over the marshes. There wasn't even the distant boom of artillery or rattle of machine-guns. Just silence.

I adjusted the binoculars and looked towards Amfreville. Oh what a marvellous sight! The American flag was flying over the château, flapping slightly in the breeze. It looked so beautiful. I recognized the stars and stripes right away. At school Mademoiselle Burnouf had once drawn it for us on the blackboard, using the last of her coloured chalks. Then she'd made us copy it. We had never worked so hard on a drawing, but we wanted to get it right because we knew that flag was a symbol of freedom. After we'd finished our drawings Mademoiselle collected them all and threw them into the fire. We understood. If anyone had been found with a drawing of the American flag, we'd have been in serious trouble. But she had also taught us to draw the British flag, and the Russian flag too, and she had promised that after the war she would teach us to sing the words of the national anthems of all the Allied countries.

I lowered the binoculars, then raised them again to make sure I hadn't been dreaming. It was true. The flag was still there. The Americans had taken the Château d'Amfreville, which must mean that the Germans had gone. Soon the war would be over – maybe it already was!

I turned to Papa, full of excitement and delight, wanting to know what had happened.

'The reinforcements arrived,' he explained. 'The troops who were coming by sea. They finally made it – and they linked up with our soldiers.'

'Our soldiers.' At long last they would have a chance to rest. How many of them had survived? All of a sudden my eyes filled with tears, and I remembered the slaughter I'd seen yesterday afternoon. They'd been murdered for nothing!

Silently I handed the binoculars back to my father and returned to the house. I went up to our bedroom and shook Claude awake.

'Claude! Wake up! The war is over! The Americans have won!'

He sat up, rubbing his eyes and staring at me in wonder.

I picked him up in my arms and carried him over to the window. From there we could clearly see the flag flying on the roof of the château.

I hugged Claude tightly – too tightly, perhaps.

'The war may be over,' he said, 'but you're squeezing me to death, Geneviève!'

I apologized and carried him back to the bed. Then I noticed his serious little face and asked him what was wrong.

'Don't you see?' he said. 'If the war's over, then we should thank God – and we ought to do it straight away, before we forget.' And he kneeled down beside the bed, his hands clasped and his eyes closed, and started to pray.

Somehow I couldn't bring myself to follow his example. After the horrible events of yesterday afternoon I still felt outraged that God hadn't stopped it. Besides, I had something much more important to do. I had to learn to be free.

I went downstairs and walked outside on to the railway line. For five days I hadn't dared stand on the tracks without fearing for my life. I gazed out at the silent marshes, wondering about my friends the ducks and other wildfowl. I whistled to them but there was no response. Just the silence of a dead world. Sadly I realized the birds were either dead or so frightened by the past few days of carnage that they had lost their voices – I would have to learn to live without them, perhaps even without the sun. Again today the sun was hidden by a thick grey blanket of cloud, like a vast shroud. What if the sun never appeared again? Would I ever learn to live without the birds and the sun? I felt a great wave of sadness engulf me.

Mama had evidently been watching me and seen me lost in my sad thoughts. She came out on to the railway line beside me and put her arm round my shoulders.

'You look as though the world has come to an end,' she joked.

I burst into tears and buried my face against her.

She patted me and murmured soothing words of comfort. 'There, there . . . You've been so brave, Geneviève. Now isn't the time to give up.'

'I called the birds and they didn't come!' I sobbed. 'And the sun's hiding too. Everything's so sad, Mama!'

'The birds will come back,' she said. 'Give them a little time to forget how frightened they've been this past week. After all, you haven't been singing either, have you? But you're still alive. And as for the sun . . . Look, the clouds are scudding past – I bet you'll see the sun again this afternoon. And when we've all forgotten what has happened, everything will be just the same as it was before.'

'Forget?' I cried. 'How can I forget? I won't ever forget!'

'Yes you will,' she said gently. 'Time erases everything. Little by little all your memories fade away – first a tiny detail, then an entire day that you can't remember. No matter how hard you rack your brain, you won't be able to remember.'

But I knew she was wrong. 'I won't forget,' I said stubbornly. 'When I'm very old, if I have grandchildren, I'll be able to tell them exactly what happened these past few days, every single detail.'

Then, because the war was over, I asked Mama if I could go to the eleven o'clock mass in Sainte-Mère-Eglise.

'Definitely not!' she exclaimed. 'Not yet anyway. No one has any clear idea of what's going on there yet – though it shouldn't be long before we find out what the situation is and whether it's safe.'

'What about my First Communion?' I asked. 'It's only two weeks away.'

'You're not going to change my mind, Geneviève, so stop trying. If you're good, I may let you go over to the Sheepfold this afternoon to visit Francis, but that's as far as I'm letting you go. You can take Claude with you, if you promise to look after him. You should see how beautiful that glider is!'

'Oh yes!' I cried delightedly. I'd forgotten about the glider. 'Wait till I tell Claude!'

While Mama went back to the kitchen to prepare breakfast, I ran upstairs to find Claude. Glancing out of the attic window en route to the bedroom, I noticed that Papa was already out in his boat, heading across the marsh waters towards the Sheepfold.

Claude was still kneeling beside the bed, praying. I waited for him to finish, then broke in:

'Breakfast's ready, Claude – come downstairs.'

He was so deeply immersed in his prayers that he simply didn't hear me. Finally I lifted him up and carried him down to the kitchen. I envied him his ability to pray with such fervour. I had always helped him to say his prayers, because I was older, but despite his tender age I knew that he could teach me a thing or two about praying.

Over breakfast we discussed the latest events, but through it all there was the constant refrain: the château's in American hands now, the war is over now! It was almost too good to be true. I had a hundred plans buzzing in my head and I started telling Claude about them, and we both got more and more excited. When I told him we might go over to the Sheepfold in the afternoon, he was almost beside himself with delight.

When we'd finished breakfast, I hoisted Claude up on to the chair between the fireplace and the old clock and started to dress him. Mama was on her knees, polishing the red tiles as she always did on Sundays.

Suddenly I heard something hit the floor. I swung round and saw that a hand grenade was rolling towards the kitchen door, which was closed against the cold morning. Mama and I both glanced at the guard: he'd had a hand grenade attached to a loop on his uniform. The grenade had gone, but the firing pin was still attached. The grenade was therefore about to explode.

Somehow I had time to think: 'How stupid! The war is over and now we're going to die because of a silly accident in our own house!' The guard who had been sent to protect us – I didn't even know his name, but I'd dubbed him 'our guardian angel' – was actually going to be our angel of death.

I hugged Claude to me and turned my back on the room, hoping my body would shield him from the worst of the blast. Mama was still on her knees, and I noticed the glimmer of tears in her eyes.

The American had been standing stock still, as though paralysed. Now he suddenly sprang to life. He ran towards the grenade, still rolling slowly across the floor because of the slight incline, and picked it up. Dashing outside, he threw it in the general direction of the swamp. A bare second later the air was torn by a loud boom, echoing down the railway line towards us.

None of us had dared to breathe. Mama was the first to react. She got to her feet and went to the door. Our guardian angel was lying face down in the yard. Poor man, I thought; he sacrificed his life to save us.

Claude followed me as I went out to the yard. Mama was kneeling beside the soldier – and suddenly I saw that he wasn't dead. His face buried in his arms, he was sobbing like a baby. Mama stroked his hair and murmured softly to him, even though he couldn't understand. But he must have known from her tone that she was trying to comfort him, and at length he got up. He towered above my mother, yet to me she looked twice as tall.

Kerry had been in the bedroom when he heard the explosion, and now he rushed through to find out what had happened. The guard explained the accident to him. Then George called the unfortunate man into the bedroom and seemed to be protesting; but when he

131

heard the full story of how the guard had risked his life to save us, he patted the man on the back and told him how glad he was with the way he'd reacted.

I tried to cut in to tell George that it was probably all my fault anyway: when I'd collided with the guard that morning I might have pulled the grenade loose from its loop above his upper pocket.

Even the old German – who, with his companion, had followed the events from the corner of the kitchen – seemed to have become human. He hobbled across to the guard and shook his hand, then his younger comrade did the same.

When things had calmed down, I asked Kerry if he would teach me how to shoot his rifle. I expected him to protest, but he simply smiled that huge smile of his and said: 'Sure!' He told me to set up an empty K-ration can on the top bar of the level-crossing gate, and then had me take a chair out and place it on the railway line so that he could rest his bad ankle.

At first I was shocked by the noise the rifle made, but I quickly got used to it. With my fourth shot I managed to hit the target, and from there on I rarely missed. Claude had been watching, and now he wanted a go. Kerry agreed, but the rifle was too heavy for Claude to hold, so Kerry stood up, laid the rifle barrel on the chair, aimed it in the right direction and told Claude to pull the trigger. Bang – a bull's eye for Claude!

Later Claude brought out his board game and invited George and Kerry to play with him. Soon the house was filled with merry laughter as they rolled the dice and moved their brightly painted little horses round the board.

Meanwhile I helped Mama clean the house and prepare lunch. Claude and I gobbled ours down as fast as we could, because we couldn't wait to set off for the Sheepfold. For once Mama said we could walk along the railway tracks – something we had never been allowed to do before – because, the lines being broken in a dozen places, there was no danger of any train coming through.

We left the house all bundled up as though it were winter and raced along the tracks towards 103. We could hardly believe it: after so long, we were at last free to run around and play without fear. Light-hearted, we leapt and scampered along the railway line, dodging the craters and the twisted metal where the bombs had landed.

But our carefree mood was quickly shattered. When we came to the bridge over the river, we literally stumbled upon two corpses: huge, bloated and stinking. Claude looked up at me, his eyes filled with horror; but I couldn't help him, I felt just as sick. And there was something that puzzled me. Mama always came this way when she was going to milk the cows on the farm adjoining 103. That meant she must have seen these two bodies lying on the path. Yet she had told us we could come this way – so had she *meant* us to see them? But why? Was it because she wanted us to see the full brutality of war, so that it would be forever engraved on our minds? She could easily have spared us this sight, by encouraging me to take the boat over to the Sheepfold. Later I asked her about it, but she never gave me a direct answer.

Those bodies stayed there for weeks, until finally, one day later in the summer, they were gone – either buried or thrown into the marshes by some person unknown.

It's up to me, I thought; I'm the older sister, I'll have to take charge. So I helped Claude over the gruesome obstacle and led him on towards the Sheepfold.

'After all, they were Germans,' I said, to make Claude feel better. 'Think of it this way: at least they can't hurt us any more.'

But Claude just stared at me with those big sorrowful eyes of his.

Fortunately we soon caught sight of the glider that had landed in the middle of a field near the Sheepfold. It was so beautiful! We ran around it, stroking it, examining every tiny detail. There wasn't a scratch on it. I wondered whether it had brought men or some other cargo. I climbed into the pilot's seat and sat there, dreaming. For one brief moment I dreamed that my wish had come true, that this was a real plane and I was a real pilot. So what if it didn't have an engine?

Francis had seen us arriving, and he came over to kiss us both.

'Come with me,' he said, 'I've got a surprise for you.'

He took us across the field to where something was sticking out of the ground. All I could see was that it was roundish and made of metal, with barbed wire strung around it.

'What is it?' Claude asked.

'Guess,' said his big brother smugly. 'Go on – guess,' he urged, turning to me.

'A bomb?' I said hesitantly.

'That's right – a bomb,' he nodded. 'One that failed to explode when it hit the ground.'

'What's the barbed wire for?'

'To keep the cows away,' Francis said. 'It might explode if they nuzzled it once too often.'

It seemed pretty small to me. I was surprised that something of that size could have done so much damage to the railway line, or made such huge craters.

'But I've got some bad news,' Francis went on. 'Blanchette's dead.'

Poor cow, I thought – then realized that this meant we'd get no more milk. According to Francis, several other cows had also been killed, either by the bombs or by stray bullets. But at least the house was intact.

'You're lucky you weren't hurt too,' I told Francis.

He nodded soberly. 'You don't know how lucky,' he said. And then he went on to tell us that that night when the plane had come looking for us – or rather, for the ammunition piled up in our yard – he had heard the plane's engines and come out to see what was happening. There was a sudden whistling noise and he felt a rush of wind through his fingers. A bomb had exploded nearby, and a piece of shrapnel had passed between his thumb and forefinger, without touching him, and buried itself in the wall behind him. He also told us that on the night of the 5th, when the paratroopers had arrived, some of them had landed at the Sheepfold, too, and he had led them down into the cellar for a welcoming glass of rough cider.

The afternoon flew past as we told each other about all the things that had happened in the past five days. Francis served us some *crème fraîche* with freshly picked apples and sugar, then told us we ought to be starting home.

'I don't want you to be out on the road after dark,' he said.

Before leaving the Sheepfold, I went up to my room and looked out to see if the steeple on the church was still standing. It was, but there was no flag flying from it. I felt that until French and American flags were flying from the church towers, we couldn't really say that the war was over.

Claude and I made a detour on our way home, to avoid the two dead Germans. Mama had been wrong about the sun coming out, but it was certainly warmer than of late. We passed the sentrybox where Papa had been forced to act as a look-out for the Germans, and again my heart froze: inside were all the men and boys that Papa and Gaby had left behind that night – dead, lying where they had fallen. Poor Monsieur Touze, I thought; he won't be popping in for coffee any more, and teasing me. 'Geneviève,' he always used to say, 'if you were a few years older and I were a few years younger, I swear I'd ask you to

12. Papa Maurice receiving the Medal of Honour and
Geneviève, America's Guard of Honour. Philippe Jutras
is on the far right. *Author's collection. Editions
Robert Laffont: Service Iconographique.*

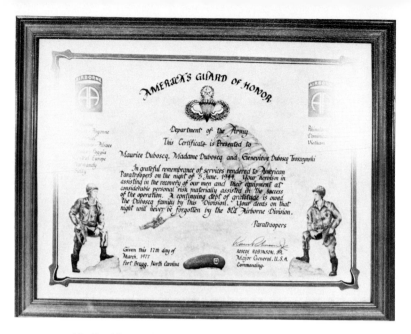

13. Certificate of America's Guard of Honour. *Author's collection. Editions Robert Laffont: Service Iconographique.*

14. Pen and ink drawing of Level-Crossing 104 on the night of June 5th, 1944, presented to Papa Maurice and Geneviève with the compliments of U.S. Major General Roscoe Robinson, Jr, and Philippe Jutras, Curator of the Sainte-Mère-Eglise Museum. *Author's collection. Editions Robert Laffont: Service Iconographique.*

marry me! A girl who can make coffee like this. . .' There was never a grain of real coffee in the pot, so his compliments were doubly appreciated.

I would have liked to call in at the farm on our way home, to see how 'our boys' were getting on. Now that the reinforcements had arrived, they would be having a chance to rest and recover. Claude and I hadn't met a single one of them that afternoon, and I realized that now the main invasion force was in France our paratroopers would probably be moving on.

But I resisted to the urge to go and see them, for Mama had made me promise to keep to the itinerary we had agreed upon. I had long ago learned to accept my father's angry blows, but if my mother had learned that I had disobeyed her and given me a slap, I think I would have died of shame.

Mama was glad to see us safely home. There was a good fire blazing in the fireplace, next to which sat Kerry and the guardian angel, deep in conversation. I went in to see George. He was propped up on the bed, several pillows behind his back.

'Tomorrow,' he said, 'Kerry is going to teach you something.'

'What is it?' I asked. 'Can't you tell me now?'

George pointed to the window; it was already growing dark. 'No,' he said. 'Tomorrow.'

Another shooting lesson, I wondered. But I would just have to wait.

Monday, June 12th, 1944

Up at the crack of dawn, I helped Mama prepare the breakfast. All five of our guests had slept well, and the older German was no longer coughing. Mama's remedy had worked again. Kerry joined us at the table, and I sat between him and our guardian angel. Mama commented on how tiny I looked between those two giants, and it was true: our newest visitor was as tall as Kerry, though dark where Kerry was fair, and he was just as nice. I told Mama that yesterday at the Sheepfold, Francis had measured Claude and me, and we'd both grown.

'In fact,' I finished triumphantly, 'I forgot to tell you yesterday – I am now three-quarters of an inch taller than you, Mama!'

'Oh dear!' she laughed. 'Now I won't be able to call you my "little girl" any more! What do you mean by growing up so fast?' Then she went on to talk about my First Communion, and how she would soon get started on my dress. 'We'll keep the white parachute that George arrived with as the material for your wedding dress,' she laughed. 'What with all these handsome young Americans around, I expect you'll be falling in love with one of them soon – and the next thing I'll know he'll have kidnapped my daughter!'

'Don't think you're going to get rid of me that easily,' I said. 'Anyway, Mama, you know how difficult I am; the man I marry will have to be very, very special.'

She smiled and suggested that before I started sewing my wedding dress I'd better get busy with the washing up. While I piled the dishes into the water, I found myself thinking about what Mama had said, although she'd been half joking. I really was growing up fast, and she had actually started to think about my trousseau.

Kerry asked me if he could borrow one of my school notebooks and some coloured crayons. I dried the dishes as fast as I could, eager to go and see what he was up to. He was drawing – very quickly and skilfully – all sorts of strange-looking objects that I didn't recognize. Soon a whole page was covered with them.

While he drew he kept up a steady stream of chatter with both George and the guard, and, although I didn't understand what he was saying, I formed the impression that he was talking about Claude and me, and that the drawings had something to do with us. When he had finished the first page, Kerry turned it over and on the back he drew something that I recognized straight away: a hand grenade, just like the one the guard had dropped yesterday.

But I still didn't understand what Kerry was doing. Beneath each drawing he wrote something in block letters, then handed me the pocket dictionary and asked me to look up the words. Claude joined me, and together we tried to work out what the drawings represented. The dictionary wasn't much help, but I did find several of the words that Kerry had written: *BOMB*, *ANTI-TANK TRAP*, *GRENADE*, *MINE*. Finally it dawned on me that Kerry had been drawing various kinds of weapons. He had drawn a mine, which looked like an upside-down dinner plate; an incendiary bomb, which had pretty blue-and-white stripes and didn't look the least bit dangerous; little anti-personnel bombs, which had wings and looked like children's toys that I'd seen; and ammunition of various calibres.

I managed to make Kerry understand that I still didn't know what he was trying to accomplish. He scratched his head, then conferred with George in English for a minute, before beckoning the guard to lend him one of his grenades. Then Kerry went out into the courtyard, motioning Claude and me to follow. I watched him place the grenade on the grass; then he pointed first at me, then to the grenade. Thinking that he wanted me to pick it up, I bent down and reached for it.

'*No!* No, Geneviève! For God's sake, don't touch it! Dangerous! Boom!'

At last I understood. Kerry was trying to show us, through his drawings and their captions, all the various kinds of weapons that we might come across, so that we would recognize them and know to avoid them. To show Kerry I understood, I pointed to his drawing of the mine, then gestured towards the grass at the edge of the railway

137

embankment and shook my head vigorously: don't worry, we won't touch them.

Back in the kitchen, I explained to Mama about the strange lesson we had just had.

'You see how kind and thoughtful they are?' she said, nodding. 'They know that when the marshes dry out, there will be lots of weapons that you might find. They want to make sure you never touch them.'

To thank the Americans, I went around and gave each of them a big kiss on the cheek. But they were so tall! Even on tiptoe I couldn't reach unless they bent down.

That afternoon a jeep drove up, stopping some fifty yards from the house because of all the bomb craters, and two Americans climbed out. They had come to see Lieutenant Wingate, they explained, so Mama ushered them into the bedroom. Apparently a field hospital was being built near 103, and tomorrow all our patients would be transferred there. Of course we were all overjoyed to know that at last George would get the proper care he needed, but I knew that their departure – George and Kerry especially – would leave a big gap, not only in our house but in our hearts.

Noticing my downcast expression, Kerry invited me for another shooting lesson, and Claude too. It turned out to be even more successful than yesterday's.

'At this rate you'll soon be winning your badge for marksmanship,' George teased us. At first I didn't understand, so he explained that soldiers had to reach a certain level of skill in shooting before they were considered qualified to use a rifle.

Papa had spent the day at the Sheepfold, digging trenches to bury the dead cows. It was hard, slow work, and when the Americans saw what he was up to they dispatched a sort of big tractor with a plough on the front – they called it a bulldozer – and within an hour or two it had dug a hole big enough to bury all the cows.

At dusk, Kerry took up his rifle again and motioned us all to follow him outside. Aiming the rifle up in the air, he pulled the trigger and emptied the barrels into the night sky, so that the darkness was suddenly lit up by a dozen brilliant arcs of light – just what I had always imagined fireworks to be.

'Tracer bullets,' Kerry enunciated carefully, and made us repeat after him: 'Tracer bullets.'

It was difficult to believe that these beautiful things could bring death.

For our last night together, Mama cooked a very special dinner. Mouth-watering smells rose from both fireplaces. In the distance we could still hear the distant rumble of artillery, off in the direction of Montebourg, beyond Fresville. We had tried to forget the war, which had moved scarcely six or seven miles on, but the constant boom of the guns reminded us how close it still was.

I looked in wonder at the strange collection of people sitting round our dinner table: Germans, Americans, French peasants – a week ago we hadn't set eyes on each other. I tried to guess what they were all thinking. The Americans seemed to project a feeling of strength and optimism, as if certain that tomorrow would grant them their dreams. I hoped they would not be disappointed. In my heart I knew the war wasn't really over, that it was only beginning for the Americans. Kerry's ankle would keep him out of combat for several more weeks, perhaps, but what would become of him after that?

Next to Kerry was our guardian angel. I hardly knew him, but he too breathed life and hope: would he survive these horrors to see his dreams come true? I felt for him, for all of them, even the Germans. The younger one especially, who was always polite; less for the older man, whose face remained a mask. What feelings lurked behind that impassive face, I wondered. Despair? Revolt? He was sitting next to me at the table and all of a sudden, glancing down at his hand on the tablecloth, for some inexplicable reason I overcame my fear of him and placed my hand over his. He shot me a glance of astonishment and seemed embarrassed. I smiled at him but said nothing, just handed him the bread basket. He merely nodded his thanks.

Several times during the meal, Papa got up to see how 'his' lieutenant was getting on in the bedroom. What would happen to George, I wondered. Would the doctors save his leg? I thought of his mother over in America, learning that her son was to be sent back home. How happy she would be, even if they did have to amputate his leg. Better to go home with one leg than not at all!

And the Germans. I kept coming back to the Germans. Tomorrow they would officially become prisoners, first interned in the American field hospital, then in some prisoner-of-war camp. After the war they would go home too. Would they have learned anything from their experiences of war, these Germans, who three times in less than a century had sown death and destruction throughout Europe, each time more bloody and awful than before?

Mama's voice broke into my daydreams. 'Your father's decided to move us all to the Sheepfold tomorrow.'

I felt a sudden surge of panic. 'Why?' I asked.

'Your father thinks the Sheepfold is less exposed than 104,' she said.

The idea appalled me. For one thing, Papa would once again have easy access to his barrels of rough cider. For another, he would have his drinking companions closer at hand. I could foresee the end of our truce: Papa would soon be using me again as a punchbag.

Mama and Papa let us stay up late that night. I knew that all good things came to an end eventually, but still I protested when Mama came into the bedroom and told Claude and me that it was time to leave George and Kerry alone.

'Up to bed now, children!' she cried.

'Please Mama,' we begged, 'just a little while longer!'

But Papa's authoritarian tones put a swift end to our pleas. Mama followed us upstairs to tuck us in. Claude had fallen asleep the moment his head hit the pillow. She gazed down at him for a long moment before she turned out the lamp.

'If I were you,' she told me softly, 'I'd pray especially hard tonight, Geneviève. I have a feeling that, after the past few days, Papa will be nicer to you in future. But I can't promise it. You should ask God for special protection.'

I didn't even want to think about it. There was no way anyone could help me when Papa took it into his head to attack me.

Tuesday, June 13th, 1944

Nothing on earth would have kept me in bed the next morning. In fact, I was the first one up, and I put the coffee on for breakfast – the last meal we would all share. I made up my mind not to worry about the future. There was no point thinking about it.

I was tying my pigtails when Mama came into the kitchen. The two Germans were awake, but everyone else was still asleep: Kerry, George and Papa, even the guardian angel. Mama set out the bowls on the table and called everyone for breakfast. That morning I managed to beat Papa to it, and before he was awake I had taken George's coffee through to him. The early bird has the advantage.

'Hello, George. How are you today?' I greeted him, in my best English.

'Very well, Geneviève,' he said, smiling. 'Very well indeed. And you?'

I went over and planted a kiss on the end of his nose, which always made him laugh.

I fixed his pillows and helped him to sit up, then gave him his steaming *café au lait*. He smiled his thanks, and I thought he looked on top of the world. The thought that he would soon be leaving us forever made me suddenly sad.

George must have noticed my expression, for he put his forefinger to my temple and said: 'A penny for your thoughts.'

'I was thinking how selfish I am,' I said in French. 'I was thinking that for the past eight days your leg wound has kept you here, in need of love and care. I was thinking that I would have liked to keep you here longer, that's all. Not a very kind thought, is it?'

'What are you saying, Geneviève? I can't follow you.'

141

'Nothing,' I told him. 'Pure nonsense. Pay no attention.'

Later that morning, Papa called out to us that some men were coming our way. I went to the window to watch them, coming from the direction of 103. They were walking in single file along the railway line. They were stretcher-bearers, carrying three stretchers.

The Germans were the first to leave. The younger one, who seemed genuinely sad to be going, smiled at me and said goodbye; the older one, as glum and taciturn as ever, left without a word.

Then it was George's turn. Mama wrapped him snugly in a blanket, for even though it was almost mid-June, it was still very cold and she wanted to make sure he didn't catch a chill, now that he was on the road to recovery.

As a present, George left Papa his paratrooper's knife and his binoculars. I was dying to go with the stretcher-bearers as far as the hospital tent, but Papa's blunt 'no' was final. Apart from anything else, I would have enough to do, getting ready for our move to the Sheepfold.

Leaning on his broom-crutch, which he seemed to have formally adopted, Kerry indicated that he didn't need a stretcher, that he would hobble along after them. I went out on the tracks to stay with them as long as I possibly could.

The stretcher with George lying on it passed me, and he blew me a kiss. 'Bye-bye, Geneviève!' he called.

There was a lump in my throat, and I could barely get the words out: 'Bye-bye, George. *Bonne chance!* Good luck!'

Kerry limped along after them, hoisting himself up the embankment to the tracks. He shook hands with all of us, his grip firm and strong. Only Claude received a kiss.

I watched him hobbling off down the tracks, his big silhouette moving awkwardly. On a sudden impulse I ran after him, calling to him to stop.

He turned back. 'What is it, Geneviève?'

'Please, Kerry, would you leave me something to remember you by?'

He fished in his pockets and pulled out an ammunition clip, loaded with bullets.

'Thank you!' I cried. 'Bye-bye, Kerry! And good luck!' And I dashed back along the tracks to the house, ran up the stairs two at a time, and placed the clip reverently in the box that contained all my other treasures.

Back downstairs, I stood on the tracks again and watched as the stretcher-bearers and Kerry slowly disappeared in the distance.

I told myself not to be sad. But it was no use. They had gone, and I would never see them again. Never. I knew the hospital tent was not all that far away but I also knew that Papa Maurice thought a field hospital was no place for children and that he would never let me go there. I knew there was no point in arguing with him.

Fortunately we had enough to do to keep our minds occupied. I helped Mama pack up our belongings, and we loaded them all into the boat. Piled to the gunwales, Papa then poled the boat across the marshes. On the other side, he and Francis would carry everything up to the Sheepfold.

When Papa had gone, Mama and I swept up the hay that had served as a mattress for the two Germans, for the American guard who'd been sent to look after us, and for my parents. While we were clearing up, Mama told me that she had a plan; she'd been thinking about it for hours. We had neither the time nor the tools to dig a proper grave in the marsh for the poor German officer who had died in my arms. What we could do, she had decided, was give him some semblance of a decent burial by surrounding his body with a fence of sticks which we could secure in the mud, then cover it with a roof of twigs and reeds. But would Papa let us use his precious firewood for the fence?

To our astonishment, when he came back from the Sheepfold, Papa not only agreed to let us have the sticks, he even offered to give us a hand. He helped us carry the sticks and drive them vertically into the mud. In less than half an hour we had built a little fence round the body. The idea was that the alluvial soil carried in the water would be deposited around the fence and build a burial mound over the body. In fact, when the floodgates were opened a short time later, the rush of escaping water took both the fence and the soil with it. But somehow the body stayed put. At that point, some good citizens from Amfreville came out and, now that the soil had dried out, buried him right there on the spot where he had died.

I folded up George's white parachute, thinking I would take it with me to the Sheepfold so that as soon as she had time Mama would be able to make it into a pretty dress for me, as she had promised.

Papa had one last boat-load to take to the Sheepfold, and it was a heavy one. The boat was already rather trickier to manoeuvre than usual, because it was so overloaded, but what made it worse was that the water level in the marshes had dropped during the past week or so. We suspected it was because someone had already opened one of the floodgates without permission. The boat kept scraping aground, but at least it was in no danger of sinking on the marshes. The river was another matter. Mama and I were both watching as Papa reached the end of the shallow marsh waters and began to cross the river, where the currents flowed faster. The water was up to the gunwales, and Papa must have made some wrong move, for suddenly the boat began to sink. Like all good captains, Papa refused to abandon his boat. We could see him going slowly down, perched on top of his heavy cargo. There was nothing we could do to help. But Papa was not one to lose his head in a crisis, and the next thing we saw was him clinging to the wheelbarrow – apparently the only item of the cargo that floated – letting the stream carry him across to firmer ground on the other side of the river. Everything else was lost.

'It doesn't matter,' sighed Mama. 'There wasn't anything in that load that was particularly important.'

I was trying to hold back my tears. 'But my wooden horse was in that boatload,' I wailed. 'The one I made for Claude's birthday.'

'Never mind,' Mama said soothingly. 'I'll help you find jobs to do on the farms around here, and over the next few weeks you'll earn lots of money, so that then you can go and buy him a really nice one for his birthday.'

We went through the house one last time, to make sure everything was neat and clean, and that we hadn't left anything behind. Then Mama closed and locked the door.

'Goodbye, 104,' I whispered to the house. 'Thank you for taking such good care of us these past few days.'

Summer 1944

Day by day the war moved further and further away from us, and gradually we began to pick up the threads of a more normal sort of life, particularly as there were now fewer restrictions on travelling around the countryside.

At the Sheepfold, our life resumed its old rhythm. After his several weeks of solitude at the Sheepfold, Francis had been able to concentrate on his studies, and now he passed his exams with flying colours. The day after the results were announced, he told me, his chest swelling with pride, that he had already found a job. I was very impressed, and asked him what sort of a job it was – but he wouldn't tell me. Later I found out: like many other young men in the area, he had been hired to bury the dead. Lots of big lorries were ferrying all the dead from miles around to the two huge fields on the outskirts of Sainte-Mère-Eglise, which had been given over to the American authorities as military cemeteries. It was such a major task that everyone had to lend a hand. I was among those who fished out all the parachutes that were still floating over the marsh waters; we cut them up and used them as shrouds. When the supply of parachutes was exhausted, we all contributed whatever we could: old sheets, blankets, anything to wrap the bodies in until the coffins arrived by ship from the States.

I realized, as we sat around cutting and stitching the shrouds, that war was still raging across France. The proof of it came with every truck-load of corpses. All those fine young men, cut down in the full flush of their youth. I wondered if the sacrifice had been worth it.

As I had feared, Papa did revert to his old drinking habits, and again I became his victim. There was nothing anyone could do to stop

145

him. But my spirits lifted somewhat with the appearance of better weather.

One afternoon, Mama asked me to go and collect some firewood. Maurice Salmon, who had been supposed to deliver us a load, had needed his cart and horse to bring in the new-mown hay, and he wouldn't be able to make the delivery for some weeks. I suggested to Mama that, instead of going round picking up dead wood from the ground, I should cut it off the trees. The fact is that dead wood that's been lying on the ground gives off a nasty, sickening taste to any food that is cooked on it; we call it 'the taste of dead wood' or 'smoky taste'. Soups and coffee were most affected. But dead wood that's been cut off the trees, or cut green and dried in a woodpile, doesn't have the same effect.

'Yes, all right,' Mama agreed. 'But for goodness sake be careful when you're climbing the trees. I don't want you falling to your death!'

So off I set. Around the Sheepfold, the hedges had a certain peculiarity: they were planted in double rows, to make a windbreak all of six feet thick. Whoever had thought up the idea deserved a medal, we thought, because it was so effective; the first row broke the wind so that the second row entirely blocked what force was left, and the horses and cows could find complete shelter in the lee of the hedge. In this way they could even spend the whole winter out in the open.

At the moment, these hedges were serving another purpose: a whole regiment of American troopers – on rest and recuperation – lay billeted beside them. Beneath the canopies of the trees, their tents blended right into the hedge itself; from the air they must have been as hard to detect as the trucks and tanks concealed beneath their careful camouflage. All I knew was that from a distance it simply looked as if the hedge was a bit thicker in some parts than in others.

I climbed up one tree not far from the hedge, a saw slung over my back. I was singing to myself, as I always did when I was working. When I reached a suitable point up the tree, I sawed off a number of branches and let them fall to the ground below. When there were enough, I would climb down and tie them into a bundle to take back to the house. We needed a lot, though, for Mama cooked everything over an open fire.

I had soon collected a fair-sized bundle of branches, but I decided to carry on – more for the fun of climbing than for any other reason. If I ended up with more than I could carry, I felt sure I could find a nice

146

soldier to help me get it back to the house. In fact, one soldier was standing at the foot of the tree, watching my every move. As I continued working, still singing merrily, he moved away and sat down a few yards away, in case I dropped my branches on his skull. When I paused for a moment, he called up to me in French, in an accent I knew at once.

'Tell me, young lady – are you a squirrel or a nightingale?'

'Neither,' I told him. 'I'm just cutting some wood.'

I slid down the tree trunk and landed a step away from him. We grinned at each other.

'You ought to be a paratrooper!' he said, extending his hand.

'My name's Geneviève,' I told him. 'What's yours?'

'Marc Levesque.'

'Oh how strange! That's my mother's maiden name,' I exclaimed. 'Are you a French Canadian?'

'I am indeed,' he said. Then he asked if I would do him a favour: would I please sing the song again, the same song I'd been singing up the tree.

So I agreed to sing him the song again if he would help me tie up my bundle of firewood.

As I had hoped, when I'd finished the song and he'd finished tying the bundle of wood, he helped me carry it back to the house.

'Who taught you to sing?' he asked.

'My mother,' I said.

'Have you ever tried to sing anything else apart from those popular songs?' I must have looked puzzled, for he went on: 'Like airs from the opera, for instance . . . Would you like to learn some?'

'Oh yes!' I cried. 'But who would teach me?'

'I would,' he said.

'Are you a musician?'

It turned out that he was a singing teacher, and he organized concerts. When he had joined the army, he had been assigned to this regiment as a tank-driver.

'But as soon as things settle down,' he explained, 'I'm going to be reassigned, to set up entertainment for the troops. Plays, concerts, all that kind of thing. If your voice is as good as I think it is, I'd like to take you with me – that's if you'd like to come, of course.'

It sounded wonderful, but I reminded him that I was only a child: 'I do have parents, you know. Especially a father.'

'Oh I'm sure I can handle him,' said the soldier.

By now we had reached the house. Mama was delighted to see all the wood I'd managed to collect and to thank the soldier for helping me bring it back, she offered him a cup of coffee. While he was drinking it he explained his idea to her.

'But she can't read a note of music,' Mama protested. 'How can you teach her?'

The Canadian didn't have an answer for that, but it was clear he wasn't going to drop the idea yet. When he left, he promised he'd be back the following day.

True to his word, he returned the next afternoon, bearing a spring-operated gramophone and two records. I greeted him delightedly.

'Oh Marc, where did you find it?'

'I bought it,' he smiled. 'It's not the best-sounding machine in the world, but let's give it a try.'

'What do I have to do?'

'Put on a record and listen carefully to the words and the music,' he said. 'Then I'll see if you're really talented.'

He had to go back to his tent then, so I looked at the records and put one of them on the gramophone. It was from the operetta *Rose Marie* – the other was from Lalo's opera *The King of Ys*.

Within an hour I felt I had mastered the words and music of *Rose Marie*.

Pretending to be looking for more firewood for Mama, I crept out and found Marc's tent, stealing along under cover of the double hedge so that he wouldn't see me coming. Then I bent down and started gathering stray twigs for kindling, and broke into song.

Marc had been pottering about near his tent. When he heard me, he stopped what he was doing and stepped over the barbed-wire fence to where I was.

'How did you learn it so fast?'

'It's not hard to learn something when you enjoy it so much,' I said.

'Well, go on, then,' he smiled. 'Sing me as much as you know.'

I sang the entire piece to him. When I had finished, he called out to his friends who were either wandering around the tents or sitting down relaxing.

'Hey, guys! Come and listen to this kid!'

Several of the soldiers wandered across to us and sat around in a semi-circle at the front of Marc's tank, while he hoisted me up and deposited me on the nose of the tank. My feet got caught up in the camouflage netting, and I had to hang on to the gun barrel for support.

And it was there, in those curious circumstances, that I performed for the first time in public. And no one could have asked for a better audience! Not only were they soldiers – and I loved soldiers – they were also for the most part Canadians, who understood the words I was singing in French. And when I'd finished, they burst into loud applause.

'Encore! Encore!'

I didn't need much encouragement. By the time I had got through the tenth song, Marc indicated that enough was enough. I could have gone on forever, but it was growing dark, and I knew I ought to get home before Papa. Reluctantly I agreed it was time to go. Marc helped me carry the bundle of kindling home, and on the way he told me about his plan to persuade Papa – tonight! No use wasting another day, he said.

Poor Marc didn't know what he'd got himself into. Papa Maurice was drunk as a lord. He barely listened to what Marc was saying, then he said a curt 'no'. But Marc persisted, telling Papa how he would make me the little princess of his theatrical company and how we would entertain the troops. Papa remained unmoved.

I wasn't surprised by Papa's attitude, but I was surprised at Marc's persistence.

'You don't realize what a talent this girl has,' he told Papa. 'A voice like hers is a rare gift, you know.'

'So what?' snorted Papa.

Finally Marc had to admit defeat; he headed back to his tent, shaking his head sadly. I tried to cheer him up by promising to spend the night learning *The King of Ys*, so that I could sing it to him and his friends the next morning.

'The whole thing?' he laughed. 'You'll never learn the whole thing. Just try to learn the princess's part, the rest is meant to be sung by men anyway.'

But I had my own ideas on that subject. The next morning I found my new friend again and sang him the entire opera, including the men's parts, passing from the deep tones of the King to the gentle dulcet tones of the Princess Rozenn.

Marc couldn't believe his ears. He called his mates over again, and again I sang to my favourite audience.

In fact, every day for the next three weeks I gave them a special private concert. 'Come and listen to God's nightingale!' Marc would cry when I arrived – he had given me that name because of my penchant for religious songs.

And then the day came when the soldiers had to leave. With the same sinking feeling that I had felt when George and Kerry left, I watched them pack up and go. Then, as I stood gazing after the departing line of tanks and trucks, I suddenly realized they didn't even know my full name. Like George and Kerry and all the other soldiers, they knew me only as Geneviève, Papa Maurice's daughter. So now I would never have any more singing lessons; I would never learn any operas or operettas by heart, I would never again perform in public. I sensed that I had missed one of the greatest opportunities in my life.

Some weeks later, on a glorious summer's day, Mama took Claude and me to mass to celebrate the feast day of Saint Marguerite. The offering of ribbons that year was more solemn and more fervent than ever before – and I've never seen one to rival it since. But, while the rest of the congregation gave heartfelt thanks to Our Lady for granting us our freedom, I found it hard to join in. I felt sad, unhappy, oppressed. Suddenly I burst into tears.

A priest, who turned out to be a missionary, saw my tears and after mass he came up and asked what was troubling me. We sat down together on the low wall that surrounded the cemetery of Neuville-au-Plain, and I opened my heart to him.

I explained how our First Communion had been postponed till the end of July because of the Allied landings. I told him how hard I had worked to learn my catechism, and how much I had been looking forward to the great day, which I expected to be the most beautiful day in my life. When our local priest had examined us on our catechism, I had come second in all the class, and as a prize this gave me the right to stand up on the morning of the ceremony, with the person who'd come first, to recite our act of faith publicly. Only the first four communicants had this right: the winner and the one in second place (me) in the morning, and those who had come third or fourth at vespers that evening. But when it was my turn, another girl whose name also happened to be Geneviève had stood up in my place. I was sure there had been some mistake, because the other Geneviève had come bottom of the class, so I had risen to my feet with her. But the woman who was in charge of us had shaken her head at me, though I could see she was upset at having to deny me my rightful place. I had been thoroughly confused. Why had the other girl replaced me?

150

As she passed me on her way back to her chair, after reading aloud a short prayer, she gave me a mischievous smile.

'Stole a march on you there, didn't I?' she whispered.

I still didn't understand, and I just stared at her blankly. After mass, as we were walking to the vestry, she came up to me again.

'Father Roulland is a man of flesh and blood, you know,' she said. 'He likes the good things of life just like everyone else. So last night Mama took him two nice chickens – and hey presto! Just like that! He let me take your place.'

My mother was even more furious than I was. During the First Communion ceremonies, the parents of all the children participating were supposed to take up a collection; everyone considered it a great honour to make a special donation to the priest. But Mama was so angry at the greedy priest that she forbade me to give him the one hundred franc note that the old lady had pressed on me when I was begging for candle money. My own anger had subsided, and I even argued in Father Roulland's defence, but Mama was not to be placated. It was the first time I'd ever seen her bearing a real grudge against anyone; she was so adamant that she also forbade me to enrol for my fifth and final year of catechism the following autumn.

The fact was that I nearly hadn't enrolled at all. My first meeting with Father Roulland had been a difficult one. In our first class he talked to us about 'Our Father in Heaven' – who, he said, was like our earthly father, who looked after us and protected us. That had been too much for me to take. I got to my feet, collected my pencil and notebook, and stalked out of the class. Completely taken aback, Father Roulland had run out after me.

'Why are you leaving?' he demanded.

'I already have one father,' I told him, 'who does anything he wants to, and that doesn't include taking care of me or protecting me. I don't need another one like that, thank you very much.'

Father Roulland seemed to understand. 'But this Father does love us, Geneviève. He loves us more than anything in the world.'

'He does?' I stopped in my tracks, dumbfounded.

'Absolutely.'

'Well . . . all right. If you say so.'

After that, Father Roulland and I had become friends. So I felt this act of treachery very deeply.

Having heard me out, the missionary did his best to console me, and indeed his words did make me feel better. Claude popped up from

151

somewhere, and I introduced him to my new friend.

'I know you,' the missionary smiled at Claude. 'I saw you offer a pretty blue ribbon this morning to the Holy Mother. In fact, I remember that your sister had to lift you up so that you could reach the statue's arm!' Then he turned to me and said gently: 'Isn't he rather young to be making a vow?'

'It wasn't his vow,' I explained. 'It was my mother's.'

'And were her prayers answered?'

'Oh yes,' I said. 'Otherwise George would have died.'

'Who is George?' asked the missionary.

So I told him the whole story – and he really seemed to care. I told him how the American paratroopers had landed in the marshes on the night of June 5th, how they had come to our house, how Papa had found the wounded Lieutenant Wingate in the marshes and brought him home, and then how he had nearly died. I also told him about the German officer who had died in my arms, and how terrible I'd felt because I wasn't strong enough to help Mama get him back to our house. And I even told him about J-Two.

J-Two was the name I had given to another friend the war had brought me. Although he was a soldier, he was so young that if he had been French he would have been classified as J-Two for the purpose of ration tickets – that is, he was no longer a child but not yet an adult. His real name was James Kimble, and though he was eighteen, he looked not much older than me. Yet he had already proved himself in battle; he had fought long and hard at the liberation of the towns of Montebourg and Valognes. When he had come to us, he had been enjoying a brief respite from the war, having been granted – along with the rest of his regiment – a short rest period of a few days.

One night J-Two had had a nightmare; he told me all about it the next day. He had dreamed that he was trapped in his tank, and his tank was on fire and he was being burned alive. And in his dream he had seen a sign that indicated this was all happening on the outskirts of a town called Saint-Lô. He'd never heard of such a place, and when I told him there really was a town by that name, he was inconsolable.

From that day on J-Two was convinced his fate was sealed. Nothing I could say or do would change his mind. He was convinced he had only a short time to live. Yet he became firm friends with Claude and me, and he seemed much more at ease with us than with the adult world he belonged to. We went for long walks together, and played games together, and generally larked about like children do. The only difference was that J-Two's toy was a huge deadly tank, armed with eight guns of various calibres that could spit fire and death.

One day, J-Two asked me if I would like a ride in the tank. He had to practise shooting that day, and if I wanted to I could go along and watch. I was thrilled at the idea, and of course once he started shooting I wanted to have a go too.

But that afternoon I arrived home in tears. Mama greeted me philosophically, wanting to know what I'd done now. In reply, I took her hand and led her outside, pointing to the skyline where the tops of six trees had been neatly shorn off.

'I did that!' I sobbed. 'All I wanted was to have a go with J-Two's guns – I only fired each gun once!'

'How many shots did you fire in all?' Mama asked.

'Eight,' I managed to tell her between sobs.

To my surprise she started laughing. 'Six direct hits out of eight! Not bad at all! But don't you go boasting about it to your father, or he'll treat you the same way you've treated those poor trees.'

The missionary must have got more than he had bargained for when he started consoling me. But he seemed fascinated by all my stories. On the subject of J-Two, though, the only comfort he could offer me was the reassurance that dreams do not always mirror reality.

'A nightmare is one thing,' he said, 'but the future is quite another.'

Then we shook hands and he headed off into the night, towards the festivities marking the end of Saint Marguerite's Day.

Claude took me by the hand and urged me to hurry up; the festivities were in full swing, and it was after dusk already.

So we made our way among the various booths and stands at the fair, but at one point I ran into some barbed wire which scratched my face. It was the last straw. Mama did her best to clean the cut and comfort me, but I was feeling very miserable indeed as we made our way home. It wasn't so much the cut on my face that was bothering me, it was my renewed concern about J-Two.

Suddenly, quite out of the blue, Claude said: 'You know Geneviève, I don't mind dying, but I hate seeing you sad.'

I bent down and hugged him fiercely.

A few days later J-Two and his regiment moved out, heading in the direction of Saint-Lô. He promised me he'd come back and see me when they had liberated the town, if he was still alive.

'Don't say things like that,' I told him. 'Of course you'll still be

153

alive! You don't really believe what happened in that silly dream, do you?'

'If I'm wounded,' he promised, 'I'll send someone to let you know.'

The days went by, then weeks, then months. J-Two never came back.

October 2nd, 1944

This morning Claude asked if he could walk with me to school. I was glad of his company, but as we were walking along he complained that his legs weren't working properly. Finally he told me he couldn't take another step. I had to carry him back home.

A few days previously he had hurt himself sliding down the wings of the glider, but no one had thought anything of it. Now Mama realized that something was seriously wrong, and she sent for the doctor. The doctor examined Claude; he could find no visible wound, but he suspected there might be a blood clot and told us that Claude would have to go to hospital.

Claude was taken to the Valognes hospital and remained there for several weeks. He had an operation to remove the clot, and a tube was inserted in his thigh to draw off the pus from his wound.

The hospital was several miles from home, but every Thursday we went to visit him, walking there and back along the railway tracks. I couldn't bear to see him in such pain, though; and sometimes I couldn't bring myself to go into his room, or even watch through a window as the nurse changed his dressings. I had to grit my teeth when I saw her take the long pair of tongs to remove his old dressing, then apply the new one. The rubber tube that the doctors had inserted to draw off the pus could not dry the wound completely, and I felt myself wince as little Claude lay there with closed eyes and clenched teeth.

Claude's absence seemed to make Papa even more spiteful towards me than ever; it was as though he held me to blame for Claude's suffering. I did my best to keep out of his way. But my friends the soldiers had all gone, and their place in the hedgerows was bare. Since the departure of J-Two and the other men of his regiment, none had come to replace them; apparently, as the armies moved gradually inland, new places were found for them to rest and recuperate.

Once again I resumed my long walks through the countryside. But life seemed dull and empty without my friends, without even Claude for company. What if Claude were to die, I kept thinking. And I knew what I'd do if he did: I'd throw myself in the river. I even knew exactly the spot I'd choose to jump in, where the river was really deep and I knew I'd quickly drown. For I had never learnt to swim. I was really serious about it: I had decided that without my little brother, life would not be worth living.

It was Papa who contributed most to my misery. He had reverted to his old habits, and he often took advantage of Mama's absences to vent his fury on me. Normally I never said a word to her about how miserable I was, but there came a time when I couldn't keep it to myself any longer.

One evening when she arrived home from her work on the farm, I sat her down and said: 'Mama, I've got to talk to you. I've done something that will probably make you angry – only I can't tell you why I've done it. But I had my reasons. Oh please, Mama, don't be angry with me!'

'What on earth have you done?' she demanded, looking alarmed.

I hesitated. 'Please understand, Mama – I did it because I had to. . .' And I removed the scarf I'd been wearing on my head.

Mama gasped. 'You've cut off your pigtails! Oh, Geneviève! But why——?'

'I told you. I can't say why.'

'Oh well,' she said, 'have it your own way. After all, it's your hair. Actually, when it grows out a little, it won't be too bad. . .' She got up and walked around me, studying the result from all angles. 'You know,' she said, 'I think it makes you look older. You look quite grown-up now.'

'But I am grown-up!' I cried. 'I'm nearly twelve, Mama. I'm almost an adult.'

Mama laughed. 'The only problem is I won't be able to grab you by the hair any more!'

I grimaced. That was precisely why I had cut my hair: not so that Mama couldn't pull my hair, but so that Papa wouldn't be able to.

Friday, October 13th, 1944

It was a bright autumn day, the lovely colours of the Normandy countryside glowing in the warm sunlight. Mademoiselle Burnouf had gone off to a teachers' meeting and given her class the rest of the day off. I knew that Papa was at the house, and since I didn't fancy spending the rest of the sunny afternoon with him, I decided not to go home. I would not show up at the Sheepfold until the normal after-school hour – that would give me several hours in which I could do as I pleased.

As I left Sainte-Mère-Eglise, instead of following the road to La Fière as usual, I turned on to a shady track that led towards the Irsa Bridge, which spanned the railway line a little over a mile from Level-Crossing 103. I had seldom been along that track. I wandered along, daydreaming about plans to spoil little Claude when he finally came home from hospital. It was clear by now that he was on the mend.

'Two or three more weeks,' the doctor had said.

I still missed him badly, but the knowledge that he'd soon be home was like a tonic to me. As soon as I heard the good news, I'd felt a surge of happiness flow over me, and I had immediately started planning all the things we could do together once he was back home again.

As I turned a corner in the track, just before the bridge, I ran slap into an encampment of American soldiers. The 'camp' consisted of a number of pup tents. In front of the nearest tent a soldier was diligently washing his metal mess kit. His back was to me, and he didn't hear me walking silently up to him.

'Good morning, soldier!'

He jumped as though shot, and turned round. He looked me up and

157

down, obviously surprised to see a young girl out by herself, and then he addressed me in French:

'Good morning, Mademoiselle. Have you lost your way?'

I shook my head. 'No, I only live a mile or two from here.'

'Then how come you're wandering about round here?'

I grinned at him. 'What if I said the Good Lord had sent me to give you a hand washing your mess kit?'

'I wouldn't believe you,' he laughed.

'Well, step aside, soldier – this is woman's work,' I told him.

'The woman strikes me as being somewhat on the small side,' he said. 'But all right – on two conditions: one, the work must be done properly; and two, you've got to tell me your name first.'

I was pleased to note that he had already abandoned the formal *vous* and lapsed into the familiar *tu* form of address.

'My name is Geneviève,' I told the soldier. 'And if you knew me, you'd know that I do everything properly. If I don't know how to do something, I ask someone to show me, and then I try my very best to do it well. It's really very simple.'

The soldier's eyes widened in astonishment at my words – and I must admit I was a bit surprised at myself too. By this time I had had a chance to size him up: he was tall, dark and handsome, and there was a sort of gentleness about him that I immediately admired. When he laughed, he got dimples in his cheeks; his eyes shone, and a delightful web of wrinkles appeared at their corners.

I felt happy to be with him. As always happens when I'm happy and busily working, I broke into song. He was pretending to be fussing with his tent, but as I sang and scrubbed his mess kit, I watched him out of the corner of my eye. I got the feeling that he knew the song I was singing, and that he was waiting to see how I handled the final notes, full and deep.

As the last note of my song died away, he whistled his appreciation. 'What a lovely voice!' he exclaimed.

Pleased with the compliment, I smiled up at him, then got on with washing his mess kit. When I'd finished, I held it up for his inspection.

'I was right to take you at your word,' he said. 'You've certainly done a good job there. Now, what can I offer you as a reward?'

'Nothing,' I said firmly. 'I didn't do it for a reward, I just did it because I like being here with you.'

'You are an odd young lady, all right,' he said.

I grinned. 'Do you really want to give me something?'

'Yes. How about some chocolate?'

'No, thank you,' I said. 'I want my own kind of reward. But I hope you won't be cross. . .' With my forefinger, I pointed to my cheek. 'A kiss,' I said. 'Right there.'

He looked even more astonished now. Poor man, just as he'd got over one surprise, along came another one! Still, he duly bent and kissed me on the cheek. I stood there with my arms crossed, as proud as punch. I'd never met such an obliging man.

'What's your name – your first name?' I asked.

'Robert,' he told me. 'Well, Isaac Robert, actually, but everyone calls me Robert.'

'Robert – that's a nice name,' I said. 'Well, do you know something, Robert? You're the first man who's ever kissed me.'

'Never!'

'Yes, it's true. I've kissed lots of men, but you're the first one to kiss me.'

'Haven't you got a father?' he asked teasingly.

'Yes – unfortunately,' I said, 'but kissing's the last thing he'd ever do to me.'

'Why?' Robert exclaimed. 'You seem like a nice young lady.'

'That's what everyone says. Except my father.'

'Tell me about it.'

'Oh, there's not much to tell really. Anyway, it's a sad story, and I'd rather not spoil things by talking about him now.'

'All right, then, we can talk about your father some other time,' Robert said. 'Now, are you hungry? Would you like a bite of something to eat?'

'Yes, if you'll join me,' I said.

'Right then,' said Robert. 'It's a deal. Why don't we put the stuff in your basket and go for a walk? You can show me where you live, the local village and the surrounding countryside.'

So that's what we did. Robert filled my basket with all sorts of things to eat, and off we set, arm in arm, as though we were the oldest friends in the world. We stopped in a field near the river, and Robert emptied my basket and spread the food out on the grass under a tree. The warm autumn sun flooded the countryside with a gentle light.

Sitting with his back against the tree, Robert handed me two biscuits covered with jam. 'Penny for your thoughts, Geneviève,' he said.

I sighed. 'I was just thinking how nice it was being here with you, just the two of us. I wish today would never end!'

He smiled, but I thought I could see something sad in his face. 'Come over here,' he said. 'I want to tell you a secret.'

Without hesitation I went over and sat beside him. He put one arm round my shoulders and pulled me close.

When he spoke again, his voice was low and sorrowful. 'You know something, Geneviève? I'm alone too. I've got no one in the world. Sometimes it's very hard to bear. Yet I'm a man, and I think it's easier for us to be alone than it is for you. But listen, you're much too young to be lonely! Tell you what, let's be friends! All right? You can tell me all your secrets and worries, and I'll tell you mine. What do you think?'

I found it hard to reply, so I simply nodded my head. A moment later the tears were pouring down my cheeks; I just couldn't stop them. Robert took my face between his hands and kissed the tears away.

It was more than I had ever hoped for: a man who was kind and gentle, a real friend, someone who really liked me. At that moment I felt a special bond between us, a deep instinctive attachment. Snuggled there in Robert's arms, I felt secure. It was a new and soothing sensation. Robert stroked my hair and I felt such a feeling of peace, of utter happiness.

'Dear God,' I murmured under my breath, 'please make this day last forever!'

But Robert had heard me. 'It will, Geneviève,' he said softly. 'It will. We'll find some way of carving happy moments like this out of every day. Agreed?'

'You mean – we'll see each other every day?'

'Yes. But only on one condition,' he said, pretending to be stern. 'You've got to stop using *vous* when you talk to me.'

I accepted on the spot.

'Now, then,' Robert smiled. 'How are we going to manage to meet every day?'

Suddenly I had an idea. 'I know! From Monday on, I won't stay at school for the evening lesson. As soon as afternoon school is over, I'll fly out the door and meet you at your camp. Then I can go home at the time I usually go home from evening school. Papa will never know.'

'What about your teacher?' Robert asked. 'Won't she be angry with you for missing her class?'

160

'Mademoiselle Burnouf? Goodness no! In fact I think she'll be delighted – she doesn't like me going home alone at night anyway. I don't usually leave school till seven at the earliest, and now that it gets dark so quickly she's even more worried. I'll do the work, though; I'll ask Mama to buy me some candles and I'll do my homework up in my bedroom after dinner.'

'Candles?' repeated Robert in obvious astonishment. 'Don't you have electricity in your house?'

'No – you see we're a long way from town,' I explained. 'And we don't have any running water either. Tell you what – why don't I show you where I live?'

'Good idea,' he nodded. 'Then I'll be able to come and visit you on Thursday when you don't have to go to school.'

I told him then that Thursdays were kept for visiting Claude in hospital. 'He's had this horrible infection in his leg,' I explained. Then I brightened. 'But he's getting better and I expect he'll be coming home soon. I know what – I'll ask Mama if I can stay at home to be with you. Then she can ride her bike to the hospital rather than having to walk all the way with me.'

'Is the hospital far away?' Robert asked.

'Over twelve miles.'

'And you walk all the way there?'

'Of course – and all the way back. And some days we don't even see him, because we can't bear to go into his room. Mama says she's afraid he might cry, and she can't stand it when he cries.'

'That must be pretty tough for you all,' Robert said sympathetically.

'Well, you see, we both love Claude.'

'Careful – you'll make me jealous!'

'Don't be silly,' I said. 'A friend and a little brother are two very different things!'

We both laughed. By this time we had gathered up the remains of our picnic and were walking towards Level-Crossing 103. As we passed the Château de La Fière, I told Robert the story of that long night of June 5th, and about Bernadette's mother being killed by a piece of shrapnel. Just then Maurice Salmon emerged from the château and started walking towards us.

'Hello, Geneviève,' he said, talking in the patois we always used together. 'I see you have a new friend.'

Answering in French, I introduced Robert as though he were an old

161

friend. The two men shook hands warmly. We walked together for a bit, then Maurice took his leave, explaining that he'd got to go and look for a stray horse. After he'd gone, Robert turned to me and asked what language Maurice had been using.

'That wasn't a language,' I said. 'It's our patois.'

'You mean the dialect you speak among yourselves in this region?'

I nodded. 'Actually, I've only been speaking proper French for four years now. And with my father I never speak anything but patois.'

'Four years? You have learned fast!' Robert laughed.

'Yes, I suppose I have,' I admitted. 'You see, I fell in love with French. What I like best is the imperfect subjunctive. I know we don't often use it, but it sounds so elegant, so beautiful. If I had my way, I'd make everyone use it all day, from morning to night!'

Robert laughed again. 'You're right, it is beautiful,' he said. 'But don't you find it difficult learning to speak another language?'

'It's just a question of getting used to it,' I told him. 'That's the problem: because we all speak patois round here, I never get a chance to practise my French, except in class.'

On and on we went, chattering all the way. I'd never talked to anyone so much in my life, and I was enjoying every minute of it. I told Robert all sorts of stories about how we children managed to enjoy ourselves. I told him how we managed to restock our supplies of sweets by rooting around in the fields to find scrap metal which the Americans collected to send back to the States, where it was melted down to make more weapons. And a double ration of sweets was awarded to anyone who found a jerrycan. I also told him how some of the children at school went out looking for the metal nose cones that were used to protect bombs when they were being transported; several of our seats at school were broken or missing, and these metal caps, with a cushion on top, made ideal – and indestructible – replacements.

When we reached Level-Crossing 103, I pointed down the line to 104, explaining to Robert that that was where we lived for part of the year. Then I took him up to the Sheepfold. At the fence we stopped and I pointed the house out to him; it looked lost amid that great thirty-acre field. I hid my basket in the fork of two branches of a nearby tree, then we backtracked towards the Irsa Bridge. When I had first come upon Robert's encampment, I had thought that it was a group of soldiers on rest-and-recuperation from the front, like J-Two's regiment, but it turned out that Robert's unit had the task of guarding the Irsa Bridge and the section of railway that ran below it.

We walked along the tracks from 103 towards the bridge, and as we walked I asked Robert if he'd mind doing me a favour. Some American soldiers that I'd met at the Sheepfold had taught me a song in English, and although I knew all the words by heart, I had no idea what they meant. So I asked Robert if he would mind translating it for me.

He agreed readily – but I'd scarcely sung the first few words than he interrupted me.

'Geneviève, don't sing that song. It's rude.'

I blushed to the roots of my hair. 'I-I'm sorry,' I stammered.

'Don't be silly,' he said. 'You don't have anything to be ashamed about. If anyone should be ashamed it's the men who taught you that song.'

To make amends, I quickly decided to sing him another song. I chose one that I particularly liked, in Latin, though I didn't often sing it because it was so solemn. When I'd sung it, Robert looked very moved.

'Gounod's *Ave Maria*,' he said. 'I love that song, Geneviève, but particularly the way you sing it.'

'I can't surprise you with any songs, can I?' I laughed. 'You seem to know them all.'

'Well, it's not so surprising,' Robert said. 'France is my second home – I lived in Paris for several years, you see.'

Then he explained that he had been born in America, of Jewish extraction. Before the war he had come to France and opened a clothes shop. But when the Germans invaded France, he knew full well what they had in store for the Jews of Europe, so he went back to America. Then, when America joined the war, he enlisted in the army and volunteered to help liberate France.

I remember thinking that this was the happiest day of my life, as Robert lifted me on to the brick parapet of the bridge in that warm October sunshine. The leaves drifted lazily down from the trees, as if they too wanted to take advantage of the last remaining days of warm weather.

From that day on, I was always the first to leave school in the afternoons. Mademoiselle Burnouf couldn't get over the change in me, for up till now I had always tended to linger at school. Robert always came to meet me, and my spirits always lifted the moment I

163

saw him. To please him, I worked even harder at my studies – much to Mademoiselle Burnouf's satisfaction, though of course she didn't know why. Mama understood, though, for I had taken her into my confidence. She hadn't raised any objection to my meeting Robert every afternoon, but neither had she encouraged me.

All she said was: 'Be careful, child. Don't go believing all that soldiers tell you.'

But her words were wasted on me. I had a blind faith in my new friend.

Day after day, Robert pressed me to introduce him to Papa – not a notion that appealed to me. Papa Maurice, who had risen so magnificently to the occasion and who I had begun to see in a new light, had reverted to his old self. That extraordinary interlude – exciting, wonderful, tragic as it had been – had been just that: an interlude. Routine, habit and the inexplicable grudge he bore me had reasserted themselves. So how could I introduce my friend to him, a man who was so totally different in character? How would Papa react to Robert? Still, I knew that sooner or later they would probably have to meet, and finally I agreed that I'd take Robert home one day when it seemed an opportune moment.

Meanwhile, quite by chance, Mama met Robert. One afternoon when we were walking through the marshes – they'd been dry for months now, ever since July – we came out on to the railway line at Level-Crossing 104. To my surprise, the house was open. Mama had come over to air the house, and dust and tidy up. She was as surprised to see us as we were to see her, but without any fuss she put a pot of coffee on the stove and heated it up, as hospitality demanded.

Before our visit was over, Robert had won Mama over completely. Not only that, he had told her of a plan that had been shimmering at the back of his mind for some time, and that he was determined to follow through. He wanted to adopt me.

I was as stunned as Mama – perhaps even more so. Yet she seemed to share my joyful reaction to this amazing announcement.

She might have been able to forget those angry words I'd hurled at her once, but I certainly couldn't: 'I'd rather die than go on living in a house where I'm treated like a dog.' It hadn't been true, of course; she and Claude were always there, and I knew they loved me. And of course she had probably realized that I was referring to Papa Maurice, and the deep, smouldering hatred that he bore me.

'The only thing is,' Robert was saying, 'I don't want to start building castles in the air. I wonder if you could ask the judge, next time you're in Valognes, whether there would be any legal problems over me adopting Geneviève.'

Mama agreed. So, the following Thursday, after we had been to visit Claude in hospital in Valognes, we paid a call on the local judge.

I was terribly impressed: I'd never met a judge before. He was dressed in a black robe, with ermine trimming, and on his head he wore a strange-looking hat.

He began by asking me some questions about my family life, and Mama encouraged me to answer him openly and freely.

'First, are you in good health, young lady?' asked the judge. 'You look a bit skinny to me.'

I grinned at him. 'I've lived like everyone else the past few years. I've often gone to bed hungry.'

The judge shook his head. 'And won't it bother you to leave your mother?'

'I'll be living in Paris, Monsieur. It's not as though it's the other side of the world.'

At this point the judge's secretary cut in.

'Watch your words, child!' she snapped. 'When you address a judge, you should call him "Your Honour".'

I blushed, then turned back to the judge. 'I'm sorry, Your Honour, I didn't mean to be rude.'

But that interruption had changed the whole friendliness of our interview. I was like a snail that had withdrawn into its shell, and the judge was furious – not with me, but with his secretary.

'When I want your opinion I'll ask for it!' he roared. 'And I'd appreciate it if you would let me conduct this interview in my own way. If your work were on a par with this child's ability to express herself – which it isn't – I'd be very pleased – which I'm not!'

Bravo, I whispered to myself; that'll teach her.

Then I immediately felt sorry for the woman: she looked so shattered by the judge's words. She turned the colour of a beetroot and her lips started quivering; I could see that she was having trouble holding back the tears.

In fact I felt so sorry for her that without asking anyone's permission I got up and went over to her, taking her hand in mine.

'I'm terribly sorry, Madame,' I said. Then I turned back to the judge again. 'I think we'd better go, Your Honour. I'm afraid things have got a bit out of hand, and I don't think we should continue our interview. If my parents decide to go through with this, we'll come back and see you another day.'

And I took Mama's arm and led her to the door. As we went out I heard the judge's astonished tones:

'Well, that's the first time in my career that a child has taught me a lesson in my own courtroom! Things have got a bit out of hand, eh? Well, I haven't finished with her yet!'

We were just crossing the courtyard when the sound of footsteps made us turn round. It was the judge. Forgetting his dignity, holding up the skirts of his long robe to keep from tripping over, he was bustling after us.

'Wait! Wait! Not so fast, young lady!'

We waited for him to catch up. I had the feeling that I'd probably gone too far and that he was about to give me a dressing down.

He puffed and panted, then finally managed to get the words out: 'I want you both to have tea with me in my chambers,' he said. 'Now, I warn you, young lady – I won't take no for an answer, I don't care how offended you are.'

I realized he was no longer using the familiar *tu* form of address that adults customarily used towards children, and I was still trying to work this one out when he started off again.

'Do I take it from your silence that you mean to refuse?' he demanded, looking me straight in the eyes. 'I really must insist that you accept. I was wrong to speak as I did, and I want to make amends.'

I don't know what came over me. 'I agree on one condition,' I said, hardly believing my own words.

'Yes?'

'You must make peace with your secretary and invite her to join us.'

'Agreed. Now you wait here,' he said, 'while I go and change my clothes and invite my secretary.'

And off he hurried as fast as he had come, still holding his robe up off the ground.

'Oh Geneviève,' said Mama reproachfully. 'You've really gone too far this time. There are some things a girl your age really should not say.'

But I wasn't having any of that. 'Mama,' I said, 'I've been through a war and occupation by the Germans, and it seems to me I've earned my right to speak my mind. The judge was unkind to his secretary – yet I know that he's a nice man really. There are such pretty colours round his head.'

To Geneviève Dubosq (in 1944) whose gallant spirit made possible the passage of the equivalent of two U.S.A. battalions via the secret passage through the flooded marshes of La Fière in order to join forces on the other side of those marshes - as stated in "Night Drop" by S.L.A. Marshall chapter 12.

A more courageous person, I have yet to meet!

Best personal wishes

Always,

Philippe Jutras

Sainte-Mère-Eglise

10 September 1977

15. A note dated September 10th, 1977, to Geneviève from Philippe Jutras. *Author's collection. Editions Robert Laffont: Service Iconographique.*

16. Papa Maurice, centre; Philippe Jutras, on the right.

17. Papa Maurice today, standing by Level-Crossing 103. *Author's collection.*

18. Geneviève wearing two medals: one awarded to civilians wounded during the war and the other awarded to her in Israel. Her children are behind her. *Author's collection.*

'What on earth are you talking about?' Mama gasped.

But I couldn't explain to her.

The judge took us to his apartment, which was near the courtroom. An elderly lady served us tea – him and his secretary, me and Mama. We told them about my little brother Claude, who'd been in hospital for so long, and we told him even more about Robert. We also talked about the adoption laws in France; the judge explained that they are very rigorous, and that any infirmity of body or mind could prevent an adoption going ahead. But it seemed that there were no obstacles in our path; if we wanted to go ahead, Robert would surely be able to adopt me.

By the time we left the judge's apartment it was already dark. Twelve miles or so home after dark might have seemed a discouraging prospect, but Mama and I actually enjoyed the long walk, buoyed up as we were by the twin strokes of luck that day. For not only had it turned out that there was little likelihood of legal obstacles to Robert's adopting me, the hospital had also told us that Claude would definitely be discharged within a day or two.

The only problem left was how to tell Papa about Robert.

My opportunity came a day or two later, one evening when my parents were discussing how to bring Claude home from Valognes. There weren't any ambulances in our part of the world, and we didn't know anyone who possessed a car. There was Maurice Salmon's cart and horse, of course, but . . .

'What we need is a jeep and driver,' I said.

Mama chimed in, right on cue: 'Do you think your friends at the Irsa encampment would help?'

'What have we got to lose?' I said, trying to keep my face straight. 'What do you think, Papa? Can I go and ask them if they'd lend us a jeep and chauffeur?'

Papa was thinking only of his young son, and how badly he wanted him home again. 'Yes, of course, child – do it as soon as possible. How about tomorrow?'

Robert was delighted to hear about this turn of events and immediately requisitioned a jeep and driver. I led them back to the Sheepfold to introduce them to Papa Maurice. I was trembling all over as we drove up to the house. How would Papa receive them? And how would he react when he heard that Robert wanted to adopt me? Perhaps after all he'd be glad to get rid of me, I thought; then all my worries would have been in vain.

Robert was so polite and so charming that he had soon won over the entire family. Denise – my older sister, who happened to be there and to whom I had confided everything – took me aside at one point.

'You've made a good choice, Geneviève,' she told me. 'He really is the nicest man. . .' Then she added with a sigh: 'Lord knows, you've earned a little happiness.' She went on to tell me her own plans for the future, and said in passing: 'Of course, when I get married I'll only come home for the occasional visit. A married woman has to live with her husband.'

'And leave her parents behind?' I cried.

'Yes, of course, you ninny.'

There wasn't room for everyone to go in the jeep, so Robert gallantly offered his place to Papa Maurice. Papa demurred, saying he didn't want to deprive Robert of a pleasant drive through the countryside, but Robert was adamant.

'Don't worry, Papa Maurice,' he said. 'Geneviève will keep me company until you get back. Your little boy will be so happy to see you; don't deprive him of that pleasure. And while you're gone I'll help Geneviève with her homework.'

So Papa climbed into the jeep with Mama and Denise, whom they were dropping off in Neuville-au-Plain.

Robert and I stood waving goodbye until the jeep had disappeared. Then we turned back indoors, happy to be alone together. The only trouble was that when we were together the time simply flew past. I tackled my homework, and Robert helped me tend the fire. He liked an open fire as much as I did, and I suspected he was as given to daydreaming as I was.

All too soon, it seemed, the jeep was back. We heard it coming, and ran to meet it. And there indeed was Claude – smiling all over his face, delighted to be home again. My parents were over the moon to have their son back, and in their euphoria they invited the driver and Robert to stay with us for dinner. We had half-expected this, and laid our plans in advance. The driver duly begged off, on the pretence that he was on guard-duty soon, while Robert allowed himself to be persuaded. Our little drama was unfolding exactly as we had planned. Yet I still felt rather nervous, for I knew that Robert planned to speak to Papa tonight. As the evening wore on I became more and more anxious, until I couldn't hide it any more. What if Papa said no? What if he blew his top and forbade me ever to see Robert again?

After dinner we went over to sit down by the fire, all except Papa, who stayed at the table with a glass of Calvados in front of him. Claude and I were sitting on either side of the big hearth, and Robert was next to me.

He leant down and whispered in my ear: 'You think I can mention it now?'

'Yes, go on,' I said. 'We won't gain anything by waiting.'

So Robert turned round to face Papa, smiling broadly. 'Papa Maurice . . . there's something I'd like to ask you.'

'Anything you like, Monsieur Robert,' said my father. 'Anything in the world.'

Papa was obviously in an excellent frame of mind. If only it would last! I felt that if my heart beat any faster it would explode.

'Well,' Robert began, 'you see, Papa Maurice, I've known your daughter Geneviève for several weeks now. I'm a bachelor, I don't have any children – and after the war I'd like to adopt her and take her to live with me. She'll have a good education, I'll make sure of that, and I'll give her everything she wants. I own a clothes shop in Paris, and after the war I mean to take charge of it again. Well, Papa Maurice, what do you think?'

Silence. Yes, I thought, my heart *was* going to burst. I glanced over at Mama; I could almost hear her heart pounding too. Only Robert seemed to retain his composure. That broad smile was still on his lips.

Finally Papa raised his eyes and looked straight at Robert. 'If you're a Parisian,' he said, 'what are you doing in the American army?'

'It's very simple. When the Germans invaded France, I turned my shop over to some friends while I went back to America. I'm Jewish, you see, and I'm sure I don't need to tell you how the Germans treat Jews.' And then Robert went on to tell Papa everything he had told me.

Papa was shaking his head. Yes, he knew all about what those damn Germans had done to the Jews, but for him the fact that Robert was Jewish was of no importance. Anti-Semitism was non-existent in our part of the world.

'Whereabouts in America do you come from?' Papa asked.

'Guatemala,' Robert said. 'That's in Central America. My parents still live there.'

'But you intend to settle down in France?'

'Yes, of course. I plan to reopen my shop in Paris, and if you agree I'll take Geneviève there to live with me.'

My father lowered his eyes for a moment and seemed to be studying his clasped hands. The seconds ticked by, each lasting an eternity. Finally he raised his head again.

'All right. I consent.'

I thought I would burst with joy. Then suddenly everything seemed to go into reverse:

'On one condition,' Papa added.

'Which is?'

'That you promise me she'll finish school. I'd be too ashamed to give you an ignoramus.'

Robert's beam spread across his whole face. 'Not only school,' he said. 'When I said I'd make sure she had a good education, I meant university studies as well. I feel very strongly about it – I entirely agree with you that education is all-important.'

A further silence.

'Well?' prompted Robert.

'In that case – yes,' said Papa. He looked over at me and winked. 'She's yours. You can take her whenever you like.'

I felt like jumping up and dancing for joy, but I just sat there next to Robert, who put his arms round me and squeezed me tight. He was as happy as I was.

'One more thing, Papa Maurice. I'd appreciate your taking care of Geneviève for me till this wretched war is over. I'll come and fetch her as soon as I'm demobilized. I'm sure the war can't last much longer. I'll ask Mama to initiate the adoption procedures as soon as possible. And I ask you, Papa Maurice, to make sure that no one does anything to harm my little Geneviève from now on. No one – you understand? If she does something wrong, let me know and I'll punish her. Can I count on you to do that?'

'You have my word,' Papa said.

'Geneviève may be coming home after dark,' Robert continued. 'We've agreed that she'll come to see me at the camp after school, and if she's a bit late some evenings, I don't want anyone to scold her. Is that clear?'

'Don't worry, Monsieur Robert. She can come and go as she pleases. She's your responsibility now.'

Papa had given his word, and for him his word was his bond. No more sudden rages; no more beatings; no more brutality. I was free!

I decided to test my new freedom. 'Is it all right if I walk part of the way back to the camp with Robert? You won't lock the door on me,

Papa, even if you're in bed by the time I come home?'

Almost gently he replied: 'Don't worry, child. The door will never be locked again, even if you don't come home till dawn.'

My eyes filled with tears. I almost felt like hugging him. I slipped into my coat and tied a scarf round my head. Robert said goodnight to my parents, and off we set in the direction of his camp, without me even taking time to run upstairs and give Claude a kiss – he'd long since gone to sleep anyway.

There was a full moon out, and it seemed as bright as day. The countryside was bathed in silver. I was silent, so silent that Robert started to worry.

'Cat got your tongue?' he joked. 'What's the matter, Geneviève?'

Without replying I just snuggled closer to him; I found his hand and held it to my cheek, then covered it with kisses. I still hadn't said a word by the time we reached the bridge.

Robert was really getting worried now. He swung me up on the brick parapet as he had so often done before, and tried to make me tell him what was wrong.

'Now look, Geneviève, you've got to tell me what's bothering you,' he said. 'You promised you'd never hide anything from me, remember?'

'You'll be angry,' I said at last.

'Why? You know I'm never angry with you,' he said. 'Come on, tell me what's wrong.'

'All right,' I mumbled. 'I'm happy that Papa has agreed to let you adopt me.'

'Great. So what's the problem?'

'But I don't want to be your daughter!' I suddenly blurted out.

Robert looked stunned. 'Whyever not?' he asked.

I had been thinking about what Denise had said to me; all the way here I'd been remembering her words to me. 'When I get married,' she had said, 'I'll only come home for the occasional visit. A married woman has to live with her husband.' Which meant that sometime, when I found a fiancé, I would have to leave Robert! Abandon the only friend I had in the world? No. I just couldn't do it. I hadn't much idea of what went on between a husband and wife, but one thing Denise had made clear: a wife did not leave her husband. So if I didn't want to leave Robert, if I wanted to spend the rest of my life with him, I would just have to become his wife. It was as simple as that.

But this wasn't very easy to explain to Robert.

171

'Why not?' he repeated.

'Can't you guess?' I asked.

'No,' he said, looking genuinely bewildered.

Scared half to death by what I was about to confess to him, I leant against him and whispered: 'Because I love you. I want to be your wife.'

I said the sentences calmly enough, I think, but my heart was pounding so loudly I was sure he could hear it.

If he had been struck by lightning, Robert could not have been more astonished. But his reaction was typically gentle and tender. Instead of laughing at me, he tilted back my head and looked at me for what seemed like ages.

'Don't you see, my sweet Geneviève,' he said softly, 'it just isn't possible. I'm much much older than you.'

'What difference does that make?' I cried. 'That won't stop you making me happy! I know I'm young – but here in Normandy we girls mature very quickly, like the summer wheat. As soon as I'm fifteen, we can get married. The war will be over by then, and we'll be together forever and ever. You'll see – it'll be perfectly possible! It'll be wonderful!'

Robert shook his head. 'I can't marry you. We're from different backgrounds. Different religions even.'

'That doesn't matter,' I said. 'Your God and mine are one and the same; you know that as well as I do.'

He was looking at me strangely. 'Have you loved me – this way, I mean – for a long time?'

'Ever since I first laid on eyes on you.'

'And you never let on. . .'

'I was afraid you'd make fun of me,' I explained. 'I'm still very young——'

'You can say that again!'

'There! You see? You *are* making fun of me! Are you angry?'

'No, I'm not angry,' he said slowly, 'but I am surprised. Put yourself in my shoes. It's the first time anyone has ever mentioned marriage to me. And the fact is, you are young – very young. . .'

'But I love you! I'll never love anyone else,' I cried. 'If you don't love me, Robert, tell me straight away. I'd rather know the truth, even if it hurts. I'll still go on loving you.'

'Yes, Geneviève,' he said. 'I do love you. More than you can possibly know, in fact. If I didn't love you, do you think I would have gone to such lengths to adopt you, to ask your parents to let me take you with me to Paris?'

'But I don't want you to love me like a father. When children grow up they have to leave their parents, and I don't ever want to leave you – not even when we're both old and grey, not even after we're both dead. I'll always go on loving you. Don't you understand?'

'Yes,' Robert said. 'But listen, Geneviève, before we make a decision we have to think about it long and hard. A lifetime – that's a long time you're talking about! And the age difference between us is a real problem.'

'I'd rather be happy with you than unhappy with a younger man,' I insisted. 'But if you want to think about it, let's sleep on it, all right? Between now and tomorrow, you think about it. If you agree, come and meet me on the path tomorrow afternoon – same as usual. If you're not there, I'll understand that you don't want me and that I shouldn't come again. We won't see each other again. It'll hurt dreadfully but . . . Anyway, it's getting late, I must go home. I want to be bright and cheerful tomorrow so I can be worthy of you at school. You'll see. If you do agree, you'll never be sorry. Now, give me a kiss.'

He kissed me. My first grown-up kiss! It lent wings to my feet as I flew home. I'd never felt so happy; I just wished my heart was bigger, to contain all the happiness that was flowing into it that night.

Papa Maurice had kept his word: the door was unlocked. I took off my shoes and tiptoed through the kitchen, past the alcove where my parents were sleeping and up the steep staircase to my bedroom. There I dropped down on my knees and prayed.

'Dear God,' I prayed with all my heart, 'look down on us and protect us both, Robert and me, no matter what the future has in store. . .'

The following morning Mama hardly needed to call me to get me out of bed. I downed my breakfast in record time and dashed off to school. I had a rendezvous today, a very important rendezvous, which might well decide the course of the whole of the rest of my life.

I hadn't slept much that night. Slowly, insidiously, the doubts crept into my mind. What if Robert wasn't on the path that afternoon after school? What if he decided I really was too young? What if he decided he didn't even want me as a daughter now? All day long the questions tormented me. When the bell rang to signal the end of afternoon classes, I was out through the door like a shot. I ran as fast as my legs could carry me to the path leading to the Irsa Bridge. There I forced myself to slow down, to walk normally, but my heart was pounding uncontrollably. With each step I took, my anxiety increased. I couldn't bear it. The tall trees that flanked the path made the relative darkness seem all the more ominous. If Robert did come to meet me, I assumed he'd be waiting for me in his usual place, at the outskirts of a tiny hamlet near the camp.

There was no sign of him as I passed through the tiny village. My heart felt like lead – then suddenly took off on a pair of magic wings. Just beyond the last house in the village, I caught sight of his tall silhouette.

Thinking I hadn't seen him, he called out to me: 'I'm here, Geneviève! I'm here!'

I ran up to him and threw myself into his arms. He held me tight against his chest.

'Did you think of me at all today, Geneviève?'

'I could think of nothing else but you!' I laughed. 'For all my good intentions, I just couldn't concentrate on my work. Mademoiselle Burnouf noticed, but she just thought Papa had been picking on me again. She tried to comfort me – and do you know what? I burst into tears like a baby!'

'Why?' smiled Robert. 'Were you afraid I wouldn't come?'

'Afraid? Afraid? I've been shaking like a leaf ever since I left you last night!'

'But there was no need – I'm here, aren't I? I did come. It's really me, in the flesh. Are you happy?'

'I wish I could tell you how much.'

He stepped back a bit and looked at me. 'Well? Now what, my darling?'

My darling! He had called me darling! I was a woman now.

'Now, my love, it's all very simple,' I said. 'You get your horrid war over, while I concentrate on growing up, and when you come back we'll get married.'

'Not so fast, young lady! Somewhere or other you've forgotten something very important: your studies. I've already told you how strongly I feel about education. As soon as the war's over, and you're ready for it, I want you to go to university to continue your studies there. Yesterday your father told me he didn't want me to have an ignorant daughter – well today I don't want an ignorant wife. If you don't go on with your studies, I won't marry you. Is that clear?'

'I'll do whatever you want,' I said humbly. 'I'll work really hard, and you'll be proud of me.'

'I'm sure of it,' Robert smiled. Then he told me that he'd been over to see my mother that afternoon, and that they had had a long talk. She had been a little taken aback by the news, apparently, but not too upset. Robert laughed. 'I think she half suspected it, you know. Anyway, she doesn't object to me marrying you – but she doesn't want your father to know, at least not for several months, in case he might not let you go. As for the rest, nothing else is changed, except for the fact that we won't have to bother about the adoption procedures now. So you've won, you little tigress! I'm going to marry you!'

'Oh pinch me, pinch me!' I cried. 'I'm sure I'm dreaming! Oh Robert, don't ever let me wake up!'

He laughed and hugged me. 'Oh yes – something else,' he said teasingly. 'Your mother wants you to make your own trousseau for your wedding. And that means you'll have to learn to sew – which I gather is a chore that might not exactly enchant you.'

'I'll learn. I could learn anything to please you!'

'And there's another thing, Geneviève. Why did you cut off your pigtails?'

'Was it Mama who asked you to find out?'

Robert nodded.

'Then I'm sorry, but I won't tell you.'

We had just come to the bridge. As usual, Robert swung me up on the parapet. Standing there in front of me, he stared at me, and it seemed to me that his beautiful dark eyes were filled with sorrow.

'You're always hiding things from me,' he said. 'Don't you trust me, Geneviève?'

'Of course I do – it's just that I don't want to hurt Mama.'

'I don't understand, I'm afraid. . .'

I hesitated. 'First you've got to promise you won't tell a soul.'

'I promise,' he said solemnly.

So I told him. The night before I first met Robert, my father had been drinking – more than usual, in fact. With Claude still in hospital, he had been angrier than ever. Anyway, he had tied my pigtails in a knot and hoisted me up and hung me by the hair from one of the beams in the ceiling of the kitchen – there were big nails in the beams to hold Papa's hunting rifle. He had left me swinging there for about half an hour. My head had hurt so much that I hadn't dared move a muscle, and I was convinced my scalp was going to peel off.

'Anyway,' I finished, 'when he let me down I cut my pigtails off so that he could never do it again. There, that's the whole story. Now do you understand why I didn't want Mama to know? She had worries enough of her own without me adding to them.'

Robert pulled me to him and held me close. For a long time we stayed like that, without saying a word. The moon was shining in his face, and I noticed the tears shining in his eyes.

'Well, I'm looking after you now,' he whispered at last. 'Your life will be different now. I promise you won't have to go through anything like that ever again.'

Several soldiers appeared just then and invited us to join them for the evening meal at the camp. It seemed I had been adopted by the whole group. And as Robert had promised, my life at home changed, immediately and completely. Papa no longer beat me. I was no longer his daughter in his eyes; I belonged to someone else now. And whatever his failings, I never did see that rough uneducated man go back on his word. Robert had asked him to look after me until he returned, so look after me he did. For the first time in my life he started worrying about me; he kept asking if I'd had enough to eat, he advised me to dress warmly when I went outside, he spoke to me respectfully, without any trace of the old roughness or anger. I found it all rather funny, but I was careful not to let him see. He was proud as punch, bragging incessantly about his youngest girl, about the marvellous man who was going to adopt her, about the endless studies she would be undertaking thanks to this man. I think it was this that made him the proudest: in fact, it was the one and only thing that ever really mattered to the poor man, who to the end of his days would never get over the fact that he had never had a chance to become educated.

December 24th, 1944

Christmas Eve. For the first time in my life we had a real Christmas tree – and I had a real present: the most unexpected yet the most dreamed of present a girl can have.

We were at the bridge again, with me sitting on the parapet, exactly as every afternoon for the past three months. Robert suddenly asked me to close my eyes and put out my hand. As I did so, I felt him slipping on my finger what I supposed to be a token ring of some sort. But when I opened my eyes I found to my astonishment that it was a real engagement ring! For a moment I just stared at it dumbly, unable to find the words to express what I was feeling. Then, as usual, I burst into song – and the song that immediately sprang into my mind was a most appropriate one.

> *When I felt your golden ring*
> *Slip upon my finger,*
> *My heart was filled with happiness,*
> *My lips were stilled – but nonetheless*
> *I knew I had to sing.*
> *In happiness or sorrow,*
> *We'll be together,*
> *One today and one tomorrow,*
> *Down the rocky road of life,*
> *Man and wife,*
> *Into the setting sun . . .*

Robert listened delightedly, then shook his head in mock disbelief. 'You always have a song to suit the occasion, don't you?'

'I do know a lot of songs,' I agreed. 'But my favourite one hasn't been written yet.'

'And what's that?'

'It's a song that I dreamed of once, called *Geneviève*, about a girl of my age – it's the story of her life and all her joys and sorrows. When people hear it they'll be moved to tears.'

'You should write it yourself,' Robert said.

'But I wouldn't even know how to start – I don't know the rules for writing songs.'

'Like everything else they can be learned.'

'But how?' I demanded. 'There isn't a library in Sainte-Mère-Eglise, and I don't often get a chance to read poetry. I've read some Lamartine, but I find him terribly gloomy.'

'I think you'll find most poets rather gloomy,' Robert said. 'But listen – let's go and show your parents your ring.'

I jumped down off the parapet and together we made our way to the house. Mama had a fire going and over it she was roasting a turkey. We all had dinner together. Papa had not been out for three days, and for three days he hadn't touched a drop of drink – almost a record! As a result we spent a very harmonious evening. After dinner we exchanged presents. I had embroidered six handkerchiefs for Robert; I'd been working on them for weeks. I had decided that it was high time I learnt to sew and embroider properly.

A day or two before New Year, Robert announced that his unit was being transferred. He wouldn't be going far, just to another post in the neighbourhood of Sainte-Mère-Eglise. The last evening before he moved, we were visiting the little bridge again – by this time we'd come to think of it as our own – when Robert suddenly made me promise never to come back to it.

'Why?' I demanded.

'Because another unit will be coming to replace us here,' he said. 'You might as well know – I'm the jealous type, Geneviève! I don't fancy the idea of you coming here and meeting other soldiers.'

'Don't worry,' I assured him. 'No matter how fond I am of this bridge, I swear I'll never come back here again.'

The day after Robert's departure, Mama and I went into Sainte-Mère-Eglise to do some shopping. On our way home I asked her if she'd mind us taking a new route – 'as a favour to me'. She agreed without query, even though the new route I suggested was a good mile longer than the usual way. I had suggested this route because I

178

thought Robert's new camp was somewhere along here . . .

I was right. About a quarter of a mile out of the village, we came upon a military installation that was just in the process of being set up. It was a much larger encampment than the one near the Irsa Bridge. Without a moment's hesitation I walked right into the camp and looked around. Lots of tents had already been erected, but the soldiers' faces were unfamiliar. Suddenly I spotted one of Robert's comrades – and as he saw me he broke into a broad grin, calling out to his friends. Within seconds they were gathering around us, and they lifted me up on to their shoulders in triumph while Mama looked on approvingly. Robert soon arrived, hearing the shouts of laughter, but at first the soldiers wouldn't let me down from my lofty perch. When at last they set me back on the ground, I immediately rushed over to Robert. But he turned his back on me, and walked across to talk to my mother.

'I know Geneviève loves me,' I heard him tell her, 'but sometimes I get the feeling she loves *all* the soldiers.'

This upset me. Of course I loved all the American soldiers! After all we had gone through together during those long days and nights, I had good reason to love them. But I had never told Robert about that time. He might have thought I was boasting, and I hated the idea of being thought boastful.

Yes, of course I loved the American soldiers. But there was only one that I was truly *in love* with.

I had been so delighted to find Robert again: how could his silly suspicions spoil my happiness? I pulled him aside and tried to explain. After all, I wasn't responsible for the way his soldier friends greeted me, was I? They had simply been glad to see me. There was no need for jealousy – although, I added, I was secretly rather pleased to see how jealous he was! For wasn't it true that one was only jealous if one were truly in love?

At last Robert's solemn expression gave way to a wide smile. He offered to escort Mama and me back home, and we readily accepted. He couldn't get over the fact that I had already found him in his new camp. As he pointed out, there were new camps going up all around Sainte-Mère-Eglise, yet I had unerringly found my way straight to the one where he was.

When the Christmas holidays were over, my little brother came with me to school for the first time in several months. His leg was

179

completely better, and it was touching to see how impatient he was to get back to school.

The New Year had brought a salutary reminder that the war was still going on. During the day, our house was always empty, what with Claude and me at school, and my parents and Francis out working. One evening Papa returned home to find the front door smashed in – the work of a pickaxe, to judge from the results. One of my uncles who lived nearby told us that he'd seen two men knocking at our door that day; he hadn't liked the look of them, so he had immediately called the Americans, stationed not far from us. The American soldiers had responded promptly, and they had caught the two men, who by then had broken into our house – when the Americans arrived they found the men putting on some of Papa's clothes. It turned out that they were German prisoners who had escaped from a nearby camp.

That same evening we were sitting round the table discussing the incident. Mama got up to light the fire before she started cooking dinner, and she noticed that some ashes had spilled out of the grate and on to the floor. She asked me to find the dustpan and brush, and she was just sweeping up the mess when the brush clunked against something hard in the ashes, something metallic.

'Maurice! Francis!' she cried. 'Come and look at this! I have a feeling those two Germans left us a little present before they were recaptured. . .'

With infinite care Papa brushed the ashes away to see what the strange object was. Mama was right: the Germans had planted an anti-personnel bomb in our fireplace. I felt a shiver run up and down my spine – and I'm sure the others in the room felt exactly the same. If Mama had lit the fire, we'd all have been blown sky high. Thank God she had noticed the overflow of ashes!

We had a cold meal that night. First thing next morning Papa would go and fetch the American bomb-disposal unit to get rid of our dreadful souvenir.

When Claude and I went to bed, Mama came up with us and made us say an extra prayer of thanks. Then, like two little angels, we fell asleep. It was not until the next day, when she was making our beds, that Mama discovered two more souvenirs the Germans had left behind: hidden between the sheets at the foot of our beds were two more bombs, the kind that explode on contact. Mama usually put a hot-water bottle into our beds for us to warm our feet on, but curiously enough the night before she had not done so. Still, it was a miracle that neither Claude nor I had touched the bombs during the night. In Claude's case, it was probably his size that had saved him; he was so little that even when he stretched out full length, his feet still didn't reach the bottom of the bed. As for me, I had been saved by pure luck: that night I happened to sleep curled up in a little ball – something I don't normally do.

After two such incidents, somehow one just has to believe in destiny.

When Robert came round that day and heard about the bombs, he flew into a blind rage. He said that an inquiry should be set up to investigate the incident, and that the two prisoners should immediately be handed over to the military police and made to face trial. They should not be tried for escaping but for attempted murder – trying to kill two innocent little children in their beds. He ranted on and on, and everyone in the house was very serious and solemn until I chimed in:

'Didn't I tell you – the Good Lord doesn't want me! As long as any of you are with me, you'll obviously be all right. I think God's afraid that if I arrive in Heaven I'll cause an absolute havoc, so He prefers to leave me down here where I'll cause less trouble.'

I said it lightly, to relieve the tension in the room, but I hadn't expected everyone to burst out laughing. We all relaxed, and after that the incident was forgiven if not exactly forgotten.

April 9th, 1945

My birthday. Robert went up to Paris, without saying a word to me, and brought me back a surprise present: a beautiful blue dress. And, in complete secrecy, he had had made for me the most wonderful bracelet I could have dreamed of; it consisted of several English silver coins, bearing the head of George V, joined together by the master silversmith who lived in our area, Monsieur Fossard. I had never been so spoiled in all my life.

But the best thing of all was that I was now into my thirteenth year. In two years, I kept telling myself, in two years I'll be able to marry Robert. That was the only thing that really mattered.

May 1st, 1945

Robert's camp had been moved again, but he still managed to visit me every day. He was now stationed at Blosville, not too far from Sainte-Mère-Eglise, so we could continue to see each other whenever we both had a free moment.

The first day of May is a national holiday, and so school was closed. When I woke up that morning, I looked out of the window as usual – and to my amazement I saw the ground was covered in a blanket of snow. In fact it was still snowing: big lazy flakes, floating to the ground. I've always liked snow. I think it dates from the time when Papa threw me out in the snow as a form of punishment – I was only about eight months old at the time.

I am convinced I remember the incident, though my mother told me the story, so it's hard to separate what I really remember and what Mama's memories were. Anyway, what happened was that, like lots of eight-month-old babies, I was cutting my teeth, and my constant crying was keeping Papa awake at night. One night, in a fit of rage, he picked up my cradle and carried it out to the fields. Then, to make sure Mama didn't bring me back inside, he locked the door and held on to the key. Mama wept and pleaded with him and threatened to call the police, but nothing would make him relent.

I'm sure I remember looking up at the night sky, watching the clouds float past the bright moon – and then it began to snow. I remember a cow coming over and peering into my cradle, and later a colt. But more than anything I remember the snow, those soft flakes falling gently round me. I also remember moments of fear as the clouds shut out the moon.

And ever since then I've loved moonlight and snow flakes and been

183

a bit scared of the dark.

Mama told me that it was dawn before she could get out of the house to come and rescue me. She rushed up to my cradle, expecting to find me frozen to death. The cradle was covered in a blanket of snow, but when she scraped the snow away, although my hands and face were blue with cold, I had been so well tucked in that I hadn't been able to loosen my covers, and so I had remained relatively warm and apparently little the worse for the experience.

This May holiday, Robert took me for a long walk through the snowy countryside. The apple trees, already in bloom, were covered with snow; the combination of the pink blossom and the white snow was indescribably beautiful. We walked until we grew tired, then sat down on the trunk of an apple tree that had been blown down in a recent storm.

'I have some bad news, Geneviève,' Robert said, taking me in his arms. 'Be brave, won't you? I know it's hard, but——'

'Don't say another word,' I said. 'You're being transferred.'

Robert nodded.

There was a lump in my throat, and the tears were welling up in my eyes. To hide my misery, I picked a daisy and shook the snow from its petals. One by one I began to pull the petals off: he loves me, he loves me not, he loves me . . . The tears started to spill down my cheeks.

Robert hugged me tightly and tried to comfort me. 'Don't cry,' he kept saying. 'I can't bear to see you cry. I promise I'll write to you. Besides, I'm sure I'll get lots of leave and I'll come and see you as often as I can. The war will be over before you know it – they say it's only a matter of days now . . . And in six months I'll be out of the army. Think of that! I'll come and fetch you straight away and take you away for ever. Be brave, Geneviève. Don't cry, darling. Promise me you won't forget me.'

'Oh Robert!' I sobbed. 'How could I forget you? I wouldn't forget you even if I never saw you again! Will you really write to me – every day?'

'Every day, cross my heart,' he said. 'And don't forget, I may show up here at any time. Just when you're least expecting me I'll pop up and surprise you. That'll make you happy, won't it?'

'How can you even ask such a question?' I shrieked at him. 'What you deserve is a snowball smack in the face!'

And that's just what he got. I picked up a fat handful of snow and flung it at him, then took to my heels across the field, with him racing after me in hot pursuit.

There are days that ought to last forever . . . But it was coming up to dusk. After a long, lingering, last kiss, the man I loved, the man who would soon become my husband, climbed into his jeep and drove slowly away, turning repeatedly to wave and cry out: 'Bye-bye, Geneviève! Bye-bye, my love. . .'

The weeks dragged slowly past. Each day the postman brought me a letter from Robert; he had kept his promise. As soon as I could I would retreat into a quiet corner with the letter, and read it alone, or sometimes with Claude beside me, sitting on the parapet of the Irsa Bridge, where I often spent hours dreaming of the happy days we had passed there together, and of the even happier days to come.

Then one evening, when I arrived home from school, Mama said to me: 'Be a good girl, Geneviève, go up to your room and fetch me some chestnuts. I need them for the supper.'

She didn't have to ask me twice. I love chestnuts. I ran up to my room with a basket to put the chestnuts in – but I got no further than the top of the stairs.

'Guess who?'

It was Robert. He'd been hiding behind the door. I dropped my basket and hurled myself at him, shrieking for joy.

'My goodness, haven't you grown – in only two months too!' he laughed. 'You've put on some weight, and you're getting prettier by the day!'

'When did you get here?' I asked.

'This afternoon. I didn't want to meet you at the school, I thought it would be more fun this way. Are you pleased to see me?'

Pleased? I was thrilled. 'How much leave do you have?'

'Three whole days,' he said. 'And I intend to spend every minute with you. Since it's nearly the end of term, your mother said you could ask permission to stay off school while I'm here. That way we won't need to be separated even part of the day.'

Claude volunteered to sleep downstairs in his baby cot, so that Robert could sleep upstairs in his big bed. For the first time my future husband and I were going to share the same bedroom.

That evening I got ready for bed first, and slipped under the sheets, pulling them over my head and pretending to be asleep. In fact I was giggling like mad. Then I sneaked a look when Robert was climbing into bed. He started to snuggle down, then threw me a look of mock

185

anger.

'Geneviève! Who made this bed?'

'I did,' I admitted, puzzled. 'Why?'

'In that case, my little chickadee, you can come right over and remake it! Unless you want me to sleep on the floor. I'm not used to being short-sheeted, and I'm not going to let you get away with it!'

Laughing so hard I was almost crying, I threw off my covers and started to remake his bed, while Robert went across to sit on mine.

'Boy, is your bed hard,' he exclaimed, pressing down on it with both hands. 'Can you sleep on it all right?'

'Yes, of course I can – I'm used to it. It's a straw mattress,' I told him.

He had noticed that all the other beds in the house had spring bases with feather mattresses on top, and wondered why mine didn't.

I shrugged my shoulders. 'Mama calls it my penance bed. She says that monks in their cells have beds that are softer than mine. But it doesn't bother me. Oh yes, of course I'd prefer a softer bed but . . . There! All done. Come on, your bed's ready for you now. Shall I tuck you in to show you how sorry I am?'

And as Robert slipped back into his bed, snuggling down without any difficulty this time, I tucked the blankets around him.

Then I bent down and whispered in his ear: 'This bed is big enough for two, you know. Why don't I climb in beside you?'

'Oh no you don't, you little devil,' he said, gently but firmly.

'Why not?'

'You will sleep with me after we're married, not before.'

'But it would be so nice to cuddle you all night! And you've seen how hard my bed is. There's plenty of room for us both in yours. Give me one good reason why I can't sleep in your bed.'

'Because I love you.'

'Oh la la! Now I really don't understand you, Robert! One minute you say you love me, then you won't do something to please me. You're mad. I've always known it – all grown-ups are mad. Never mind, I love you just the same.'

Robert pulled me down on the bed and wrapped his arms around me. 'Listen,' he said. 'You've got to trust me. I want you to believe me when I say that I'd be even happier than you if you could share this bed with me tonight. Grown-ups aren't as mad as you think. Sometimes they have to put duty before pleasure – and there are times when it's very hard to do that. So don't go making it harder on me than it already is. I know you don't understand, but go on back to your own bed. Think of it as a favour you're doing me, something to show how much you love me. All right?'

I could tell from the tone of his voice that he was absolutely serious.

'All right,' I said. And without another word I went back to my own bed and climbed in.

A solitary child, living in the countryside, for all my natural curiosity I had never really thought about how the human species reproduced itself. I hadn't a clue about the physical bonds that unite man and wife. Which may have been just as well, in fact; given that I had such a curious nature, I might have wanted to try it out on the spot. But Robert was a gentleman; even if I had wanted to try it on, he would certainly have refused.

I woke up before him next morning, sneaked downstairs and brought him his breakfast in bed.

'Come on, lazybones,' I teased him as he ate his breakfast. 'The sun's up already. I want to take you for a walk.'

'Where?' he asked between mouthfuls.

'I'll give you three guesses.'

'Oh go on – tell me!'

'Irsa Bridge,' I announced triumphantly.

'I thought I made you promise not to go there again,' Robert said. 'Are you telling me you broke your promise?'

'You told me not to go as long as there was an army camp there,' I retorted. 'Well, there hasn't been a camp there for ages.'

'And how would you know that if you hadn't gone there yourself, young lady?'

'Because,' I said, my temper rising, 'Papa works over in that area sometimes, and he told me. And there's something I want to get straight,' I added, now barely able to control my anger. 'I *always* tell the truth and I *always* keep my promises. Just you remember that!'

He was instantly contrite. 'I'm sorry, Geneviève. Come here——'
He held out his arms, but I didn't budge. 'Look, I told you I was the jealous sort, Geneviève, but it's only because I love you so much – sometimes I get so jealous I can't control it.'

'Promise you'll never hurt me again?'

'Cross my heart,' he said, keeping his face straight. 'I'll be the perfect husband.'

'You'd better be! Otherwise I'll . . . I'll eat you up!'

187

I flung myself on the bed and started nibbling at his ears with mock fury. He laughed and fought me off, calling me his little Norman savage.

Every detail of those three wonderful days remains engraved on my mind. Three days of fleeting happiness . . .

August 14th, 1945

It was nine o'clock in the morning. Claude and I had come to my usual haunt, the Irsa Bridge. We decided to climb down to the railway line below so that we could play around on the bed of stones that flanked it; we'd often gone there with Robert and his army chums when their camp had been nearby. It was an ideal place for a spot of target practice, and the soldiers had set up all sorts of makeshift targets and given us shooting lessons – once they even let Claude fire a machine gun.

I'd rather neglected my little brother recently, but he wasn't one to take offence. In fact, he seemed pleased to see me enjoying life so much.

One day recently he had looked at me seriously, shaking his head, and said: 'Even if you'd married the lord of the manor and become the grandest lady of the village, Papa would never have treated you with such respect.'

And it was true: tough old Papa Maurice had mellowed, at least as far as I was concerned. It was all because of Robert.

Anyway, this particular morning I was daydreaming as usual when there was a sudden cry from Claude.

'Geneviève! Can you help? I'm stuck!'

He was lying on the ground about thirty yards away, flat on his stomach on the stony bed of the railway tracks. I ran across to see what had happened.

'Are you hurt, love?' I cried.

'No, I'm all right,' he said. 'I just tripped. A piece of wire got caught in my shoelaces – see?'

I tried to work the piece of wire free but I couldn't. Finally I bent

189

down to get a better grip on it, and tugged at it with all my might.

There was the most tremendous explosion.

Later on I learned that the wire had been attached to a land mine, and by pulling it I had set it off. In fact, it turned out that the whole area under the bridge had been mined. It was astonishing that none of them had gone off before, for Robert and I had often gone there when he was still stationed near the bridge.

The explosion sent Claude and me flying through the air, but in different directions. I landed not far from the tracks, and by sheer willpower I managed to crawl the few yards to the railway line; I even managed to make it across the little drainage ditch and up the embankment. I was determined to reach the telephone that I knew was on the telegraph pole the other side of the tracks. But I simply couldn't make it. Despite all my efforts, I couldn't even crawl beyond the first line.

I was entirely conscious, fully aware of what had happened to me. As I collapsed on the tracks I examined myself almost clinically. I was completely naked: my clothes, even my shoes had been blown off my body. From a gaping wound in my right side, my intestines had begun to spill out on to my thigh. My hands were burned and cut all over. The little gold ring that Robert had given me had melted; it was encrusted in the flesh of my finger. I reached down and tried to push the intestines back into the hole in my abdomen. They were blueish-purple; I remember being amazed at this. Then I realized that my legs were broken – in fact there were several fractures. The tibia of my right leg was sticking out like an arrow that had embedded itself in my flesh. My right kneecap had completely gone; there was just a hole there now. My face and hands were burned, the skin virtually vanished. It felt as if my right eye had been gouged out, but actually it had just been pierced by shrapnel from the blast. And I knew I'd been hit in the throat, too, for every time I opened my mouth a jet of bright red blood spurted out.

Yet the curious thing was that I felt no pain.

I heard the whistle of a train approaching from the direction of the Chef-du-Pont station. If I stayed where I was on the railway line, the train would soon finish me off. I had to move. My mind gave the order, but my body refused to obey. I was too weak now to pull myself across the tracks to safety; I couldn't even crawl another inch. Then I realized that if I leaned over the side of the embankment, gravity would pull me down. With all my waning strength, I leaned towards the edge of the embankment – and toppled down into the drainage ditch below.

The ditch was dry, and its steep sides protected me from the hot sun. I just lay there, passing in and out of consciousness, I suppose – at least, I don't remember hearing the train go past. All sorts of strange things went through my mind. At one stage I decided that Robert would never be able to love me if he saw me in this state, so I would just have to die. No two ways about it. I wouldn't want to live without him so I would quite simply die. Then it came to me that this was August 14th: tomorrow was the birthday of the Virgin Mary. The idea that I would arrive in Heaven on Her birthday amused me. I just hoped that my soul was not as damaged as my body, or God might have trouble recognizing me. Then I almost laughed out loud as I pictured Saint Peter's expression when he saw me arriving in such a mess. I could even imagine what he'd say:

'*Now* what have you done, you little ninny?'

I wanted to fall asleep, but I knew I had to fight against this. I still felt no pain; I was relaxed, almost cheerful. I was sure I was going to die, but it didn't bother me at all.

All I could see from my position in the ditch was the little bridge where I had spent so many happy hours. It looked particularly beautiful, bathed in bright sunlight. I tried to remember the last song I'd sung there for Robert: what was it? Come on, think. Oh yes – that song from the Lalo opera. Robert had been amazed at the way I switched so easily from singing the part of the Princess Rozenn to that of the King. 'You have gold in that voice of yours,' he had said seriously. 'It'll make you rich and famous one day.' I had laughed and said: 'Don't worry, I'll never sing for anyone but you. You might get jealous!'

If I had to die that day, I was glad it would be here, in this place I loved so much. Silently I thanked God for His choice . . .

I lost consciousness for a while. When I woke up I was trying to remember what Robert had told me one day about the origin of the English word 'goodbye'. It seemed very important to me. What was it? 'Take me closer to You, God.' No, that wasn't right. 'I'm going to Thee, God.' No, that wasn't it either. I couldn't remember. I drifted off again . . .

A man was bending over me. 'What happened?' he asked. 'Did you fall off the train? What's your name?'

'Geneviève – Papa Maurice's daughter,' I managed to tell him. 'My mother's on guard duty at Level-Crossing 103.'

Every time I opened my mouth to speak, another bright red jet of blood spurted out.

The man looked horrified. 'Don't talk any more,' he said. 'I'm going to telephone for help. We'll bring a railway trolley down the line for you. Don't worry. You'll be all right.'

I heard him scramble up the embankment and cross the tracks to the telegraph pole on the other side, where the telephone was. Funny, I thought: why did he tell me not to worry? I'm not worried. I'm going to die, that's all. And I knew it was all going to be very easy; I knew now that those who have suffered a mortal wound don't feel any pain.

The man was back. He laid his blue working jacket over me and told me he was going to fetch my mother from Level-Crossing 103; he would soon return, he said. I noticed he was crying.

'Don't cry, Monsieur,' I said. 'Dying's not so serious. What's your name?'

'Maurice. Maurice Friouze,' he said. 'But please don't try to talk, child. Don't worry, I'll be back before you know it.'

I was thirsty and tired – so very tired . . . He had promised to be back soon. But Mama wouldn't be able to come with him. The railway company's rules were very strict: no employee could leave his or her post for any reason whatsoever. I didn't mind; I didn't want her to see me in this state anyway.

The August heat was causing the blood to clot on my wounds. The only place where I could still feel myself bleeding was in my throat, and then only when I opened my mouth. I had no notion of time passing. How long had I been in this ditch? I felt so sleepy . . . but I fought fiercely to stay awake. I wanted to hear the last beat of my heart.

When I next came to, my father was leaning over me.

'Do you understand me, child?' he was saying. His voice sounded muffled, as though he was speaking through a thick wall.

The question struck me as so ridiculous that I hesitated a moment before answering. Then:

'Of course I understand you!'

'Then tell me where Claude is,' Papa said.

'He's over there – on that stony patch under the bridge. Go on, go and help him, Papa. I'm beyond help, I'm dying. . .'

Two other men bent over me, and started trying to lift me out of the ditch. But one of the men had to turn away and I heard him being sick.

I must have been the most gruesome sight. Swarms of flies had gathered all over my body, no doubt to lay their eggs in my open wounds.

The men lifted me on to a stretcher and carried me up the embankment to the railway tracks. There was a trolley on the line, and they placed me on it. As they lifted me, the pain suddenly hit me, and I screamed. Why oh why hadn't they left me in the ditch? I'd been so comfortable down there, in no pain at all.

Once on the trolley, it was even worse. Every time the trolley lurched forward it caused me such agonies that I screamed aloud for them to stop. Finally the men lifted me off the trolley; it seemed they had decided to carry the stretcher all the way to the Chef-du-Pont station. Even that was an agony. I kept begging the men to put me down, to let me die, to take me back to the Irsa Bridge to find my little brother. At the head of the stretcher, walking backwards and therefore facing me, was kind-hearted Monsieur Pottier; he was sobbing like a child.

Eventually an American army truck was commandeered to take me to hospital in Cherbourg. I was drifting into a state of semi-consciousness, but I remember them having difficulty getting the stretcher into the back of the truck. My vision was getting blurred, but I watched their every movement. And I remember them discussing what to do, then deciding that my two stretcher-bearers should go back to the Irsa Bridge to help search for Claude. The county chief had arrived, and he asked two other men who happened to be there – Monsieur Legoupillot and René Lemaire – to join the search team. The more searchers, he said, the more chance of finding the boy. Papa was sitting beside me in the back of the truck, hunched up on a wooden bench. On my other side sat a young American soldier, who had said he wanted to come to the hospital with me. I still had both hands clutched to my abdomen, trying to keep my guts from spilling out; I wanted to beckon the young soldier to come closer, but I didn't dare move my hands. Then the soldier saw that I was trying to make some kind of sign and he knelt down at the head of my stretcher.

'You're a very brave girl, Geneviève,' he said.

I could hardly summon up the strength to speak but I managed to ask him the time.

He glanced at his wristwatch. 'It's ten past one,' he said.

Ten past one. The explosion had been about three and a half hours ago.

I was barely conscious now, but my mind was struggling to focus on something: I had suddenly remembered the origin of the English word 'goodbye'. It used to mean 'God be with you'. I felt very pleased with myself for remembering.

The pain was agonizing. I kept thinking how sad Robert would be if he knew, and was glad he didn't. Over on his bench, Papa was crying silently. Did that mean he loved me – just a little bit?

With every jolt as the truck drove along those country roads, I yelled aloud, despite every effort I made to bite the screams back. The pain was too much to bear. The young soldier was still kneeling beside me, his face close to mine. I looked up at him one last time, and whispered:

'Geneviève is dying. Bye-bye, soldier. . .'

The tears were pouring down his cheeks. I wanted to console him, to tell him not to cry, but I was sinking fast. The last thing I remember is thinking of Robert. Goodbye, Robert . . . goodbye, my love . . . I'll love you till the end of eternity . . .

Everything was going dark. Then I heard his voice, close to my ear – or was I imagining it? His gentle voice, tender as always, was saying as he had so often said before:

'Bye-bye, Geneviève.'

And then nothing. Darkness. I slipped into a coma that was to last for nine days.

August—December 1945

When I woke out of my coma, the first person I saw was a tiny nun, dressed entirely in white. I knew I was small, but she was even smaller than me. I was in an enormous room containing about twenty beds, most of them occupied by girls of about my own age.

Seeing that I was awake, the little nun came bustling over to my bed. She put a finger to her lips.

'So you're awake then? Good. But you mustn't speak, child – no, you mustn't even try. You have a bad wound in your throat, and if you try to talk you'll start it bleeding again. Just nod your head if you understand what I'm saying.'

I nodded.

'Good.' She smiled. 'Very good. Now just relax, don't try to move. I'm going to get Doctor. He wants to talk to you.'

And away she bustled. I stared after her, still amazed that a grown-up could be so small and even more astonished by the speed with which she moved. She was back only moments later, accompanied by a man also dressed in white, aged about fifty.

'Hello, Geneviève,' he smiled. 'I'm your surgeon. I'm glad to see you're awake now. But I must warn you that you've got a bad wound in your throat, and if you want me to save your voice, you'll have to help me by not trying to talk. Not yet anyway. You must be patient. In a few days we'll give it a try. Do you understand?'

Again I nodded.

The surgeon then started to ask me a whole string of questions.

'Are you still going to school?'

I nodded.

195

'Did your teacher teach you about fractions?'

What a funny thing to ask, I thought, but I nodded again.

'So if I talk to you about a ten per cent or twenty per cent chance of something happening, you'll understand what I mean?'

More and more intrigued, I nodded once more.

'Good. Now here's what I wanted to say. You've been very badly hurt, Geneviève.'

I wondered if the man was all there. I know I've been badly hurt, I thought; you'd have to be blind not to know that I've been hurt. Luckily he couldn't read my thoughts.

'You can get better,' he went on, 'but only if you listen to me very carefully. Eighty per cent is up to you. My medical science is worth about ten per cent. The other ten per cent we'll have to leave to God. How does that seem to you?'

With my right hand, the only one that was free, I made a sign to him that I wanted to write something. The girl in the next bed was writing on a slate, which the surgeon borrowed with a piece of chalk. He puffed up the pillows and helped me to sit up, then handed the slate and chalk to me. But I couldn't hold the slate and write on it at the same time. He had to hold the slate for me.

'I understand. I'll do whatever you want me to do,' I wrote.

He read what I had written and then glanced at me in approval. 'Good girl,' he said. 'You'll be here a long time, but I have the feeling you're going to make it. You and me together – we'll see you get better.'

I shook my head. I pointed to the large crucifix the nun was wearing and held up three fingers.

The nun started laughing. 'She's right, Doctor. Not the two of you – God as well!'

Then I started writing on the slate again. 'Where's my little brother?'

'I don't know,' said the surgeon. 'Ask your mother. She'll be coming in to visit you every Thursday afternoon.'

'What about Robert?' I wrote.

'Who's Robert?' the surgeon asked.

'He's her future stepfather,' the nun chimed in. 'Her mother told me she was going to be adopted by an American soldier. The adoption papers are being processed now.'

The surgeon shook his head as if he thought it was highly unlikely the adoption would now go ahead, with me in such a condition.

The nun turned and went into a little cubicle that I later learned served her both as office and bedroom. When she came back she was carrying a letter, which she handed to me. It was from Robert – I could tell by the handwriting. The postmark on it was from a little place in the north of France.

'Do you want me to read it to you?' asked the nun.

I shook my head, covered the letter with kisses and slipped it inside my nightgown, next to my heart.

'He really means a lot to you, this Robert, doesn't he?' said the surgeon.

I nodded, then pulled the slate forward again. 'He's my only reason for living,' I wrote.

'That's not being very nice to God,' commented the little nun.

'There's no need for God to feel jealous,' I scribbled, 'He is and always will be my only reason for dying.'

The surgeon burst out laughing. 'Well, I'm glad to see you've got a sense of humour, Geneviève! As long as you can keep that, I'm sure you'll survive.'

Now I scribbled on the slate: 'How bad am I?'

'Pretty bad,' said the surgeon with a grimace.

'Tell me,' I wrote.

He shook his head. 'Not today. You need to rest, my girl. Don't you think so, Sister? No, Geneviève, you get some sleep now, and I'll answer all your questions later.'

'Can I read my letter first?' I wrote.

'I think you'd be better off getting some sleep first,' he said.

So I acquiesced, and handed him back the slate and chalk. The nun straightened my pillows and I lay back, my hand on Robert's precious letter. My eyes were already closing, but I heard the surgeon say to the little nun:

'What a child! I think she'll pull through all right. In fact, if willpower has anything to do with it, I'm sure she will.'

When I awoke again, the same little nun was bending over me, one finger on her lips.

'Don't forget,' she said. 'No talking – not yet anyway.'

I nodded, to show I hadn't forgotten what I'd been told.

The surgeon was standing a few beds away, tending a girl who I later discovered had been operated on for appendicitis. He saw that I was awake again, and came across to speak to me.

197

'Well, Geneviève, you never do things by halves, do you? You've
been asleep a full twenty-four hours! And a very good thing too, in my
opinion. You must be feeling much better. Here – I've brought you
this notebook and pencil. Now you can write down any question you
want to ask me.'

I took the fat notebook and pencil and immediately wrote: 'Please
can I read my letter first?'

'Yes, of course,' he said, and offered to open it for me.

I handed him the letter, the envelope all crumpled now because I'd
been lying on it. The surgeon smoothed it out as best he could, then
took out a pair of scissors – attached to his waist by a piece of string –
and snipped off the top of the envelope and handed me two pages
covered with the firm, strong handwriting that was so familiar and so
precious to me.

The letter was dated August 22nd, 1945.

> *My darling little Geneviève,*
>
> *I have just learned from your mother of the terrible accident
> that happened to you and Claude. I can't find the words, my
> darling, to tell you how terribly sad I am at the news, and to
> know how you must be suffering. But I want you to know, my
> angel, that you have to go on hoping, and understand how
> much you have going for you. Modern surgery is making
> enormous strides these days. We'll make you well again, of
> that I'm sure. As soon as I got your mother's letter, I asked to
> be discharged from the Army at the earliest opportunity. The
> paperwork is going through now, and I'm assured that I'll be
> out in three or four months' time at the latest. As soon as I'm
> out, I'll be with you just as fast as I can make it, and I'll stay
> with you forever. You'll see, my darling, with time and
> patience we'll make you as good as new. Meanwhile, make
> sure you do all the doctors tell you, even if it's painful
> sometimes. You must be brave and obedient. Remember, your
> whole future is at stake. You must accept everything, no matter
> how difficult it is at the time. Above all, remember that I love
> you more than anything in the world, and I want you better
> soon. You must do everything in your power to that end. If you
> can, please write to me as soon as possible; if you can't, ask
> your Mama to write a letter for you. Just make sure you don't
> leave me without any word of you. Hurry and get well,*

darling. I must end this letter now, but I'll write again soon.

With all my love,

Your Robert.

P.S. As soon as I can get leave, I'll be there to see you.

I closed my eyes for a minute or two. So, despite everything that had happened to me, Robert still loved me. That was the best reason in the world to get better quickly.

The surgeon made no attempt to interrupt my silence until I started to cry.

'Now, now, Geneviève – don't cry,' he said. 'I hope the letter didn't bring bad news?'

I shook my head, trying to wipe away the tears that were spilling down over my bandages. Then I pulled the notebook and pencil towards me and started writing again:

'My soldier friend is trying to get leave soon so that he can come and see me. I think it's time you told me exactly what's wrong with me now.'

'What do you want to know?' asked the surgeon.

'Will you have to cut off my arms and legs?' I wrote.

'I'm pretty sure we can save everything,' he said. 'Your arms are fine. If you can't move your left arm, that's because of the needle there – stuck into your arm at the end of this rubber tube, see? As soon as you can eat properly, I'll unhook the needle and take this thing away, then you'll have the full use of your arm. As for your hands, apart from a few broken bones, there's nothing we can't mend.'

'What about my legs?' I scribbled.

'Well, your right leg is coming along fine,' he said. 'I had to cut off a bit of the tibia when I set it, but that won't affect the length of your leg, and I don't foresee any problem with it. I can't be so sure about your left leg, though. Where it was enough to apply a simple splint to your right leg, as you see I've had to put the whole of your left leg in a plaster cast. I don't like having to plaster over any broken flesh, but in your case I had no choice. Anyway, we'll have to keep an eye on that leg. If you feel anything odd about it, let me know at once, even if it doesn't seem very important to you. All right? You'll have lots of pretty spectacular scars, but you'll get better. You'll soon be able to walk again, if you really work at it. As I said, your recovery depends largely on yourself. Are you still game?'

199

I nodded, then scribbled something else: 'What about the rest of me?'

'Of all your wounds, the one in your tummy will probably heal fastest.'

'Which part of me will take longest to get better?' I wrote. He hesitated for a second, so I added another line to the notebook: 'Please, Doctor. I must know.'

Slowly, as though reluctant to let the words escape his lips, the surgeon told me that my face would take the longest to heal. In fact, he said, he would have to call in the plastic surgeon, because he couldn't do any more for my face.

I raised my right hand to feel my face. It was covered in bandages, with holes for my mouth and eyes. I patted it, trying to feel through the bandages.

Then I took up my pencil again: 'Please take off the bandages and give me a mirror.'

'No, Geneviève,' he said firmly. 'You're not well enough yet. Wait a few days.'

I sat up on one elbow, nearly pulling the needle out of my arm in my determination to show him how strong I was. 'I want to see now,' I wrote. 'If you don't do it, I'll take the bandages off myself.'

The surgeon was very reluctant but when I kept insisting he finally gave in.

'Very well then,' he said. 'But first I want to tell you that plastic surgery can do wonders nowadays – and I'm sure it will work wonders for you too. And there's a new drug available – I'm going to try to get some, so that we can use it to fight the infection in your legs.'

'What's it called, this drug?' I scribbled.

'Penicillin,' he said. 'An English scientist discovered it only recently – about ten years before the war. They call it a miracle drug.'

But I wasn't going to let him delay the awful moment any longer. 'Now will you take the bandages off?' I wrote.

'Now listen, Geneviève,' he said, 'I don't want you to be upset when you see what's happened to your face. Whatever you do, don't cry out. If you want to save your voice, you mustn't utter a single sound now. All right?'

I nodded. Then I picked up my pencil again: 'Will I be able to sing again?'

'Yes, of course,' he said. 'There's no reason why not. Your vocal cords are intact. A piece of shrapnel hit you in the throat, and sliced a bit of it away, but it's healing nicely now. I just don't want you talking or crying out yet. You see? We'll wait a few days before we let you use your voice.'

At last he started to unwind the bandages round my head. My heart was beating faster and faster. The little nun brought me over a hand mirror. The surgeon leaned over me.

'Remember, now – no using your voice, no matter what. Keep telling yourself: I'm going to get better. Promise me you'll do that?'

I nodded. If it hadn't dawned on me before, it certainly dawned on me now that what I was going to see would be dreadful, shocking. I hesitated for a second. Maybe it's better if I don't look, I thought. Then I took a deep breath. I remembered all the soldiers I'd met over the past few months, who had found themselves in a similar situation and faced up to it bravely. I had to be as brave as they were. There was no going back now.

I seized the mirror and stared at my face. It was the most horrible sight. It bore no relation at all to the features I remembered. The burned and bruised and swollen flesh that I saw in the mirror wasn't me; it wasn't even human. My mouth and chin were more or less intact. The worst part was my cheeks, though the skin was beginning to reattach itself to the bones. I looked so frightful it was all I could do not to throw up.

The surgeon took the mirror from me. 'You're a brave, brave girl, Geneviève,' he said. 'You handled that like a true soldier.'

I wrote: 'That's the nicest thing you could have said to me. And I *will* get better, I know I will. But please will you do something for me?'

'What's that?'

'I don't want Robert to see me like this. He might not love me any more. And if he stopped loving me I would want to die.' And, I added to myself, I wouldn't want him to have to feel sorry for me.

'Well now,' said the surgeon, 'I'm sure we can handle that. When he comes to see you, we'll put the bandages back on. All right?'

I nodded.

Then the surgeon went to talk with the little nun in her cubicle. When he came back he told me they were going to give me a drink, to see if I could swallow properly.

'What would you like?' he asked.

'Coffee,' I scribbled.

A few minutes later the nun trotted up to my bed with a strange-

201

looking mug which had a lid on it that looked like a duck's bill.

'We call this a "duck",' she smiled. 'Because of its beak, you see. It makes it easier for you to drink when you're lying down.'

She helped me into a semi-sitting position, and slipped the beak between my lips, gently raising the mug so that a little of the warm liquid trickled into my mouth. As the first drops reached the back of my throat, I let out a scream of pain.

The poor nun got such a shock she dropped the mug and it broke on the floor.

The surgeon, who had moved on to attend the girl in the next bed, rushed over to me. 'Please, Geneviève – you mustn't scream!'

But it had hurt me so much I hadn't been able to stop the scream. I was sobbing uncontrollably.

The surgeon opened my mouth gently and looked inside. The pain was so bad I was convinced I must have torn something, but he told me there wasn't any bleeding.

'Well,' he said, 'I think we'll forget the drink for today. Try and get some sleep. We'll have another go this evening, when I hope you'll feel a bit better. It's just that I don't want to keep feeding you through that thing for much longer.' He nodded to the bottle of liquid that hung from the stand beside my bed.

I knew beyond all doubt now that my road to recovery was going to be a long and rocky one. For a minute or two I lapsed into self-pity; I felt sorry that I hadn't died. It's so easy to die, so hard to go on living. I envied the little girl in the next bed to me. According to the nurses' conversation that I had overheard, she had burst her appendix and was on the point of death; there was nothing they could do to save her. She was ten years old, an only child, as pretty as a picture, and her parents doted on her. Why did she have to die, while I had to live? It didn't seem fair.

For consolation I turned to Robert's letter again. Robert – my only reason for going on, for fighting to get better. How I wished he were here with me. But he'd soon be out of the army, he'd said, in two or three months perhaps. Two or three months to wait, then we could be together for always.

Suddenly I realized I didn't even know what day it was. I scribbled something in my notebook and handed it to the little nun, who was engaged in sweeping up the mess where the mug had broken on the floor.

She read my question, and it seemed to amuse her. 'It's August

28th,' she smiled. 'You've been here for two weeks now. Is that what you wanted to know?'

I nodded and took back the notebook. 'What did you do when I first arrived?' I wrote.

'Well, first I called for a priest,' she said. 'I told him to come very quickly so that he could administer the last rites to you.' She smiled again. 'But as you see, that wasn't necessary.'

'I could have told you that you were wasting your time,' I wrote. 'God doesn't want me.'

'Why do you say that?'

My pencil flew across the page. 'Because I've nearly died lots of times, and each time God has shaken His head and said no. I'm such a nuisance that I think He'd rather keep me down here than let me go up to Heaven – more's the pity.'

'Why?'

'Because life down here isn't much fun. If I had my way, I wouldn't waste another day down here, I'd go up to Heaven straight away.'

'I know what you mean,' the nun said gently. 'Considering the state you're in. But life is a precious gift from God, Geneviève, and we must just take it as it comes.'

'It's not much of a gift,' I wrote. 'It's more of a burden. And I think there's worse to come.'

The nun smiled at me sadly. 'Don't despair, Geneviève. It'll all work out all right. You'll have to try to keep cheerful, that's all, or you'll never get better. Now, what about trying to get some more sleep?'

So I settled back in the bed again. Just before I fell asleep I remember coming to a decision. I was going to get better. I would have to treat my body like a machine that needed repairs, and I'd do my best to get it back in working order. And I made up my mind not to let it get me down; I would never again think about how much I'd prefer to be dead.

The nun woke me up, asking if I felt strong enough to try another drink.

I nodded, but indicated that I wanted to use a spoon rather than resort to that mug again.

So she brought me a spoon and held it to my lips. I tried to lap the coffee from the bowl of the spoon, the way I'd seen kittens do. The result was less painful than before but it still hurt. At least I had achieved something: I hadn't screamed.

'Well done, Geneviève,' smiled the surgeon, coming over to me from the bedside of the girl with appendicitis. 'That's victory number one. I'm sure there will be many more.'

He examined my throat, and then explained to me exactly what had happened. At the moment of the explosion I had probably opened my mouth to scream – it was a reflex reaction, he said – and at the same moment a piece of shrapnel from the land mine had struck my throat, slicing everything on its way. The wounds were deep, he said, and it would probably be a while before I could manage to eat anything by myself, and I might have to learn how to use my vocal cords all over again.

That night I heard the little girl next to me calling for the priest; she must have known she was dying. The priest hurried in and duly administered the last rites. Her parents had been called, but they arrived too late. She had gone. The last I saw of her, her face was wreathed in a lovely smile.

Seeing I was awake, the priest came over to speak to me.

I asked him to give me my notebook, and in it I wrote: 'Is she dead?' He nodded.

'She's lucky,' I wrote. 'Why her rather than me?'

'I don't know, child,' he said. 'We propose; God disposes. Perhaps He has such arduous work for you to do in your future life that He is preparing you by teaching you now how to bear suffering.'

'But I don't see what He wants of me,' I wrote.

'It's not for us to understand His ways,' said the priest. 'Let Him do as He sees fit. You keep telling yourself this: "His will be done." That will make things easier – you'll see.'

We were interrupted then by the mother's loud sobs from the bedside of her dead daughter.

One afternoon in early September, just as I was preparing to settle down for my usual nap, the surgeon came in to see me and sat down on the edge of my bed. By now I had discovered that his name was Doctor Blanchard.

'I'm going away on holiday,' he told me. 'But before I go, I think we ought to try a little experiment. We're going to test your vocal cords. All right? Now this is what I want you to do. Raise your head so that you're stretching your neck – that's right – and when I tell you, I want you to say just one word: "fine". Understood?' He placed his fingers on my throat. 'All right, say it.'

'Fine.'

The sound that emerged from my throat was a harsh croak. But Doctor Blanchard smiled.

'That's good, Geneviève,' he said. 'Let's try it again – but without forcing.'

I took a deep breath and tried again: 'Fine.' Then for good measure I added: 'Everything's fine.'

'That's enough, big mouth!' laughed Doctor Blanchard. 'When I want you to improvise, I'll tell you. Now open your mouth and let me take a peek inside to see what effect those sounds have had . . . Good. Looks as if my little repair job is holding up. Did you drink any coffee this morning?'

I nodded.

'Try to tell me in words,' he said. 'If it hurts too much you can stop.'

So I told him. 'I . . . drank . . . a little coffee . . . this morning . . . and at lunchtime . . . Two teaspoons.'

The sounds that were coming out of me were horrible. I must have looked worried.

'Don't let it upset you,' said Doctor Blanchard. 'That will get better. More important, does it hurt?'

'When I drink, yes; when I talk, no.'

'I'm sorry to hear it hurts you to drink,' he said. 'I had hoped to take you off the bottle before I left.'

'When are you going?'

'Tonight. I'm a tired old man.'

'Yes, you must be tired,' I said. 'You stayed up all night with that girl who died, and you've been around all day too.'

I was speaking very slowly, and the words sounded very strange to me, but Doctor Blanchard seemed to understand. At least he was letting me go on talking.

'How do you know all that?' he asked.

'I have eyes.'

'One eye, Geneviève – only one.'

'I only use one now,' I said. 'But I still have two.'

'Geneviève,' he said softly, 'I'm afraid that your other eye will never be able to see again. It was filled with shrapnel. Doctor Cau did all he could, but it was no use.'

I was stunned. 'You mean . . . I'll never see again with that eye? Why didn't you tell me before?'

205

'I'm sorry, Geneviève,' he said. 'There were so many things wrong with you that I just forgot to mention your eye.'

'What else have you forgotten to mention?'

'Nothing of any importance.'

'Tell me.'

'Well . . . I haven't told you before that you'll be a human pincushion for the rest of your life. There are hundreds of little bits of metal in your body.'

'Can't you remove them?'

'Not all of them,' he said. 'There are just too many. But we will remove all the ones that are painful.'

'So I'll be walking around for the rest of my life with all those bits of metal still inside me?'

He nodded. 'That's right. And if what they say is true, you'll grow up stronger than Popeye.'

I didn't understand.

'They say that iron is good for children,' he explained.

'Oh very funny,' I croaked. 'Look, Doctor – I'm not a child any more. I'm a young lady.'

'I was only joking,' he said. 'And don't you start thinking that because you can talk now, you can make remarks like that to me – otherwise I'll be sorry I agreed to let you start talking.'

I asked him if there was a risk my voice might go again.

'Well, yes,' he admitted. 'There is a risk. With all the cuts inside your throat, it's a miracle you can talk at all.'

And he explained that he hadn't been able to remove all the pieces of shrapnel that had lodged in my throat. There were still a dozen or so tiny splinters of metal in my gums, for instance – but he hadn't wanted to remove them for fear he might ruin my 'beautiful teeth'.

'I'm glad you didn't then,' I said. 'That must be the only beautiful thing I've got left.'

He must have detected the bitterness in my voice, for he smiled at me gently. 'Try not to brood, Geneviève,' he said. 'That will only make you depressed, and depression will stop you getting better.'

After a moment's pause I asked him about the little girl with appendicitis. 'Why did she die?' I said.

'Because her parents brought her to me three days too late,' he said. 'They thought it was an ordinary stomach ache, and that it would go away. Peasants are hard people, Geneviève. They don't always respond to a child's cries.' He shrugged. 'I did everything in my power to save her but . . . There are days when I wish I'd never decided to become a doctor.'

'Now who's getting depressed?' I said. 'I'm glad you became a doctor – after all, where would I be without you?'

'There are other surgeons,' he said.

'Yes, but it was you who saved my life.'

He smiled. 'That's true. It was certainly touch and go for a while. I couldn't believe my eyes when I saw the state you were in – covered with flies and larvae, after you'd been lying out in the sun for four hours.'

'What did you do?' I asked.

'First I gave you a warm bath, to get rid of the larvae that were beginning to eat you. Then I had you taken to the operating theatre, but I didn't know quite where to begin.'

'Well, thank you for everything,' I said. 'I think you did a super job, Doctor.'

'My only mistake was repairing your vocal cords.'

I looked up at him in horror – then saw that he was smiling. 'Do I talk too much then?'

'You certainly seem pretty good at it,' he grinned.

'Wait till I start singing again,' I told him. 'Then you'll really have something to complain about.'

'Why's that?'

'I sing all the time, morning, noon and night. I hold the world record for singing – you'll see! And I've got a range of six octaves.'

'How do you know?'

So I told him about the American soldier who'd appointed himself my music teacher, and given me a gramophone and two records, and wanted to take me with him on his concert tours.

'But my father wouldn't let me go,' I finished.

'Then how come your father is letting your friend Robert adopt you?' Doctor Blanchard asked.

'That's different,' I said; as far as Papa was concerned, Robert was adopting me after he was discharged from the army.

'Aren't you happy at home?'

'Not really,' I said. 'Papa is always drinking, and when he drinks he always . . . Never mind. I'm just lucky that Robert wanted to adopt me. He loves me like a real father, and I love him. He wrote to tell me that he didn't mind about me being disfigured; he said he'd still love me. But I've got to try to get really well – I want to be as good as new

207

again, so that he won't ever feel ashamed of the way I look.'

Doctor Blanchard received all this in silence. Then he said thoughtfully: 'I don't know whether I ever mentioned this before, Geneviève, but I have a daughter who's about the same age as you. Every time I see her I think of you, and I tell myself how lucky she is. You're the bravest person I've ever met, Geneviève, and I can say that even after seeing all the victims of this war. We'll all work together to make sure you get completely better. There are a lot of people round here who love you, Geneviève.'

The little nun popped her head round the door and interrupted. 'Doctor – your replacement is here. He'd like a word with you in your office.'

'I'll be with you in a minute, Sister.'

I asked him to do me one last favour before he left. 'Please will you unhook me from that machine?' I begged, pointing to the bottle of precious liquid that dripped into my arm. 'Then I'll have to start feeding myself, won't I?'

'What if you can't?'

'I'll manage.'

He looked at me sceptically. Then, without another word, he went round my bed and unhooked the bottle. He gently withdrew the needle from my arm, and nodded at me.

'Yes, I think you will be able to manage,' he said, and turned to leave the room.

'Thank you, Doctor!' I called after him. 'Have a lovely holiday!'

I was exhausted after our long conversation – the first I'd been able to have since arriving in hospital. I felt like going to sleep for days. But I was glad to have my voice back, even if it did sound so strange. Soon I'd be able to sing again . . . And on that thought, I fell asleep.

It was the new doctor who wakened me. He was considerably younger than Doctor Blanchard, but he looked just as nice – which only goes to show how misleading first impressions can be.

He began by removing the rubber tube draining fluid from my right leg, then unwrapped the thick bandages and cottonwool. The open wound at the top of my thigh was covered with a thin piece of gauze, which he now ripped off. I winced, but worse was to follow. He started pulling off all the bits of gauze that still covered the numerous cuts and wounds on my body, and with it he took whatever thin layers of skin had been starting to form over my wounds. I couldn't help it: I

208

had to scream.

The little nun, who was assisting the doctor, tried to comfort me, and told me not to ruin my voice or I might never be able to sing again. Her words fell on deaf ears.

My wounds were bleeding again. The doctor was rubbing at them heavy-handedly, cleaning them, pulling them, tugging them. By the time he had finished, I was almost fainting from pain.

Next the doctor turned to the plaster cast on my left leg. Where's that revolting smell coming from, he wanted to know. Sister explained that part of my kneecap had been blown away in the explosion, and that the wound it had left was infected. He stood there a moment, scratching his head, then ordered Sister to go and fetch the male nurse.

'That cast will have to come off,' he said.

The male nurse arrived bearing an enormous pair of shears, like those used to cut sheet metal. He slipped one blade of the shears beneath the end of the plaster cast; then, to get more leverage, he leaned with all his force on my upper leg. I stifled my cries. Then, the lower blade, working its way down inside the plaster cast, entered the hole where my kneecap had been. I fainted.

When I came to, Sister was washing my wounds, very gently. The doctor had gone. Apparently there had been an emergency elsewhere in the hospital, and he had had to go. As it turned out, I didn't see him again for several days.

That same afternoon, Mama came to visit me. She seemed pale and thin, and she was dressed all in black. The sadness in her face lifted somewhat when she saw that I was awake. She took me gently in her arms, and we stayed like that for a long time without speaking.

Then I asked her about Claude.

'He's in Valognes Hospital,' she told me without hesitation. 'Same ward as last year. He's still on the critical list. I'm afraid he's even more poorly than you, Geneviève.'

I immediately reached for my notebook, tore a page out, and started writing him a letter. Mama promised me she would deliver it on her next visit to Valognes. In the letter I told Claude to be brave, and promised him that I'd get better as fast as I could so that I'd be able to come and visit him.

The new doctor's second visit nearly ended in catastrophe. When he arrived, the bandages on my left leg were covered in pus, and he

209

announced on the spot that he would have to amputate the leg.

Sister tried to reason with him; if the bandages were soiled, she said, it was just because I'd been a bad girl.

I started to protest, then she caught my eye and I realized she was trying to help. Dear little nun, she was a rotten liar! She was blushing all over her face. But her lies saved the day: the doctor agreed to give me one day's grace before amputating.

'If the discharge has begun to go by tomorrow,' he said, 'then I won't amputate. Otherwise. . .' He turned to me and added: 'You'd better behave yourself, young lady. If not, you're the one who'll suffer.'

When the doctor had gone, Sister gave me a conspiratorial smile. 'I thought you were going to give me away,' she said. 'I'm sorry I had to say what I did – but that doctor will amputate at the drop of a hat. Corns, bunions, anything – he'll take your leg off. No, no, I'm exaggerating. But we must do something to stop him. I'm sure Doctor Blanchard can save your leg when he gets back. The trouble is, he won't be back for a few days yet . . . I know! Yes – the very thing! Listen, Geneviève, this is what we'll do. Doctor G——— always makes his rounds at the same time each day. Half an hour before he's due to arrive, I'll come in and wash your wounds, then apply fresh bandages. What he doesn't know won't hurt him.'

I objected that the doctor would be bound to ask questions, though, and then Sister would have to tell more lies.

The little nun shrugged her shoulders. 'It'll be worth it if we can save your leg,' she said.

I was astonished that a nun would deliberately tell lies. She must have guessed at my thoughts, for she went on:

'The chaplain will give me absolution. Lies do exist, you know, dear. But we should only use lies to protect people, not hurt them. Now then, let's make our plan. I'm a bit worried that you might give the game away by screaming out when I change your bandages. So I'll give you an ether mask, all right? A few whiffs of that and you won't feel a thing. No one will be any the wiser.'

'What about the other girls in the ward?' I said doubtfully. 'They might see what's going on and tell the doctor.'

'I doubt it,' said Sister. 'But to make sure, I'll let them in on the secret and pay them to keep quiet. I've got a big stock of sweeties that the American Red Cross gave us. That should do the job.' Then she gave me a worried look. 'What about you, Geneviève? You won't say anything to anyone, will you?'

'Of course not!' I croaked.

'The only reason I mention it is . . . you do talk a lot.'

'Only with people I like,' I told her. 'And that doesn't include Doctor G———.'

Our little game worked beautifully, and the next few days actually passed quite quickly. When Doctor Blanchard walked into the ward again, we all breathed a sigh of relief. The first thing he did, after examining my left leg, was to order a new plaster cast to be applied. Without a cast on the leg, he told me, there was even less chance that the few remaining fragments of bone that had been my kneecap would be able to 'knit', even if the price we had to pay was at the expense of the other wound on my leg.

One day I mentioned to Doctor Blanchard that I was sorry to be missing out on school. He immediately had the answer.

'What if I brought you my own children's school work each day? Then you could keep up with your class.'

I was so pleased with this solution I flung my arms round his neck and hugged him. The poor man looked completely stunned.

From that day on, he treated me almost as his own daughter. He found all sorts of things to keep me happy. Knowing that I liked flowers, he gave me a tiny vase, and he kept it filled constantly. As soon as one little bouquet began to wither, he replaced it with another. Even better: with the complicity of Sister, he devised a scheme to attract birds to the windowsill near by my bed. Our rations were pretty meagre, but what with the breadcrumbs I salvaged from each meal and the occasional bag of grain that Doctor Blanchard produced, we were able to scatter some sort of bird food on the windowsill every day. I couldn't get out of bed to see them, of course, but by twisting and turning my head I managed to watch the antics of the birds as they fluttered about on the windowsill.

One day I had a visit from a teacher from Sainte-Mère-Eglise, and with her she had brought a big doll, stuffed with straw, as a present. How was she to know I hadn't played with dolls for years? Anyway, Doctor Blanchard found a use for the doll. He said that I should use it as a sort of surgical record: each time I had to be operated on, he said, I should make an appropriate incision on the doll's body, and afterwards I should sew it up as carefully as possible. So when I left hospital I would have a complete record of all the operations I had

211

had. It might seem a rather ghoulish diversion, but there wasn't much else to keep me amused.

I wrote to Claude every day, and each Thursday when she came to visit me Mama would collect my mail. She posted my letters to Robert and personally delivered the ones to Claude.

Time began to pass more swiftly. I did some school work every day, and Doctor Blanchard would take it away to be corrected, then return it to me the next day. Gradually the end of the year was approaching, and I was counting the days till Robert was discharged from the army and came to take care of me. Each day I was getting stronger. I still had a plaster cast on my left leg, and the rubber tube in my right leg, but I wasn't in as much pain now. My face was still a bit of a mess, but at least it had become more acceptable. They told me I might need skin-grafting operations on my face, but not yet; I decided to let Robert make that decision. The grafts would have to be done in a hospital in Paris, they said, by which time Robert would have his clothes shop again, and he would probably be able to come and visit me every day in hospital. The future was looking brighter and brighter.

And to top it all, Christmas, the happiest season of all the year, was just around the corner.

December 22nd, 1945

From my bed I could hear Christmas carols floating up from the chapel on the floor below. The choir was rehearsing. Doctor Blanchard still wouldn't let me sing; he kept postponing the day, time and time again. But when I heard those carols, I couldn't bear it any longer. I begged him to let me go down and rehearse with the choir. I could easily be taken down on a stretcher, and I could sing perfectly well even when lying down. But he wouldn't hear of it.

I began to suspect that he was keeping something from me. I asked him to tell me the truth – there and then.

He seemed flustered and upset, but finally he stammered out that my voice – as far as singing was concerned – was a thing of the past. No matter what he had done for me, no matter what he would continue to do, he could not give me back my singing voice.

I refused to believe him. I loved singing; I had always loved it, for as long as I could remember. It just wasn't possible that I would never sing again. I burst into floods of tears.

Doctor Blanchard was almost as distressed as I was. He tried his best to comfort me, telling me that if I put as much effort and hard work into learning to sing again as I had put into overcoming all my suffering, then perhaps, after all, I might manage it. Who could tell what might happen?

I clung to this tiny shred of hope he offered me, but my instincts told me it was false. Still, the thought that I just *might* be able to sing again comforted me and calmed me, and I decided not to waste another minute: I wanted to start trying to sing right away.

Alas, instead of those sweet vibrant notes that had once come to me so effortlessly, the sounds that grated from my open mouth were scratchy and discordant. That was the best I could manage. I was desolate.

It's no use, I caught myself thinking. I might as well give up, I might as well be dead . . .

December 23rd, 1945

I was expecting a visit from Mama. She would be bringing not only my Christmas present, but also – I hoped – news of Robert's impending arrival. I was counting the minutes impatiently.

What would she say when she heard I would never sing again? Would she understand the depths of my distress? Surely Mama would be able to comfort me, perhaps even give me some slim hope to cling to . . .

When the visiting hour came, I got the shock of my life. Despite my plaster cast and all the restraining bandages, I shot upright in bed – previously I had always need help when I wanted to sit up. The man walking across the ward to me, his step heavy, his cap in hand, was someone I hadn't seen for over four months: Papa Maurice.

He was dressed in his Sunday best. There was a black ribbon in his buttonhole, and his new shoes made a creaking noise as he walked towards me. He stopped at each bed and peered at its occupant, then moved on, until he reached me.

Something.kept me from opening my mouth, even to ask him why he'd come. I sensed that his visit meant trouble.

We stared at each other in silence for a moment – me struck dumb by his arrival, and him apparently at a loss for words as he gazed at my bandaged head. Then he pulled up a chair and sat down beside my bed. I noticed that he was nervously fingering his cap as he began to talk.

Then it all came out in a rush. He seemed to have no notion of the distress his words caused, he just rattled on and on.

'I'm fed up with the stupid games they're playing with you in here. Your brother Claude is dead. He didn't survive his wounds. Your

215

mother didn't want you to know. But I'm telling you now, because I hold you responsible. You were told to take care of him, so you're to blame. That's how I see it. And I don't see why you should be spared. If you lived to be a hundred years old and had a life as full of suffering as Job, it wouldn't be enough to punish you for the sin of my son's death. Your punishment begins today. Your soldier won't be coming back for you. In the state you're in, the adoption wouldn't be able to go ahead anyway. I've forbidden him ever to lay eyes on you again. He tried to make me change my mind, but I wouldn't listen to him. I've sent him packing – said I'd get him arrested if he persisted. You'll never see him again. Understand?'

I suddenly saw my father in an entirely new light. It was as though I was seeing him for the first time. He was no longer the cruel, mean man that I had known, he was just a poor broken father, stricken by the death of his beloved son. His coming here to tell me all this was simply an effort to try and make his aching heart feel better. I felt sorry for him – but I couldn't find a single word to say.

A welter of thoughts were pounding through my mind. 'Claude is dead. It's your fault.' And it was true: by pulling at that wire I had caused the land mine to explode. I couldn't have foreseen it, but the fact is that I did it. Now my little brother was dead. And Robert would never be coming back. Ever. Yesterday I learned that I would never sing again. Today I had lost my little brother and my future husband. It was too much.

As I collapsed, the girl in the next bed called out to the nurses. Two of them raced across to my side. Sister reached for my pulse.

Through a wall of cottonwool, distantly, I heard her cry out: 'The child is dying! Sister Augustine, run and find the chaplain – and Doctor Blanchard! Hurry!'

I heard her muffled footsteps receding, then Doctor Blanchard was at my side.

'What happened?' I heard him ask the girl in the next bed.

'That man you passed just now, the man carrying a cap in his hand. He was talking to her – he told her that her little brother was dead, and that her stepfather would never come and see her again.'

'Who was the man?'

'I don't know,' said the girl. 'I couldn't hear everything he said. I got the feeling he was suffering terribly. He was crying as he left.'

In my semi-conscious state, I remember taking note of this extraordinary detail. Papa had been crying.

The nurses were pulling screens round my bed. Screens! That meant I was going to die. At long last! Far from frightening me, this thought comforted me. My suffering would soon be over.

Doctor Blanchard was sticking a needle into my left arm. Intravenous, I thought, proud to remember the term; they're the only sort of injections that don't hurt. The reaction the injection produced was almost immediate: I opened my eyes. Kneeling at the side of my bed, Sister was cradling me in her arms, pressing my head against her chest. The big silver crucifix she wore hung down and dangled in front of my eyes. I gazed at it fixedly . . .

Then everything grew dark again. I could scarcely make out the chaplain who was administering the last rites. Sister was crying. I could feel the warm tears dropping on my hands.

'It's over, Father,' I heard her muffled voice telling the chaplain. 'Poor child – but she'll suffer no more.'

And that was the last I remembered as I sank into the welcoming darkness where memories that break your heart can no longer have any effect.

Epilogue

Yet again, Death rejected me. But to say that I soon recovered would be an exaggeration. When I came to, I was completely blind. Later, when I was well enough to be transferred, they sent me to the Cochin Hospital in Paris, for treatment under the renowned eye specialist, Doctor Offret.

Months later, this marvellous man had restored to me the sight of my left eye. But my mind was a blank. At first I took this to be straightforward amnesia, but they later told me that some of my brain cells had been destroyed during those minutes when my heart had stopped beating that December day. And the fact is that I've never fully recovered the alert intelligence I had possessed as a child.

But here I must pause and thank Papa Maurice for his contribution: he forbade the surgeon in charge of my case either to give me ECG treatment or to perform brain surgery, even when it seemed that I would never come out of the coma. Papa maintained that only time and my iron constitution would prevail. And he was right.

It took me months and months of effort and self-discipline before I recovered what I had lost. But at the end of that time I found I could piece together the disorderly fragments of memory floating through my head. I undertook this re-education process by myself, immediately after I left hospital, and no one helped me except Mademoiselle Burnouf. At the age of fifteen I even managed to pass my Certificat d'Etudes at Sainte-Mère-Eglise.

Today, from the time of the accident, I have spent a total of five years in hospital. I have undergone thirty-three operations. There is still one I might have to face: an operation on my right eye. But as yet there is no French surgeon who dares to perform it. A pity: if it were to succeed, my vision would be almost normal.

As Doctor Blanchard predicted that autumn of 1945, I am a veritable human pincushion. There are still over three hundred bits of metal stuck in various parts of my body, ranging from the size of a pinhead to the size of a walnut. Plastic surgery has indeed restored something of my face, though it still won't express my feelings the way it did when I was a child. And, again as he told me, my singing voice has gone forever. In fact, there are times when my vocal cords seize up altogether, and I cannot speak at all. Then, without apparent reason, my voice returns.

Cruellest of all, I lost my beloved Robert. Despite all Papa Maurice had said, Robert went on trying to see me again, until my mother told him of all the complications I'd suffered, giving him to understand that my case was hopeless. Then he gave up – not only me, even his plans to recover his clothes shop in Paris. He went back to his parents in Central America, and later I heard he had married a local girl. It was the only reasonable thing to do. I still shudder today at the thought of him ever seeing me in the physical condition I was in. I had wanted his love; I could never have endured his pity.

To while away the endless hours in hospital, I started writing letters to pen-pals all over the world. Just getting a letter, even from someone I had never met, made life a bit easier. Among them was a Frenchman of Polish extraction. In the course of our correspondence, he revealed that some months earlier a woman had broken his heart, and he in turn learned from my letters that I was reluctant to return home when the hospital finally discharged me. He wrote to me proposing marriage. I accepted without a moment's hesitation, even though we had never laid eyes on each other. I was seventeen years old at the time.

We both knew from the start that our hearts would never be whole again, after the fearful blows we had both received. Still, we thought that together we could build a marriage that would endure, even if it were not very passionate.

The birth of our first child with a stomach defect brought us together for a while, but when the baby died after two agonizing months of life, something in our relationship also died. We struggled on for several more years, and had five more children. Then one day my Polish sailor weighed anchor and left his home port behind, never to return. I was left with the task of supporting and raising my five children.

It must have been about this time when I really began to understand something Papa Maurice had said to me so many years before, that night when we had perched unsteadily at the top of that great elm tree in the gathering dusk. He was not there to lighten my burden, but to prepare me – albeit unwittingly – for the years of Job-like misfortunes that lay ahead. Without the Spartan upbringing he forced on me, I would never have survived. And I can now say that my childhood – which I have described, I think, not unfairly – was despite all its trials and tribulations the only time in my life when I enjoyed spells of real happiness.

Papa Maurice has mellowed in his later years. He drinks less now than he used to. However, after thirty-six years of marriage, he and Mama finally decided to go their separate ways. Of all his children, I am the only one that Papa ever visits. Now it is he who cries when I arrive. I do my best to surround him with comfort and tenderness, but he can't manage to forget the past. They say that Time heals all wounds, but I have learned that this isn't entirely true. Certain things can never be forgotten. I myself can never forget the people I once knew and loved, and who have long since died – not least those American soldiers, who had come to rid us of the Nazi yoke and who died out in the marshes around our house. Were we worthy of their sacrifice? It's a question I still ask myself today.

And of course I shall never forget Robert, as he has never forgotten me. Twenty years ago now he wrote asking if he could be godfather to my daughter Stephanie, who I named after his daughter. Now, as I write, both our Stephanies are grown-up and married.

No, Time certainly cannot heal all wounds – particularly those of the heart. The man I once loved so dearly, the man I have never stopped loving, is happy now; the knowledge that this is so does bring me some measure of solace and shared pleasure, as do the letters he sends from Central America. When I think of the few short months we were together, I marvel that so deep a love could have been forged between us.

Fortunately we still have eternity to look forward to.

On Christmas Eve 1945, I travelled all the way to the Gates of Heaven only to be turned back. There must have been a reason for that. I have done my best to make sure that all those around me can enjoy a happiness that I have so rarely known. Occasionally depression stalks me, but it has never conquered me. The handsome big house that I built myself has no lock on the door; anyone who walks in is always welcome. Strangers have come to me, exhausted, cynical; they join us for family dinner, and when they go I can see they leave with renewed belief in the qualities of love and friendship.

Sometimes, when the weather is bad, my old injuries play me up, and it can be painful just to move around the house. But nothing can compare with the memories I have of what tortures those American soldiers endured before they died, those young paratroopers whom the Germans deliberately and in cold blood massacred beneath my very eyes that day in June 1944.

I am still waiting, with a certain degree of impatience, for the day when God will find Himself obliged to nod rather than shake His head. It will happen sooner rather than later.

Such remarks upset my children. Stephanie frowns at me as if to say: 'Will you never learn to be serious, Mama?' Perhaps it's simply that I have never really grown up. I'm still as curious about things, as prone to ask incessant questions as when I was a child.

One of the questions I still ask myself, each time I reread this very moving poem, is this: who was it, Monsieur Lamartine, that hurt you so; what indelible wound were you referring to when you wrote these lines:

> *The Book of Life is the highest book,*
> *It can neither be opened nor closed as we choose;*
> *For the parts we love there is no second chance*
> *Not even a peek, not even a glance,*
> *While the page of death turns itself.*
> *No matter how hard or how often we look*
> *To relive that moment of glory, we lose,*
> *While the page of death turns itself . . .*

With grateful thanks from the Major General

Dear Maurice and family,

Thirty-three years have passed since the night that began the liberation of Europe. In that interregnum several generations of soldiers have passed through the ranks of this Division. Those of us who follow the men who spearheaded the liberation continue to look to that night as the epitomization of the airborne spirit. Their sufferings and successes are our heritage, and we jealously continue to share them.

We know, just as they knew that night, that our successes were to no small part the result of the help we received from many French men, women and children who risked and gave their lives with us in pursuit of the common cause. Many of you were not known to us at the time; and the Duboscq family, although long known to us by deed, has only recently been identified by name. We knew that you collected, sheltered and led our soldiers to their comrades. We knew as well that you told us of the land and where the enemy lay. We knew that in your small boat, Maurice, you collected our supplies. Only now can we offer thanks to all of you for that help. We suffered then your anguish over the loss of your son and the wounds of Geneviève; only now are we able to say so.

The invaluable aid that the Duboscq family provided on the nights of 5–6 June, 1944, and the sacrifices you made, are a part of the heritage of the 82nd Airborne Division.

ROSCOE ROBINSON, Jr.

Letter from Major General Roscoe Robinson, commanding officer of the 82nd Airborne Division, to Papa Maurice and family in 1977.